THE HOLOCAUST OBJECT IN POLISH AND POLISH-JEWISH CULTURE

THE HOLOCAUST OBJECT IN POLISH AND POLISH-JEWISH CULTURE

Bożena Shallcross

Indiana University Press / Bloomington & Indianapolis

This book is a publication of

Indiana University Press
601 North Morton Street
Bloomington, Indiana 47404-3797 USA

www.iupress.indiana.edu

Telephone orders	800-842-6796
Fax orders	812-855-7931
Orders by e-mail	iuporder@indiana.edu

♾ The paper used in this publication meets the minimum requirements of the American National Standard for Information Sciences—Permanence of Paper for Printed Library Materials, ANSI Z39.48-1992.

Manufactured in the United States of America

Library of Congress Cataloging-in-Publication Data

Shallcross, Bozena.
The Holocaust object in Polish and Polish-Jewish culture / Bozena Shallcross.
p. cm.
Includes bibliographical references and index.
ISBN 978-0-253-35564-5 (cl : alk. paper) 1. Polish literature—20th century—History and criticism. 2. Polish literature—Jewish authors—History and criticism. 3. Holocaust, Jewish (1939-1945), in literature. 4. Holocaust, Jewish (1939-1945)—Poland. 5. Reality in literature. I. Title.
PG7035.J48S53 2011
891.8'509358405318—dc22
2010031793

1 2 3 4 5 16 15 14 13 12 11

To my mother, Elżbieta Mądra,
who was a slave laborer in Berlin 1940–1945,
and in memory of my nephew Hubert Mądry (1982–2010)

CONTENTS

THE HOLOCAUST OBJECT IN POLISH AND POLISH-JEWISH CULTURE

The Totalized Object: An Introduction

We are crammed, surrounded by things, objects, furniture, clutter,
this dead fauna which increases over the years, disturbed at the
time of moving house, considered indispensible for life. Never
before, during this war, was man so brutally fleeced of the
surroundings of things among which he lives.

—Kazimierz Wyka

Knowledge must indeed present the fatally rectilinear succession
of victory and defeat, but should also address itself to those things
which were not embraced by this dynamic, which fell by the
wayside—what might be called the waste products and blind spots
that have escaped the dialectic. . . . Theory must deal with
cross-grained, opaque, unassimilated material, which as such
admittedly has from the start an anachronistic quality, but which is
not wholly obsolete since it has outwitted the historical dynamic.

—Theodor W. Adorno

The Holocaust Object as Text

We associate the Holocaust with human tragedy. Hence, mounds of objects,
looted from their murdered owners, seem much less important, their tales ig-
nored. Over the course of time, however, the physical remains of human victims—their jewelry, shoes, clothes, and even their hair—have become the
Holocaust's dominant metonymy. Housed in museums or memorial sites and
arranged by professional curators, these objects now stand out as the Holocaust's most persuasive and tangible reality. These surviving objects attest to
the fact of genocide, if one respects their authenticity; ordinary and humble,
these objects are endowed with unique representational power: pillaged or
exchanged for the victim's life, they trigger numerous Holocaust narratives.

Usually, the biography of an object continues as long as it maintains its capacity to serve its owner. One disturbing effect of the objects on display in Holocaust

museums is produced by the reversal of this order: beholders confront lifeless items that were in usable condition at the moment of separation from their owners and, thus, encounter in these vestiges not only their owners' tragic end, but also stories of violated proximity and forced separation. Since the Holocaust already exists at a temporal remove, its proximity diminishing into memory, both its material vestiges and immaterial traces manifest their past immediacy mainly through metonymy, which allows these fragments to speak on behalf of past wholeness. The tension between such gathered material vestiges and their initial integrated functionality underscores the great power of metonymy: this tension connects memory of the Holocaust with diverse processes of the post-Holocaust era, during which the surviving shreds produced narratives about human lives and how these lives ended. The beholder approaches the material legacy of the Holocaust in order to read its metonymic configurations and, in so doing, to pose questions about its graspable meaning.

The now institutionalized display of these objects at sites of death clashes with both their initially intended use and the way in which they attest to the powerful human desire to live; after all, their owners carried these possessions to places of destination and destiny, as objects intended for use in a future life at these locations. Anyone who contemplates the material legacy of Auschwitz-Birkenau is struck first of all by both its shabby everydayness and the simple utility of the objects on display—a utility determined by the demands of survival. Amid the chaos of suitcases, kitchen pots, footwear, one will not find canvasses painted by old masters or other precious collectibles. Today, this clash between the former owners' hope to live and their imminent death continues to produce the symbolic core meaning of Holocaust objects.

At the point when the victims, forced to leave their homes, had to make quick and irrevocable decisions regarding what to take with them, their needs were indeed basic. One took warm clothes, food, and symbolic mementos such as family pictures, but left behind furniture. Jewelry and hard currency were kept close to the body or hidden in its crevices. After reaching the ghettos, extermination centers, or concentration camps, the victims and their belongings were subjected to yet another process of segregation and elimination.[1] They first were deprived of their belongings, and then their lives. The resulting mass of plundered objects was again sorted before being sent, under the supervision of the special forces, to the Reich. Some of these leftovers, stored in barracks across Hitler's Europe, were looted after the war and, later, in diminished yet still terrifying immensity, have served as material evidence that the Holocaust was not a figment of some collective imagination.

The illegal processes of enriching the Reich in order to further its war efforts blurred otherwise clear distinctions that existed between collection and accumulation:[2] while the acts of collecting gesture toward the cultural sphere, those of accumulation and amassing signify more mundane needs. According to Jean Baudrillard, surplus and disorder are both inherent in accumulation.[3] This chaotic regrouping of artifacts hoarded by the Nazis, intermingled with aggressive anticultural notions, culminated in the 1942 Paris burning of a huge number of works of art produced by leading avant-garde artists.[4] Cultural critics John Elsner and Roger Cardinal do not distinguish between collecting and accumulating, because for them the mechanism of collecting is an inherent part of totalitarian systems in general and of Nazism, in particular. Therefore, they argue that "the Holocaust is collecting's limit case."[5] For them, the perverted Nazi impulse to accumulate is limited solely to works of art and reified human beings; this approach overlooks Nazi plans for the accumulation of everyday things. I argue, however, that when the Nazi project of "collecting" turned into amassing and recycling looted everyday items and even corpses of victims, such collecting degenerated into unaccountable accretion.

A new turn in Holocaust analysis of the material object-world emerged in the 1990s, when, due to systemic changes in East Central Europe, the previously stalled process of restituting Jewish property gained momentum. The convoluted problem of legal ownership and doubtful provenance of artifacts shook the art world, prompting both museum studies and art management methodologies to scrupulously track and reconstruct the provenance of museum holdings. Legal actions resulting in some dispossession were complemented by eventual repossession.[6] In Poland, the restitution began in earnest in 1997, only to slow again in recent years. There, the process had to do mainly, but not solely, with the return of real estate to Jewish communities; the holdings involved were primarily cemeteries and synagogues, which require special care and further negotiations regarding future use.

Given that objects typically serve as metonymic representations of their owners and users, a closer inquiry into what constitutes the identity of a culturally specific object—or, for that matter, a Jewish object—becomes pertinent. Unless an object is geared for a specific clientele, the production process usually defines the cultural and ethnic designation of artifacts. During the Holocaust, however, the cultural or national provenance of ordinary paraphernalia was defined rather by ownership: objects were Jewish because their owners were Jewish. Nazi science understood race as an essential trait of human subjects, yet from the practical vantage point of this science, Jewishness was not inherent in either corpses or objects. With the notable exception of religious artifacts, Jewishness was quickly stripped from the identity of everyday objects in order to facilitate the redistribution of these types of stolen goods across the Third Reich. In this context, Emmanuel Levinas's remark that the identity of an object does not constitute its primary structure takes on new relevance. According to his claim, the processes of circulation—the exchange, sale, and purchase of an object—disperse the permanence of its identity into the "anonymity of money."[7] A fundamental discursive change must be noted at this point. When the objects of Holocaust victims were circulated, initially they signified their owners' death, yet their gradual transformation stripped them of any association with their owners; thus, the objects were ready for reuse. Extreme forms of recycling, such as melting, resulted in a complete erasure of a product's shape, cultural identity, or function. For instance, the amassed gold teeth, melted into bullion, conveyed a radical dissociation from their human users. Recycling de-essentialized such objects and produced them anew.

I maintain that the Holocaust, with its agenda of human extermination, promoted a fetishization of objects; the acts of looting, amassing, and sorting gave unprecedented centrality to the fragmented material object-world. The re-signification of material objects, which had to do neither with some phenomenological return to things nor with any sort of philosophical materialism, resulted simply from the debased wartime economy. The new meaning invested in these material objects was informed by the processes of looting, recycling, and accumulation through which some of them passed en route to physical destruction.

One of the recurring themes of my analysis is the concept of ownership and property. Jeremy Bentham, founding father of the modern civil code and author of *Theory of Legislation*, succinctly elucidates the fact that "property and law are born together and die together. Before laws, there was no property; take away laws, and property ceases to exist."[8] Clearly, Bentham's definition explains that the birth of the concept of property is entirely defined by law and sheds light on the extent to which property functions as a legal notion. One could argue that German jurists had a clear understanding of Bentham's concept of property, since the legal changes introduced in the Third Reich allowed the appropriation of German Jewish property precisely because the law was circumvented: there was no law regulating or delegalizing this process. And since there was no such law, the ongoing illegal expropriation of Jews was guaranteed by the state of exception introduced in February 1933, as well as by the concept of Aryanization of Germany formulated in the 1935 Nuremberg Laws.[9] These initial concepts enabled the Germans to gradually dispossess the non-Aryans (read Jews) using indirect means, for example, through extremely heavy property taxation rates, which inevitably resulted in foreclosures.

Even the regulatory step undertaken by the Nazis—the Decree Regarding the Reporting of the Jewish Property, introduced by the Reich Minister of Justice after the annexation of Austria on April 26, 1938—did not set forth the notion of dispossession, but required every Jew to report the value of his or her entire foreign and domestic property.[10] This regulation set in motion a further hypocritical process that led to complete expropriation of Jewish property in both the Reich proper and in annexed Austria. As the war unfolded, the methods of solving the expropriation varied in the occupied countries. When the western and most economically advanced part of Poland was incorporated into the Third Reich, it was treated in a similar manner: property was not sanctioned by law. The formation of the Generalgouvernement and incorporation of the remaining part of Polish territory into this administrative body resulted in the confiscation of all state property, followed by the conveniently ambiguous January 1940 decree, according to which "private property could be taken over when such an act was justified by the 'public interest'" (Gross 1979, 94). To invoke just one aspect of the ongoing economic exploitation, the eviction of both Polish Jews (and some Poles) from their homes started very early in order to provide better housing and higher standards of living for both the occupiers and the local German population. Those later confined in ghettos were subjected to exploitative and prohibitive regulations and decrees that pertained to every aspect of their existence. These included further relocations, forced labor, food rations, and property regulations; the decree regarding the latter was nothing but a joke, given the ongoing plundering of people's homes and frequent instances of mugging.[11]

These references to the larger historical and legal framework offer the necessary perspective and backdrop against which I can view the objects of my interest—the kitchen utensils, clothes, bedding, and other such trivial artifacts, which constitute the "stuff" of everyday existence. This background also helps to illuminate the true scale of the bare life during wartime, when so much depended on overlooked items that had trivial monetary value.

A further investigation of the Holocaust's material object-world foregrounds ontological and epistemological differences between Holocaust and post-Holocaust materialities and temporalities and their subsequent impact on both periods' objectives and types of representation. This temporal distinction returns my analysis to its original source and context: capturing the immediacy of the genocide's extreme experience and its history in the making without, however, validating the artistic (mainly literary) expression of that time as the only authentic one. Authenticity is a value characteristic of the post-Holocaust perspective; within the Holocaust, the main value of any written testimony, including a literary one, was its incrimination of the genocide.

When approaching the factuality of the Holocaust, researchers often employ a shift in perspective, transforming the totality of mass murder into a gruesome mass of facts and numbers.[12] Such objectification displays the cold statistical truth of the Holocaust on museum walls in a format akin to entries in a telephone directory. Thus, one type of reification is followed, this time out of necessity, by another. On the one hand, the representational method employed by curators inevitably brings the fragmented messages of the detritus to the level of abstraction. On the other, however, it points to the mounds of objects' raison d'être: the representation of the totality of the Nazi extermination project that visibly demonstrates and perpetuates their agency in controlling the material object world and implies mass murder.

The Holocaust Text as Object

> I can say that the existing book, the existing sheet of paper, have
> a special sense, they are animated by an intention. The book with
> its paper pages, its cover, etc. is a thing. To this book there does
> not append a second thing, the sense; but instead the latter, in
> animating, penetrates the physical whole in a certain way.
>
> —Edmund Husserl

Nazi policy in occupied Poland demonstrated an awareness of the word's material basis through acts of censorship and the destruction of written testimonies. Because every materially preserved inscription is constituted as a physical object, it can be investigated from a perspective different from the one that regards it as mere "intellectual property." Indeed, in a manner unprecedented in Western culture, Holocaust inscriptions insisted on their own materiality and, frequently, on the materiality of that which they represented. This twofold materiality (though the latter one is without matter) enabled each manuscript and each copy of these object-oriented works both to tell its own story, and also to refer to the story of its author. Writers and artists caught in the whirlpool of war and unfolding genocide tried to secure their paintings, prints, and unpublished manuscripts in every possible manner, burying them, depositing them in safe places, or entrusting them to relatives and acquaintances who lived outside of confinement or in quieter parts of the country.

In this book, I take pains to describe the ontology and the status of the Holocaust text as both material thing and written document. In order to account for this conceptual synthesis, I apply to it the term *precarium*, which in its original legal context describes the deposit of items slated to be returned to their owners upon a positive change of situation.[13] Another meaning of this condition implies precariousness, a shaky, unstable status, which with great accuracy reflects the Holocaust text's wandering and threatened existence, the way it changed hands and places in diverse chance-driven scenarios. In my interpretation, the term embraces both meanings.

Since the precarious object perpetually oscillates between existence and obliteration, because of both its ownership and its physicality, *precarium* predetermines the Holocaust text's ontology. More than by anything else, the precarious existence is triggered and augmented by the fact that the Holocaust text is permeated by a unique historic meaning. In approaching writings, artifacts, and works of art from the Holocaust, I necessarily encountered instances of erasure, of texts deliberately destroyed precisely because they recounted acts of genocide, either factually or fictionally. Although it is not the only principle governing this effect, *precarium* sets apart the Holocaust texts from postwar writings because their incriminating messages endangered them, as well as their authors and keepers.

Acutely aware of this condition, Russians during the Stalinist terror memorized their texts. The tradition of memorizing texts is equally strong in both Polish and Jewish traditions, but the mass genocide undermined the possibility of safely preserving a text in individual memory. For all aims and purposes, providing a material sort of protection was a better solution, as proven by many incredible post-Holocaust discoveries.[14] During wartime, *precarium* is intensified, and the Holocaust produced *precarium* on an epidemic scale. Of course, the Holocaust text shares this characteristic with other artifacts, all of which require material preservation. Those pieces that were preserved on paper, however, were particularly fragile. The contingency of these texts is closely, if not intimately, connected to their creators' threatened status, as well as to the whole range of extreme situations in which they were created. For this reason, their destructibility exceeds in both manner and degree the universal vulnerability of matter.

The principle of *precarium* emphasizes both the text's material foundation and the degree to which this foundation is exposed to chance. The text, as a fragile material object, usually embraces the phases of its creation: preservation, itinerancy, archiving, and, in the final postwar process, commitment to a museum. All these stages seem self-explanatory under normal circumstances. However, conditions of terror, extreme censorship, and a type of deprivation that made writing tools scarce or deemed their possession illegal transformed the whole process of writing into a hazardous preoccupation. As Emanuel Ringelblum, historian of the Warsaw Ghetto, wrote: "People were afraid to write at that time, because they anticipated searches."[15] These ongoing searches undoubtedly affected "the survival of written documents from the war period" (Ringelblum 1988 471). Despite the fact that searches on the Aryan side were less frequent, the mechanism of terror and fear also forced many individuals to destroy their accounts. During a Gestapo search in her apartment building, the prominent writer Zofia Nałkowska quickly burned in an oven her "second diary," a priceless recording of the annihilation of the Warsaw Jewry, rescue efforts, and other risky observations made from the perspective of an engaged Pole. Yet, some of Holocaust Ur-writers penned their texts with hope, trusting that their Word would survive. This indicates a greater concern about the continued existence of their creations than of their own lives. The basic desire to leave a written trace of truth and, thereby, mark one's existence prevailed.

Despite the scarcity of paper products, "everyone wrote: journalists, literatis, teachers, community activists, young people, even children" (Ringelblum

1988, 471). Notwithstanding serious efforts to protect them, many manuscripts were destroyed or lost. Jacek Leociak's excellent study of the writings produced in the Warsaw Ghetto supports this conclusion.[16] It is still surprising that many letters, diaries, memoirs, and chronicles survived. Written in both Yiddish and Polish, both outside of and within ghettos, these were mainly nonfictional, historical, and testimonial accounts.[17] In contrast, poetic and fictionalized autobiographical writings were produced, and later recovered, in proportionally small numbers. For example, among the few wartime poems written by Zuzanna Ginczanka, only one refers directly to the extermination of Jews and to the poet's Jewish experience. I wish to draw attention to these inscriptions in times of war in order to focus on their disturbing and incriminating message.

The physical vulnerability of Holocaust poetry lent unexpected and prophetic validity to Osip Mandelshtam's belief that a poem is like a message found in a bottle. Although his simile, taken literally, is not entirely adequate to the Holocaust text, which was never thrown into the open, but buried and hidden like treasure to be discovered by future generations, it retains a certain relevance. The very fact that these poems have reached us, though their authors and the entire world in which they were written have perished, verges on the miraculous. The convoluted fate of these poems was shaped by numerous historical circumstances, but I find that *precarium*, which involved a chance movement between the fragile material foundations of works, their incriminating message, and historical events, is crucial for a larger understanding of the Holocaust text.

The fate of the Holocaust inscription as a material object is intimately connected to the physical surfaces used for writing: any inferior or accidental surface that substituted for paper was transformed by the text and its intrinsic aspect. The Holocaust thus forced the revaluation of detritus—such as wrapping paper, old receipts, bottle labels, cement bags, walls of confinement, and even scraps of toilet paper—into the carriers of priceless messages. The preservation and archivization of written Holocaust accounts lead us to question what was actually collected and archived by the handful of dedicated individuals who undertook this labor. For example, Ringelblum's inner circle had a distinct approach toward archiving their finds. Unlike today's archivists and museum curators, who attempt to preserve the Holocaust as past history, the Oyneg Shabes archivists collected the documents, as they recorded what happened in their authors' immediate everyday experience, to be remembered.[18] In so doing, both the archivists and authors were driven by the daunting desire to serve as witnesses to themselves and, by extension, to their nation.

Archiving mass genocide—understood as a necessary protective measure—they resisted extreme methods of Nazi policy as well as the usual destructive forces of the elements and time. Since archives, as collections of incriminating records, were perceived as hazardous and vulnerable in this period, they had to be hidden in protective places, outside of the public space and its gaze, because this sphere was itself dangerous.[19] The archivists of the Holocaust were not afforded the relative luxury of archiving according to the controlled openness characteristic of public institutions. Although the task of archiving did not preclude that the archived items would be either destroyed or partially damaged, as was the case with a portion of the *Chronicle of the Warsaw Ghetto*, it was pervaded by a strong positive intent.[20] Resisting *precarium*, the very gesture of archiving displayed hope that the documents would resurface at a time when they could bear witness not against their authors, but, instead, both on their behalf and against the perpetrators. In this sense, Holocaust writings that had once been threatened became *survivors*. Can one speak of the *survival* of texts without lapsing into personification? Amy Hungerford warns against such personification of texts about the Holocaust.[21] Although I agree with the author that the Holocaust was first and foremost about the destruction of human life that paved the way to further destruction— that of culture—I do not separate them in any radical manner, but argue for the complex interaction of life and culture in informing the word.

Today one encounters only the remainders of Holocaust texts. Described as a treasure by one of the men who buried the Oyneg Shabes archives,[22] these vestiges of those who were obliterated by the genocide are now preserved physically in the best possible way. Since, for the most part, we cannot directly access these remnants, we must rely on mediation by microfilms, photographs, and computerized images. By excluding touch as a means of contact, this separation transforms our already limited relationship with the victims' messages into a purely visual form of communication. This severance doubles the distance between researchers and witnesses. It makes one aware of how much has already been irrevocably lost; one can never reconstitute tangible realness, but only a form of the past based on the language of traces.

The phenomena of proximity and vestige order the Holocaust object's temporality by bracketing a time span of more than sixty years. In order to understand the Holocaust as proximity, one should dwell on the sense of separation, enhanced by the increasing temporal distance, which transforms the Holocaust into its own trace. Levinas never tires of reminding us that proximity is not based solely on spatial relations, on intentionality, or even on the sensuous contact through which touch overcomes spatial determinism.[23] Nonetheless, proximity is delineated here *also* as a temporal, spatial, and emotional position, which requires separation; through separation proximity is better understood. Moreover, through separation, reinforced by the passage of time and the workings of the elements, proximity eventually metamorphosed into the trace or the vestige, a fragile site of disappearance that safeguards the past presence. Mainly because of the Holocaust inscription's material base, I embrace both meanings here: the trace and the vestige. Yet neither of them is merely a fragment, although in their openness they function like one. Rather, they are what remains: a remnant and a signifier, both of which constantly negotiate absence and presence.

Some of the traces of the Holocaust are not endowed with the self-effacing character because their gradual disappearance is conditioned by external elements and the passage of time.[24] However, Derrida's reassessment of the complex notion of trace and foregrounding of its spectral nature gives a useful conceptual tool for a scholar of the Holocaust.[25] The spectral quality of the trace/vestige defines both the Holocaust's material and immaterial remnants, whether they are held in memory or in an archive. One of the most palpable examples of this spectrality is captured in the extant snapshots from the Auschwitz crematorium, taken despite a strict order forbidding photographing in death camps.[26] These were taken by a member of the Sonderkommando, hidden in an emptied gas chamber. The black void of the gas chamber frames two moments of the genocide in the making: a group of naked women pushed around before their death, and the burning of the gassed bodies. Taken from afar, these two stages of killing occur in broad daylight in the open space outside Crematorium V. Blurred contours of the faces and bodies in motion, the framing effect of the gas chamber as the implied place of their inevitable death as well as the point of view of the photographer managing the camera while risking his life, are juxtaposed with the other snapshot revealing a pile of corpses and the smoke coming from the burning bodies. The eerie quality of the events, enhanced by the shaky visual imprints taken from a hidden camera, speaks of both the spectral and the specular quality of these material shreds deemed to represent the very core of the Holocaust.[27]

The Represented Holocaust Object

In order to situate the represented Holocaust object within its processes of circulation, (ex)change, (dis)possession, and recycling, I consistently approach every poem or short story or novella as a cultural text. Therefore, when I engage in textual explication, it constitutes only part of my interdisciplinary reading, which emphasizes equally the representational schemes and their historical aspects. The texts I discuss in this volume were primarily created during the war and therefore retain some proximity with the past. On two occasions, I analyze short works by Zofia Nałkowska and Tadeusz Borowski who, although active writers throughout the war, wrote and published these particular stories shortly after the Holocaust, when, as the saying goes, the memory was still fresh. For this reason alone, they were not endangered by *precarium* and call for an approach different from current Holocaust discourse, with its emphasis on post-memories.

The precarious status of the Ur-author and his writing forced him or her to place in the text the near-totality of what he or she experienced. The Holocaust Ur-text speaks of the pressure to record, to articulate firsthand knowledge directly and with an immediacy of experience. The urge to bear testimony to posterity often shifts to the authors' impulses to *share* their shocking experience with others. Literature represents the genocide more vividly. It can achieve this through the language of objects, materiality, and matter written by intuiting humans with no less precision than historiography.[28]

In drawing a distinction between literature *of* the Holocaust and literature *about* the Holocaust, David Roskies emphasizes a shift in authorial point of view between the perspective textualized during the Holocaust and after, "so that anything written after the fact is colored by the new reality."[29] The critic's gesture of distinguishing the *sensu stricte* Holocaust artistic production from the logic governing its later representation is relevant to my examination. Therefore, I reiterate the question: what constitutes a Holocaust text? First, it is a text that carries an "incriminating message," engaging both perpetrators and victims as actors. The perpetrators fear incriminating texts that would disclose their monstrosity; the latter fear the impending destruction of incriminating testimonies and, with them, their own existence. Besides the engagement of certain Holocaust themes, such as the incriminating message, the Holocaust text is lacunary and often object-laden. Its removal to a safe place of stasis as well as its quite opposite itinerant biography are conditioned by *precarium*.

I have briefly discussed the status of the Holocaust object as text and the inversion of that phenomenon, the Holocaust text as object. These related formulations are, obviously, two sides of the same coin. The third element, the Holocaust object as imagined in literature, enriches this constellation and brings us to the question of how objects are represented in Holocaust texts. Generally, I believe that the nature of this genocide is representable, even though those who lived through it, and first spoke of it, were given no real opportunity or time to master strategies of representation that would express their experience. This representation occurs more vividly when the Holocaust experience is evoked through ordinary objects.

The factuality of the material object-world reflected in Holocaust literature reveals a dramatic relationship between people and the items they carried to camps and ghettos. Tending toward stark realism and privileging the use of everyday objects, many Holocaust narratives reveal an intensified state of subject–object unity that defies a Cartesian understanding of the divide between subject and object. Related to each other in a distinctly unifying manner, these fleeting moments inform the sense of episodic object–subject proximity as triggered by the threat of death or dispossession.

When the critical theorist Bill Brown calls on us to study "the privileged modes of physical transgression, destruction and resuscitation," he also gestures toward the nature of our engagement with the violated material world during mass genocide.[30] This project concerns both the nature of that material world and its contribution to the literary construction of the Holocaust. Accordingly, I investigate the trajectory of objects based on their diverse relationship to people. This story of repossession belongs to an emerging theme in post-Holocaust discourse.

At the same time, for the sake of greater precision, I attempt to delineate major patterns of representation by which Polish and Polish-Jewish writers communicated lessons derived from objects during or shortly after the Holocaust. Here it is important to give a brief sketch of these major, often overlapping strategies, which I distill into several dominant paradigms: the mimetic, the metonymic, the agalmatic, and the transformational.

While most Holocaust testimonies engage objects as the flotsam of brutal realism, this mimetic model assumes that one can recognize historical veracity in represented reality. Although the mimetic pattern prevails in my discussion of Jerzy Andrzejewski's and Tadeusz Borowski's writings (chapters 5 and 6, respectively), it overlaps with the other types of representation and informs one of the main goals of my overall culturalist reading.

This study also reads the texts in which the represented objects speak of their owners' identities, shed light on their broken lives, and point out the looters' greedy desires in a way that supersedes the strictly mimetic function of these texts. I deploy the metonymic model of representation in reading the poetry of Władysław Szlengel (chapter 1), who invoked human destinies through objects and vice versa. Some of his poems are so saturated with objects (even as the human presence is erased) that they acquire the quality of object-poems. Because of the great possibilities inherent in this model, metonymy is widespread and, indeed, omnipresent in diverse Holocaust genres as an authorial strategy, although it comes to the fore in postwar literature where it mediates past human tragedy.

Related to these representational methods is the violation of intimate parts of the body and the corpse in search of gold and diamonds, a daily routine in death camps. In addition to hiding them in other ordinary and inconspicuous looking containers and places, which were nonetheless scrupulously searched, the human body became a site of both concealed valuables and violent search. Given the fact that these and similar searches were widespread practices, paramount to the story of the Holocaust object, I name this mechanism of material desire and safekeeping agalmatic. The coinage, like many other words in English, derives from the Greek to agalma (treasure or glory), used in reference to ornate figurines of gods, which ancient Greeks hid and found in small drawers located inside sculpted busts of the proverbially ugly Sylenus. Conceptualized in this manner, the perpetrators' search for treasures allows me to discuss the tragic and complex perspective of one victim—the Polish Jewish poet Zuzanna Ginczanka—subjected to extreme persecution triggered by both her identity and her material possessions (chapter 2). Here, I discuss her poem-testament, which envisions how greed on the part of her persecutors led them to murder her and to destroy her belongings, such as couches and pillows, in search for the real treasures supposedly hidden in them.

Most narratives of the Holocaust object involve the murder of the victims followed by the recycling of their possessions and a radical transformation/re-cycling of their bodies into material goods, or human soma, a paradigm I identify as transformational. In order to more fully understand this practice, I investigate the Nazi practice of commodification and recycling of human corpses using a reportage by Zofia Nałkowska (chapter 3); these processes fore-ground the writer's questions regarding somatic impermanence and waste as devoid of religious underpinning. I continue the discussion of the transforma-tional paradigm via the remarkable apocalyptic poems written by Czesław Miłosz (chapter 4), in which he witnesses the destruction of the Warsaw Ghetto and contemplates the after-death fate of human soma and its decom-position as engaging broad eschatological perspectives.

This book attempts to seek the meaning of *precarium* as it conditioned the fate of manuscripts; of shifting identities, both human and inanimate; of the recycling of objects, including the human *soma* that belonged to the leveled-down material world of the time; of the ashes and their preservation of so-matic, and by extension, pneumatic markers. This highly nuanced creative legacy of objects as texts and texts as objects yields a disturbing and unique reflection upon human lives. Through my excavation, I attempt to recover this legacy in the hope of distinguishing—at least partially—the obliterated dead and restoring the living connection between object and reader.

ON JOUISSANCE

CHAPTER ONE

A Dandy and Jewish Detritus

I who am not, who only was once,
There where the road led to the camp gate.

My trace, a diary hidden between bricks.
Perhaps someday it will be unearthed.

—Czesław Miłosz

T HE NAZI WAR ECONOMY sustained itself not only through production, exploitation, or looting, but also through substitution and replacement, which took the form of a whole range of ersatz products, cheap fakes, and impermanent copies. For example, an inferior food product made from sugar beets replaced marmalade and its proverbially bad taste was long remembered after the war. These imitative products were a part of larger processes of emulation summed up by Kazimierz Wyka in the phrase *życie na niby*, "life as if lived, life not quite lived."[1] One encounters the same bitter resentment in the expression *życie-ersatz*, "ersatz life,"[2] coined by Władysław Szlengel, the Polish-Jewish poet (1914–1943), to whom this chapter is dedicated. The expression aptly refers to his existence in the Warsaw Ghetto.

This ubiquitous substitutive force had its parallel within the domain of Holocaust representation, mainly in its wide use of metonymy and synecdoche. When objects entered the frame of representation, playing the role of protagonists while signifying their absent users, they performed only one role among the many available in the metonymical paradigm. Paradoxically, this entrance into the sphere of representation gave trivial things their maximum agency.

An ordinary item, such as a pair of shoes, introduces us to the world of the Holocaust. It should be surprising that shoes perform this function, but it is not; the shock they cause comes from their sheer quantity. Moreover, shoes achieved a stunning career through literary strategies of substitution. Though a pair of shoes is just a pair of shoes, their inside is a reversed image of the feet which they protect. Together with their outside peculiarities, they inform an imprinted "portrait," and, by extension, a metonymic image of the individual who, long absent, made this "footprint."[3] Likewise, the worn surface of a tool

contains an impression of the hand that used it for various chores. One is intrigued by the visual details inscribed on the surface of objects: the older the
object, the more intricate the traces and texture of use and abuse. A single ordinary item—a pencil, suitcase, or penknife—can stand for the larger whole of
historical processes. Once again, the Holocaust comes to mind, engaged, as it
is, repeatedly and stubbornly, in the dynamics of miniature and massive accumulation. An indispensable item such as a pair of shoes, accumulated in
camps as detritus, became part of a common series of things that were regu-
larly thematized in Holocaust texts. One of them, entitled simply "A Load of
Shoes," was written by the Yiddish poet Abraham Sutzkever on January 17,
1942, in the Vilna Ghetto. In an attempt to reach beyond an amassed and unspecified pile of shoes, "transported," as they were, "from Vilna to Berlin," he
questions the "objectual heroes" of his poem about their owners—"where are
your feet?" or "where is the child / who fit in these?"[4]—and emphasizes the
forced separation of these things from their users, whose demise they, then,
suggest. While the poem tends to personalize the shoes in a sentimental fashion, it also attempts to dispel a sense of the all-encompassing and chaotic anonymity of their pile. This is clearly the case with a pair of women's Sabbath
shoes, which are identified as belonging to the poetic persona's mother. This
moment of recognition communicates her death.

A written account, perceived in terms of a physical object, reveals a similar
logic. Here a poem stands for its author, implying both the person and his or
her lived experience. When considered within the context of mass genocide, a
poem enters a stage of contradiction: it stands as a testimony to the dying
human presence, but also to its own, often accidental, survival. A single episode from the posthumous peregrinations of Szlengel's oeuvre is sufficiently
evocative. After the war, Ryszard Baranowski, a man from the town of Józefów
near Warsaw, found a typed collection of Szlengel's poems in the double top
of an old table Baranowski was demolishing. The collection bore the poet's
handwritten inscription with the date 11.2.1943. Hence, these were some of the
last poems Szlengel wrote before his own death. Although it turned out that
these were merely copies of the poems that were, for the most part, already
known, their endurance triggers one's apocryphal imagination to narrate and
fill in the gaps of the poet's biography and the copies' separate history. Most
likely, the owner of the copies, who received them from the author, uncertain
of his own fate or aware of their accusatory message, entrusted his precious gift
to the table. The table, like all possessions owned by Jews, went through its
own precarious adventures before its existence nearly ended under Baranowski's axe. Today the collection, along with all other archival materials related to
Szlengel, is deposited in the archives of the Żydowski Instytut Historyczny[5] in
Warsaw; its completed journey stands metonymically for the poet.

In order to analyze the representational and poetic side of Szlengel's object lessons, one must situate his poems within multiple perspectives that are, at times, oppositional and, at others, overlapping. These poems deal, in turn, with street grammar and dandyism, *jouissance* and voluntary death, as well as with the miniature and the monumental. For the poet, creating a metonymic object pattern to represent the Jewish world inside the Warsaw Ghetto was not a goal in itself, since he was never prone to the cult of things. Szlengel retreated to this repertoire in order to give the Holocaust word its highest degree of historical urgency and textual palpability. In his poetic writing about history, he was careful to speak from a specific moment and place, from the unrelenting *hic et nun* as he lived it in the Warsaw Ghetto. To this end, the poet modified and expanded the time-honored device of metonymy in a manner that placed small, even miniature material things in dialectical tension with their large-scale surroundings. The outcome of Szlengel's poetic project intensifies the sensation of the destruction of everyday life, which comes across in the multitude of its individual forms. By juxtaposing the minute to the large—and even the immense—the poet indicates the central, albeit absent, protagonist of the process: the unrepresented or only indirectly represented human figure or the diminishing human presence. Contrary to the formalist view that metonymy communicates that which is tangible and concrete through abstract terms,[6] Szlengel's metonymy communicates the concrete through the most concrete. He develops a language of objects which, in its precision and specificity, assesses historical events from a perspective both collective and individualized. This language reveals the proximity or association between both points of view. Its method, wherein correlations are made in a specific manner and where a physical object stands in for the user, ultimately reinforces the substitutive logic of Holocaust literature.

Let us look at a volume of Szlengel's Tyrteian poetry, entitled *Kontratak. Wiersze z dni ostatnich. Tomik trzeci. Luty 1943* (Counterattack. Poems from the last days. Volume three. February 1943). It was written in Warsaw during the first wave of resistance to the Nazi liquidation of the ghetto; in terms of its style, the volume displays how well grounded Szlengel was in Skamander poetry and its neo-traditional sense of form. The specificity of the title indicates a manner of dating poems by the month, day, and even by hour, a frequent practice among "ghetto scribes," to use David Roskies's phrase. By citing the date of the volume in its subtitle, Szlengel aimed to create a sense of immediacy and urgency for the reader's gaze—a sense that pervades his poetic reportage of what was then the most recent chain of events in the ghetto. Despite its precise date, which coincides with a concrete historical event, the volume's subtitle produces another, somewhat prophetic, effect: it suggests that *these* poems could be the poet's last and, therefore, the last ever written in the Warsaw Ghetto, which was, at that point, doomed for destruction. In fact, Szlengel's premonition that the ghetto would be completely destroyed was realized only two months later.

Szlengel's poetic project during the last months of his life was simultaneously personal and universal, radically dramatizing the way in which material possessions were caught up in the whirlpool of history. Written between September 1942 and his death in April 1943, these poems are also his most mature, transforming the voice of this former cabaret performer into a dark cry of despair. The manner in which he chronicled and bemoaned the demise of the Jewish community of Warsaw earned him, after the war, the honorary title of "the bard of the Warsaw Ghetto." This title betrays—on the part of those who bestowed it upon him—no fear of the pathos so foreign to Szlengel, who, for the most part, served the muse of light entertainment. Prior to the war, he wrote satiric and jocular poetry, as well as cabaret songs, one of which, entitled "Tango Notturno," was a hit. But the events that he described and that later became known as the Holocaust, drastically darkened the tonality of his lyrics. Those included the poems in his collection *Co czytałem umarłym. Wiersze getta warszawskiego* (What I Read to the Dead. Poems from the Warsaw Ghetto),[7] which commemorate the trauma of everyday life in the ghetto and lament the poet's growing isolation and certainty of death.

Szlengel became known for his detailed descriptions of various methods of violated existence and the suffering these processes caused. For Irena Maciejewska, otherwise appreciative of his poetry, "These are more documents then artistic works" (Maciejewska 1977, 27). Always clinging to the concrete, Szlengel's poetic notations in *Co czytałem umarłym* also tell stories of how ingeniously and successfully frantic people constructed hiding places in the ghetto.[8] Again, the bunkers signify their unquenched desire to survive: "Carting of cement, bricks, nights reverberate with the din of hammers and axes. Pumping of water, constructing of underground wells. Bunkers. Mania, running, the neurosis of the heart of Warsaw Ghetto" (*What I Read to the Dead*; Szlengel 1977, 49). The word *ghetto* was forbidden by the Nazis, who allowed only the use of the periphrastic term *dzielnica zamknięta* (closed neighborhood), but the poet disregards the imposed limitations of censorship and does not mince words to call the ghetto by its own name.

> Light, underground cables, making the exits,
> again bricks, ropes, sand . . . Lots of sand . . . Sand . . .
> Board-beds, bunk-beds. Provisions for months.
> (*What I Read to the Dead*; Szlengel 1977, 50)

Those cleverly disguised shelters, tunnels, basements, and burrows, which Frieda W. Aaron eloquently calls the "architecture of despair" (Aaron 1990,

100) were in response to the "liquidation" of the ghetto. People moved from the places they inhabited above the ground to new shelters underground. For the builders, the construction of the bunkers bespoke hope. For the pursuers, these hiding places were a demonstration of the Jews' subversive attitude. For Szlengel, despite his praise of the ingenuity and resistance of the ghetto's inhabitants, these spoke of an utterly debased lifestyle, which humiliated him. Those condemned lived the atavistic existence of burrowing creatures, of "moles"[9] deprived of basic conveniences. Only the most indispensable utensils accompanied them in these tight places: kitchen pots or some bedding. People were forced to operate within a new kind of practical arrangement that was devoid of the achievements of civilization to which they were accustomed. In this sense, the poet anticipated an important strain in the discourse of the Holocaust that understands Nazi practices as a new form of attack against civilization in which, in this case, the result of the attack is forced solely upon Jews:[10]

> Crossing of electricity, water pipes, everything. Twenty centuries crossed out by the whip of an SS-man. Cave age. Cressets. Village wells. Long night. People are returning underground. (*What I Read to the Dead*; Szlengel 1977, 50)

To enhance this and earlier stages of regression, Szlengel singled out certain objects that belonged to the previous order of things and, thus, to a different lifestyle: door buzzer, window, and telephone used to be taken for granted in prewar life. Several poems are structured around these everyday objects because these unsublime poetic themes represented a past life that Szlengel wished to sentimentalize. In order to do so, the poet retreated to an adaptation of the pictorial genre of the still life, creating, arguably, the most expressive of his objectual configurations.

Today, post-Holocaust literature of a highly sophisticated aesthetics is, sooner or later, viewed with suspicion, as if aesthetization were something unbecoming. Szlengel, like many of his contemporaries, demonstratively operated beyond these limitations. His critic, Maciejewska, wrote with considerable admiration for his wide range of poetic forms and artistic means. Although Maciejewska did not fear that the text–image comparison would transcend the ethics of a Holocaust philologist, she did not discuss Szlengel's translation of the painterly genre of still life into the textual sphere in terms of ultimate aesthetization. The pictorial genre fit Szlengel's poetic project, perfectly complementing the metonymical figuration and controlling one of its main characteristics—the exclusion of human presence. This is a genre requirement, which dictates that a still life is primarily constituted through a more or less complex arrangement of inanimate objects in an artificial setting.[11]

In another time and place, this type of visual sensitivity of a poet toward the world of concrete, casual objects could indicate the represented world's prosperous stability and order, or even its beauty. In contrast, Szlengel appropriated the characteristic features of the still life to narrate an impoverished world in which lives were disrupted and destroyed. A voyeuristic glimpse at the interiors of houses after Nazi "action" grasps those moments through observing and listing discarded things:

> In the abandoned flats
> scattered bundles,
> suits and comforters,
> and plates and stools,
> fires are still dwindling,
> idle spoons lie about,
> thrown out in a hurry
> family photographs....[12]
> ("Things"; Szlengel 1977, 127)

Any Dutch still life that portrays the disorder of, for example, a table after a feast or an interior after an excessively jubilant night[13] would share some of its aspects with the images of objects portrayed by Szlengel: a half-empty glass, an open book, flatware tossed away. Obviously, the lack of human presence within the space of Szlengel's still lifes connotes a different preposterous history of these images, to refer to Mieke Bal's concept, encompassing the violation of normalcy of a domestic abode that has been destroyed and whose inhabitants have just embarked on their last journey. He captures the pathos of their departure only by conjectural signs, referring to the scattered utensils that communicate the abruptness of that which has happened in those surroundings. In such a way, he also renders these preposterous and unportrayed events frozen and, moreover, dead.[14] Szlengel's compositions of the empty domestic interiors after "action" evoke a double meaning of deadness and rupture. The first relates to murdered people, while the second recalls useless things. Only the metonymic suggestiveness of the detritus does not allow the lingering human presence, in its everydayness, to be entirely erased.

Szlengel engages objects to talk about the debased and disrupted lives of the owners from which they were wrenched. On the level of extreme poverty and dispossession, synecdoche enters the frame of the poem in an equally limited manner. For example, in the poem "Pomnik" (Monument), a simple kitchen utensil, a single pot, is elevated to the role of a headstone and monument for a Jewish woman. This sole material vestige is all that remained after she, a housewife and mother, was sent to die in a camp. Reminiscent of the simple still lifes depicted by twentieth-century painters, the image is minimalist and understated in its realism evoking "Her cold, dead pot."[15] Imprinted with her personal history, this ordinary object testifies to her past proximity, her bygone touch, and the pot's everyday usage which, as seen above, has granted it, as an object, meaning vis-à-vis her nourishing presence. While the mapping of the life–death dichotomy onto the sensual polarity of heat–cold is not necessarily original, this pot as a solitary material sign is not an empty and abstract item; at least in this case, the object is pregnant with symbolic meaning, since, in a final gesture, Szlengel endows the object, which, during the woman's life, embodied nothing more than its use value, with a commemorative function. In devising this conclusion, the poet, who used to thrive on clever punch lines, rewrites the poetic message to shift its metonymic logic to the level of an homage.[16] In a double entendre, he moves the memory of the dead woman into an ellipsis of pathos.

The shift from a single object to a plethora of objects serves Szlengel's objectual idiom by indicating a disturbed equilibrium or an emerging threat. This strategy functions much like an exception posited against a general rule. His exceptional objects, juxtaposed with a nebulous abundance of equally unspecified objects, demonstrate the main dichotomy of the Jewish community's precarious state. "Rzeczy" (Things)—a poetic study of gradual dispossession and demise—intensifies this logic and, along with it, the metonymic principle of representation. Historically, the poem refers to the several stages during which the territory and boundaries of the Warsaw Ghetto were revised and diminished according to Nazi specifications. The poem focuses on the results of such grand revisions—that is, on the forced relocation of the Jewish population to the ghetto and their repeated transfer within the constricted space from one street to another, from flats to single rooms. These motions are represented as several "material events," in which objects, as if carried by invisible hands, imply the erasure of their rightful owners. The quantitative logic of the poem encompasses seriality and rupture: every time the Jews were ordered to move, they carried less with them; furthermore, whatever remained in their possession became smaller and less valuable.[17]

> From Hoża and Wspólna, and Marszałkowska Streets
> the wagons were driving . . . the Jewish wagons . . .
>   furniture, tables and stools,
>   small suitcases, bundles,
>   chests, caskets and bedding
>   suits, portraits,
>   linens, pots, rugs
>   and wall hangings.
>   Slivovitz, glass jars,
>   cups, sterling, kettles,
>   books, trinkets and all the rest
>   is driving from Hoża to Śliska ("Things"; Szlengel 1977, 125).[18]

"Things" is a quintessential thing-poem, a Rilkean *Dinggedichte*, devoid of human presence, sarcastically referred to as *zgraja ponura* (gloomy bunch); through metonymy it narrates the process of the gradual destruction of the ghetto inhabitants. The long poem is dominated by the contradictory rhythm of objects' presence: they grow more expansive and important as their quantity decreases.[19] Each time, reorganized into a poorer and more rudimentary new whole, these things are reassembled only to gesture back, with each new configuration, to their original wholeness.[20] Szlengel's handling of an enumeration, an ancient figure of speech, defines this separation, and, subsequently, amplifies the separated things. On the other hand, enumeration is a figure that involves a degree of ordering, since to divide objects means, by definition, to bring certain order. Artful as it is, the trope of ordering/dividing depends on listing, that is, on imposing a new sense of control over that which is fundamentally disordered. Such manipulation of things through the type of enumeration seen in "Things" restores, as in other Holocaust texts, the importance of objects in projecting anonymous human death.[21]

It is the unrelenting logic of subtraction that structures the enumerations of detritus; eventually, even the last small item is taken away and with it the life of the last Jew. Szlengel presses his dramatization to the zero point, at which nothing remains but a pill with which to kill oneself. What the poet deliberately omits from representation is the final push on the part of the Nazis, through which the material possessions were constricted to the ontological zero. Instead, he envisions a vengeful return of animated Jewish possessions, their final appearance filled with the restored power of justice ends the poem.

One step in the diminishing procession was the so-called *kocioł* (cauldron), a colloquial name for the method of corralling people in the streets. The Germans called such operations *Einkesselung*, and Szlengel refers in "Things" to the specific *Einkesselung* organized on Ostrowska Street, which was only an episode in the colossal liquidation of the ghetto. This *Aktion*, which started on September 6, 1942 and lasted until September 11, was the stage during which thousands were deported to Treblinka.[22] The detritus and trash, which Jews left behind during the tumult of liquidation, pervaded the emptied streets and homes.

In his "Cylinder" (Top Hat), Szlengel attempts to counterbalance or, at least, to resist this process of human degradation

> I'll put on a top hat,
> a tuxedo I'll put on—
> a tie with a panache . . .
> I'll put on a top hat,
> a tuxedo I'll put on,
> I'll walk up to the sentry.

> The gendarme will stagger,
> the gendarme will dread,
> maybe he will hide . . .
> maybe he'll think,
> maybe he'll think,
> that someone has gone mad. (Szlengel 1977, 96)

This imagined death of a ghetto inhabitant turned dandy is conceived in terms of the defiant act of a provocateur who thrives on the extravagant superiority of his clothing. Balzac, who had an expert knowledge about dandyism, noted critically that "Dans la vie élégante, il n'existe plus de supériorité."[23] Later on, Baudelaire remarked on "the pleasure to surprise others" in his ruminations on dandyism.[24] In the case at hand, this has the effect of making an impression on the Nazi guard. A dandy knows his power to stun, and the poetic persona, in his gesture of challenging death, intends to capitalize on this effect by putting on a white bowtie and black tuxedo, an outfit that echoes Beau Brummel's dazzling signature piece attire. This insight into constructed superiority of appearance prompts the question of what, in Szlengel's creation of the Jewish dandy, resists and negates the perpetrators' approach to the Jew as a reified man without substance.

If it is the tragic itself that offers resistance here to the reduction of the poetic self to a sophisticated surface, nothing resonates more among the poem's paraphernalia than Szlengel's top hat. Through this single article of clothing, Szlengel calculates how best to impact his executioner and, perhaps, even force the latter to remember him. This is why the poetic persona's transformation, his nonchalant pose and formal evening attire, elaborate his staged suicide in terms of the dandy performative role. The greater his control over the show and its appearances, the closer he comes to achieving sheer aesthetic perfection and, ultimately, having an impact upon the blank-faced Nazi. The poet's stated intent is to inscribe surprise and confusion on that face.[25] Yet it is the seemingly unforeseen consequence of a situation so carefully arranged by the dandy that is curious. In doing his job, that is, by killing the strange apparition of the Jewish dandy, the gendarme fulfills—unbeknownst to him—his victim's unspoken wish. Here the poet reverses the Hegelian interdependence of master and slave. The master, turned into Sadeian executioner, labors for his slave's satisfaction, thus completing the Jewish dandy's project without any self-gratification of his own, that is, without his own dose of sadistic *jouissance*.

The unfulfilled sadistic joy of the dandy's executioner aside, "Top Hat" relates to Roland Barthes's discussion in *The Fashion System*, in which fashionable outfits are construed in terms of a transformational myth of one's exterior that contain a self which, according to the myth, desires a disguise.[26] For Szlengel, who, unlike Ginczanka, was confined in the ghetto, an obfuscation of his origin was pointless, except for, notably, his final gesture, in which his clothes transformed his identity. Otherwise, he was marked not only by his address, but also by a Star of David band and by his poor, emaciated appearance and ragged clothing. Therefore, to perform this symbolic act of identity transformation meant, for Szlengel, to wear, for the last time, what was, in prewar years, his own skin: an elegant tuxedo standing out in and against abject surroundings. It also meant to walk in the measured pace of a trochee and amphibrach, of the brisk beat of the master of a regular six-line stanza, in the rigorous armor of word repetition, which would overshadow the poem's final line.

This dandy transformed the event of showing his elegant costume into a provocative and risky "splendor of heroism" (Konody 1930, 134). Yet this transformation was not quite so simple in Szlengel's case. Jewish identity in the Warsaw Ghetto was part and parcel of the language of street visibility, of clothes and appearances, of the peculiar look of impoverishment, and of both exhaustion and resignation. This new poise, combined with a revived flamboyance and an elegant outfit, radically erases these undesirable symptoms and markers. All the same, the identity status becomes fluid and dependent on borrowing items from the material world through which one's identity can be reinvented. Here personal and intimate accessories represent the shifting markers of Jewish identity or, rather, markers of the shifting, fluid identity that can be invented and dressed up, seemingly at will.[27] Despite the context of a war wherein Jewishness had become dangerously accentuated and controlled by various regulations, it was once again possible to establish a fixed textual space in which Jewishness could be represented anew and against prevailing ideological notions.

Szlengel's use of the future perfect tense of reiterated verbs connotes the finality of the poet's performance and the scale of his obsessive desperation. In stark contrast to the reality of the Warsaw Ghetto, he imagines his death in terms of an elegant dream of nonexistence, projecting himself through the dandy's language of clothing, surfaces, and appearances. The space of the ghetto is obviously not conducive for the dandy, but Szlengel's self-construction reinvents his old self, that is, his prewar profession as a cabaret performer in Warsaw's famous cabarets. In fact, he continued to perform even in the ghetto, most frequently in the Café Sztuka (translated as "Art"). In this sense, his top hat, the glamorous *vesteme* fetishized in *The Blue Angel* as a signifier of the whole European modernist cabaret culture, recreates Szlengel's past professional incarnation. In addition, his poem directly recalls the lightest possible image of a jovial and debonair entertainer, that of Fred Astaire in his role with Ginger Rogers in the 1935 dance musical *Top Hat* directed by Mark Sandrich. There is evidence in the text that Szlengel, who in his poetry often made learned allusions to American cinema, had seen the movie and may have had it in mind while writing the poem. Besides the title, it is the line—"I am putting on a top hat"—from the song "Top Hat, White Tie and Tails," composed by Irving Berlin, that is quoted and ironically inverted by the poet. However, it should be mentioned that in his reach for a functional intertext and for the past, which, after all, was not so distant, Szlengel recalled the world not entirely care-free and elegant. In Astaire's performance of the song, there is a sudden change of joyful tone when the singer, abandoned by the chorus and with his smile erased, is surrounded by the ominous darkness.[28]

Laughter—in its cruel, vulgar, sarcastic, or liberating varieties—was not an infrequent presence in both ghetto and camp life. People were all too familiar with the therapeutic effect of folklore humor that spontaneously expressed emotions in the ghetto that ranged from irony and revenge to despair, and, yes, *jouissance*.[29] Mary Berg maintained persuasively that "It is laughter through tears, but it is laughter. This is our only weapon in the ghetto. . . . Humor is the only thing the Nazis cannot understand."[30] Shimon Huberband's collec-tion of ghetto jokes and puns ranges from laconic to detached, as in the follow-ing: "God forbid that the war last as long as the Jews are capable of enduring" (Roskies 1988, 401). Although I would not venture to argue that post-Holocaust comedies are made in remembrance of such Holocaust laughter, the spirit of Jewish wit, as collected by Huberband, is reflected in them.[31]

Entertainment—as the more formalized side of ghetto *jouissance* and often as a matter of business—was a sphere in which Szlengel's name appeared frequently. He was drawn to popular forms of amusement in the ghetto out of both a need for employment and a desire for artistic expression. Besides the top hat, he wore many other hats. As an actor, a lyric writer, a master of ceremonies, he ran what was described as a one-man show entitled "Żywy Dziennik" (Live Daily), an ephemeral program in Café Art. In all these incarnations, he practiced the art of detachment.[32] Although Szlengel, like every Jewish person during this period, lived under the constant threat of death, his poems are devoid of anxiety about the unknown: they express his freedom to die on his own terms. While Szlengel's fantasy of controlling his final moments describes a unique, singular death—that of a poet—it also describes the manner in which objects become quintessential survivors, albeit ones thoroughly lacking in triumph.[33] But it is the return of the pleasure principle to these lyrics, or rather the return of that peculiar combina-tion of vengeful enjoyment and agency-restoring voluntary death, that shifts this poet's fantasies to a different sphere. In doing so, the poet puts into practice the commonly shared belief that wit can soothe the effect of the real.

On Things Small and Round

The top hat is among the seemingly unique objects that, upon closer scru-tiny, belong to a distinct series of accessories (such as caps, hats, and berets) intended for the protection or beautification of the head. In addition to this functional similarity, these objects share formal and aesthetic similarities. The top hat is not, after all, so exceptional. What marginally exceptional nature it possesses derives only from the emphasis it places on the wearer's class distinction by virtue of its elegance. However, besides participating in this configuration, Szlengel's top hat poem also enters into a different series of objects. Along with the pill, the pot, the bullets, the German "Juno" cigarettes,[34] and other round things, it belongs to the chain of signification that symbolizes a radical change of fortune.

Szlengel does not refrain from amusing himself with the dramatic oscillation of the bad luck of the Nazi soldier, killed in action, and the fate of his top hat. As a poet who always displays a great deal of self-awareness in his writing, Szlengel weaves these episodes and their material texture together in order to express the guiding principle of his poetic universe: "Okrągło wszystko się toczy" (Everything goes round and round; literally: "Everything is rolling over roundly"; i.e., changing).[35] This geometric concept is built upon the iconography of the wheel of fortune and the understanding that the fates of both humans and objects are determined by pure chance, albeit devoid of a fatalistic outlook.

> Let the guard shoot
> as I hum,
> o, meine Kinder . . .
> let the
> shining top hat
> roll to the hard boots. . . . ("Top Hat"; Szlengel 1977, 97)

The movement of this single prop of death is premeditated and conditional, real yet never actualized within the frame of the poem. The unpredictability of this and all other small, rolling objects—frequent props in his mise-en-scène—constitutes the core signification of fate in Szlengel's poetry. This is always associated with the unpredictable roll of the dice/fortune and with the notion, deeply ingrained in Polish culture, of life as a game of chance, which one can win or lose in a wink. As Anna Wierzbicka observes, the Polish word for fate ("los") "evokes the image of a great lottery, where different people draw different tickets."[36] Furthermore, the same Polish word connotes a lottery ticket, which places the emphasis on the unpredictability rather than on the uncontrollability of life (Wierzbicka 1992, 75).

The concept of unpredictability can be employed for its cinematic effect. The macabre aesthetics of the rolling top hat anticipates a constellation of images in war and postwar cinema that advanced an absurdist notion of human destiny expressed through the chance movement of round and small objects.

For example, in *Citizen Kane*, released in 1941, the dying Kane loses his grip on a glass ball, which then drops and rolls; Kane's death delimits the suspense of this segment. Or think of the scene in Roman Polański's *The Pianist*, in which the protagonist Władysław Szpilman (Szlengel's colleague in the ghetto) drops a can of food. The camera follows the can as it rolls to a stop in front of the Nazi officer's boots. In a split second, Polański reverses this ominous sign to a happy coincidence, in that Szpilman is rescued in the following scene. In a less famous, but more conceptually interesting, scene from Krzysztof Kieślowski's *Przypadek* (Blind Chance), a rolling coin triggers three different linear scenarios according to which the protagonist's life could unfold. Although worlds apart, these images explore the accidental movement of objects and the link between this release of haphazard energy and the fear of death that triggered their release. They are united in the unpredictability of their motion, yet the ensuing randomness is delimited by death in each case.

If murder, as Thomas De Quincey and others believed, can be perceived and understood in terms of artistic, subliminal creation, then suicide, as imagined by Szlengel, becomes its ultimate performance, buttressed by the rigid and consistent form of the poem. Suicide became the only luxury he could afford (in real life, he died in the way he had desired so strongly to avoid).[37] Sublimation is, after all, most effective within a creative process. Even Lacan, otherwise so reluctant to grant the possibility of complete sublimation, has admitted as much. Furthermore, if we follow Slavoj Žižek's reading of Lacanian sublimation in *Looking Awry*, the process also implies a movement from biological forces to a linguistic one. Such a shift is of special relevance to the present discussion, concerned as it is with the linguistic force of poetry.

If Szlengel sublimates his death, should it matter where his bloodied body lies? It is nowhere, and yet is viscerally bound to the very shape of the poem. Szlengel's poem invokes neither corpse, nor any unsightly somatic fragments, the type of which preoccupied other poets as they envisioned their own death.[38] His bloody and abject body is concealed by both a tuxedo and the shining silk of his top hat, rolling directly toward the Nazi's boots. The image that draws Szlengel's performance to a close also neatly summarizes the strategy he employs in his elegantly designed death. At this point, the delicate accessory and hard leather would be in terrifying proximity. Thus, this cinematic effect serves to excise the head from representation, completing the poet's symbolic suicide: instead of his head, his top hat rolls over on the pavement. Once again, it is Szlengel's understanding of metonymy that negates the rigor mortis imagery and recedes it from representation. A staged encounter and chance, the provoked finality of death, and the moment of suspense caused by the rolling top hat: these are the conflicting rules of the game that Szlengel's poem lays down.

A Digression on Dignity in Death

Within the gruesome lexicon of the Holocaust's material world, the dandy's appearance creates a jarring contrast, entering its usual depiction of both the traumatic and the commonplace from somewhere outside the sphere of representation bounded by these two axes. Even someone aware of the existence of places of entertainment in the Warsaw Ghetto may be surprised by Szlengel's choice of image, asking why the poet would employ such a superfluous figure in a narration of his suicide. Solitary, singular, impeccably dressed, and, above all, in sharp contrast with his environment as a whole, the dandy both observes and is observed by his anonymous executioner, whose eye becomes the mirror whose presence the dandy relies upon. This scenario restores perfect dignity to the poet's death, reinforcing his own *jouissance* to such an extent that it entirely permeates the image. It is this *jouissance*, then, that enables him to overcome the communal, ugly, humiliating nature of the death prescribed for him.[39]

In his book on suicide, the writer and survivor Jean Amery launches a serious critique on the term *self-murder*, preferring instead the more neutral expression *voluntary death*. This latter word more adequately reflects his larger philosophy wherein suicide becomes a gesture of both self-liberation and self-realization.[40] Nonetheless, the matter is more complicated in terms of those who provoke or manipulate others into acting as executioners. In Szlengel's "Top Hat," despite the elegance with which he projects his interiority as something heavily (in)vested in exterior fashion, we must deal with the brutality of a suicide in which the trigger is pulled by another person. For this reason, I would rather treat this act as "self-murder," on the grounds that it gestures toward two opposite types of death: suicide and murder. Being both suicide and murder—and yet neither of them exclusively—"self-murder" falls between these two categories. As a violent removal of the self, it is complicated further by an element of violence directed toward the guard in forcing his hand.

Furthermore, Szlengel's authorial performance of suicide draws on two clashing sources: the ancient Stoics' quiet acceptance of a death imposed by society and the utter desperation of bare life wielded by an external sovereign power. The same type of despair that would force some concentration camp inmates to hurl themselves onto electrified fences could easily drive them to provoke the guards to kill them. The Nazi system of power, under which those crowded into ghettos and concentration camps took their own lives in order to escape being killed, allowed a type of suicidal exit that preserved dignity at all cost. Suicide proved stronger than the desire to continue an undignified life. The paradox of these solutions stems from the limitations imposed on the individual's will, where the only choice available to the inmate becomes the choice between one death and another.

The question of suicide always reminds us of Socrates, forced by the Athenian judges to end his own life by drinking hemlock. His conduct in the last moments of his life has become the prime example of the stoic philosophical approach to death. In *Phaedo*, Socrates faces death without fear, jokingly asking to sacrifice a cock to Asclepius. When the servant comes to Socrates to remind him about his approaching hour of death,[41] the philosopher continues to control his emotions and, in doing so, is praised by the servant.[42] Socrates, a condemned man who laughs before his own death, thus becomes both actor and spectator in the final act of his life. He is dying and yet, simultaneously, observing the process of his death. Devoid of self-pity, the philosopher is already detached from his life.

By and large, in hearing or reading of suicide, we struggle to accept or justify the decision on the part of the person who has committed suicide. In order to address the form of suicide that occurred during the Holocaust, however, the notion of this kind of death must be qualified differently. The Holocaust suicide often speaks of a compulsory decision to die by his or her own hand when death is both imminent and omnipresent, which, indeed, forces the decision. This will to die is often paired with an angry desire for ultimate liberation and, therefore, with a certain amount of courage. In this manner, the Holocaust suicide restores the individual's freedom and agency. In fact, it functions as the sole means whereby one can regain one's lost humanity. The voluntary death of Dr. Janusz Korczak is noteworthy in this respect because through this act he actually cemented his solidarity with children from the orphanages under his control.[43] A man of his social status could have survived the liquidation of the Warsaw Ghetto, especially given that the underground made attempts to rescue him. He was, however, determined not to abandon "his children," the ghetto orphans, and went with them to Treblinka. As a friend and co-organizer of cultural events in the orphanage on Śliska Street, Szlengel witnessed Korczak's march with the orphans and described it in his reportage-poem "Kartka z dziennika 'akcji'" (A Page from the Diary of "Action"). Within the Christian theological context, Korczak's gesture would qualify him to be a martyr. Outside this context, however, one sees in his decision a display of self-recognition and an awareness of his Jewish roots. In his action, the European history of *Bildung*, with which Korczak was so concerned in his own pedagogical writing and practice, came to a sharp conclusion. In giving up his educational mission and his belief in Jewish acculturation to Polish non-Jewish culture, Korczak turned his back on the century-old illusion of emancipation through transformation. If Korczak found another community, it was with his people and was formed through death.

The inhabitants of the ghettos had a great deal to say about the distinction between a death carried out with dignity and one lacking dignity in which the doomed knew how they would die. Suicide was paired with dignity in "Song for the Last," whose anonymous author lamented that the condemned were weaker than moths, in that the latter were at least capable of throwing themselves into the flames (Roskies 1988, 497). Chaim Kaplan, a Hebrew educator who managed to smuggle his memorable diary to the "other side" before he perished in Treblinka, voiced a similar outrage while observing the Gęsia Street cemetery. He saw "Mostly naked corpses . . . removed from the wagons, without even a paper loincloth to cover their private parts."[44] Shocked by the sight, he felt that "simple human dignity had been insulted, the dignity of man" (Roskies 1988, 497). Kaplan's approach is remarkable in that it reveals his high understanding of funerary respectability. Finally, one should also listen to what Borowski says about death in Auschwitz: "communal death, disgusting and ugly. . . . The same gas chamber, only an even more hideous, more terrible death. . . ."[45] In the death that awaited inmates, humiliation was undeniable. For those living in the state of bare life, bare death was inevitable unless they chose suicide. Therefore Auschwitz, Giorgio Agamben notes, "marks the end and the ruin of every ethics of dignity and conformity to a norm."[46] This revision, wherein dignity is predicated upon un-dignity, informs his understanding of a new post-Holocaust ethics.

In this discussion, it is worthy to recall the comments made by the survivor and the literary scholar Michał Głowiński about suicide and dignity. Recalling his grandfather's suicide, he writes in his valuable memoir:

> One often hears about a "dignified" death in connection to the genocide, one often hears the opinions that are unwise and frivolous. Everybody who died sentenced by criminals, died with dignity. And one has to say this even if one would find that Brutus in the Shakespearean *Julius Cesar* is right when just before taking his life with his hand he says: "Our enemies have beat us to the pit: / It is more worthy to leap in ourselves / Than tarry till they push us." There were only different styles of dying. The styles of victims who allowed themselves to be led to gas chambers without protestations and the styles of those who preferred to die in action. Some, like the ghetto insurrectionists, resisted; others committed suicide. A man as old as my grandfather could only choose suicide.[47]

For Głowiński, suicide is triggered by a lack of choice, which sounds like a classic definition of a tragic position. This puts him at odds with Amery, who glorifies voluntary death as a liberating act. Głowiński's is a totalizing claim, according to which every unjust death is dignified. This assertion, however, is borne out neither by the testimonies I have mentioned above nor by accounts pleading for dignity in death. Arguably, the most controversial in Głowiński's ruminations on the subject is his use of the word *style* in reference to death. Voluntary death, as espoused by Głowiński, is too irrelevant a testimony, if relegated to the realm of mere style. The reality of genocide was radically in-commensurable with that of aesthetics. The bare life seldom afforded its sub-jects the liberty to stage an action of any sort, including that of a suicidal death, much less the opportunity to reflect on death in aesthetic terms. If one's end was constructed in a stylized fashion, it happened in the realm of the symbolic, as we see in Szlengel's lyrics.

Yet another option of exercising dignity existed for those who rebelled. In Szlengel's "Counterattack II," his detachment signaled in the bitter phrase "Bunt mięsa, / BUNT MIĘSA, / ŚPIEW MIĘSA!" (The revolt of the fodder, / THE REVOLT OF THE FODDER, / THE SONG OF THE FODDER!) (Szlengel 1977, 139), shows that the Warsaw Ghetto insurrectionists, reduced to meat, to mere mat-ter, were shockingly capable of revolt. The poet, aware of the extent to which the Nazis utterly reified his people,[48] indicated how the dignity regained through armed resistance and revenge undermined the reifying forces: death in battle became another alternative for restoring agency to human subjects. But this was an option available for just a few—and certainly not for the *Musel-mann*, who reached the point beyond voluntary death.

Texts

"Top Hat"

I'll put on a top hat,
a tuxedo I'll put on—
a tie with a stripe . . .
I'll put on a top hat,
a tuxedo I'll put on,
I'll walk up to the sentry.

The gendarme will stagger
the gendarme will dread,
maybe he will hide . . .
maybe he'll think
maybe he'll think
that someone has gone mad.

I'll put on a top hat,
and without a band
in my head an orchestra
in my head a fantasy
and in my heart a zeal
as if it were for the New Year.

I'll put on a top hat
and I'll make it to the sentry
if he wants he can shoot,
I'll put on a top hat
and I'll put on a tuxedo
so that . . . they can see . . .

So that they can see . . .
so that they can know . . .
the cads, the simpletons
that a Jew isn't only
a ragamuffin with a band,
a stake from a picket fence.

Such fantasy,
such zeal
so I took this fancy
and look in surprise,
I'm walking in a tuxedo
with a white bowtie . . .

Let the guard shoot
as I hum,
o, meine Kinder . . .
let the
shining top hat
roll to the hard boots . . .

"CYLINDER"

Włożę cylinder,
smoking założę—
krawat z rozmachem . . .
włożę cylinder,
smoking założę,
pójdę na wachę.

żandarm zdębieje,
żandarm się zlęknie,
może się schowa . . .
może pomyśli,
może pomyśli,
że ktoś zwariował.

Włożę cylinder,
i bez opaski,
we łbie orkiestra,
we łbie fantazja,
w sercu ochota
jak na sylwestra.

Włożę cylinder,
dojdę do wachy,
jak chce, niech strzeli,
włożę cylinder
i włożę smoking,
żeby . . . widzieli . . .

żeby widzieli . . .
żeby wiedzieli,
dranie półgłówki,
że żyd nie tylko
łapciuch w opasce,
brudas z placówki.

Taka fantazja,
taka ochota,
tak mi się chciało,
patrzcie zdziwieni,
chodzę w smokingu
i z muszką białą . . .

Niech żandarm strzeli,
kiedy zanucę,
o, meine Kinder . . .
niech się potoczy
pod twarde buty
lśniący cylinder . . .

CHAPTER TWO

The Material Letter *J*

... because the Jew, you know, what does he have that belongs to
him, that isn't lent, borrowed, never given back ...

—Paul Celan

THE SEMANTIC OF PROPERTY denotes both a character feature and material
goods. In either case, property is something that belongs to and defines a subject or an object. In close relationship to it is propriety, which defines a more
specific character trait such as decency as well as ownership, and generally
refers to the human world. Thus, the meanings of property and propriety overlap when one considers the relationship between and attribute of a human
subject and ownership. The Holocaust saw an extreme manner of intermingling of the terms. Never before had a more simplified relationship existed
between material goods and their owners, between property and its proprietor.
Within the sphere of representation, this interrelationship, reduced to an
equation, erased and replaced the neo-Platonic practice of subjectivity projected onto objects in highly individualized, almost infinite manners.

Identity, as a perennial and universal problem, is often revised and constructed
anew by political and scientific discourses. If one considers the discourse according to a more particular practice, that of Jewish identity, one observes its historical trajectory from essentialism through its erasure in the name of Difference to
the reemergence of the moderate Essential Design in recent years. Historically
speaking, narratives about identity and material culture attained epic dimensions in such disciplines as cultural anthropology and archeology. An interpretation of material objects within disciplines of anthropology, ethnography, and
archeology is reevaluated in a manner parallel to understanding local contexts.
Usually, the interdependence between an object and its context (be it national,
ethnic, cultural, historical, or economic) has a circular character. A material object is used to define a cultural context and identity and, in turn, such an object
is defined through a meaning present and is retrieved from its context.[1] I would
like to pick up one minor, yet telling, thread from the rich history of this interrelationship as linked to the infamous German archeologist Gustaf Kosinna

(1858–1931), who extracted his conception of the relationship between ethnicity, nationality, and material objects from a reading of Herder's and Fichte's philosophies. *Volk*—as the principle that organized this discourse—led Kosinna to believe that the Aryan and early German cultures were superior because they were marked by a high level of cultural productivity.[2] Since he overvalued their cultural productivity, he consequently and with relative ease relegated non-Aryan cultures to an inferior position.

Another step that paved the way to the premises of genocide was taken in the discourse of German jurists, who interpreted the concept of sovereign power and its interdependence within the state of exception. Carl Schmitt opened his *Political Theology* with the well-known definition of authoritarian power as one that decides on the state of exception as indispensable to society.[3] The most palpable results of these politico-philosophical notions were the introduction of the state of exception and, prompted by Hitler's ascent to power, the Nuremberg Laws. While the latter can be viewed as a phase in the process of essentialization of race, the Laws also produced a clear racial distinction between the German-Aryan citizen and the German-Jewish citizen. Furthermore, considering German Jews only "nationals" and proclaiming that they therefore had no political rights, the Nuremberg Laws excluded Jews from the society of the Third Reich.[4] With the change of this legal status, the German-Jewish rights of ownership were abolished in praxis, although no law legalized the dispossession of this part of the Jewish-German population.

The perception of these people as culturally and racially inferior, excluded from the protection of law and, simultaneously, subjugated to law in matters of death and punishment quickly led to further racist distortions. Over the course of history, Jewishness was characterized in various ways, most often through engagement of the categories of religious faith and ethnicity. In the 1930s and 1940s, the biologically construed form of Jewish identity was projected—no matter how shifting this identity proved to be—on everybody who fit the precisely defined racial criteria and, by extension, on the world of their material possessions. In this way, property and propriety became one.

In the light of these legal, cultural, economic, and political processes, which were applied in various ways in the territories occupied by Germany during World War II, we will now consider the following object-driven poem. It is an important representation of how individual property and propriety were negotiated at that time.

> Non omnis moriar—my proud estate,
> Meadows of my tablecloths, fortresses of indomitable wardrobes,
> Spacious sheets, precious bedding
> And dresses, light dresses will be left after me.

I did not leave any heir here,
So let your hand ferret out the J things,
Chominowa, of Lwów, brave wife of a snitch,
Sly informer, mother of Volksdeutch.
Let them serve you and yours, why should they serve strangers.
My dear ones—not a lute, not an empty name.
I remember you, and you, when the Schupo were coming,
You also remembered me. Recalled also me.
Let my friends sit down with a goblet
And toast my funeral and their riches:
Kilims and tapestries, serving dishes, candlesticks—
Let them drink the night through, and at first light's dawning
Let them search for precious stones and gold
In couches, mattresses, comforters and carpets.
O, how they will work, like a house on fire,
Skeins of horsehair and sea grass,
Clouds from torn pillows and feather beds apart
Will cling to their hands, will change both hands into wings;
My blood will glue the oukum with fresh down
And will suddenly transform the winged to angels.[5]

The undeservedly little-known author of the poem, which entered the public domain through a single copy that emerged under mysterious circumstances, was Zuzanna Polina Gincburg, a young Polish-Jewish woman poet, who published under the pen name Zuzanna Ginczanka. In broad strokes, the brief trajectory of the poet's life began in Kiev, where she was born in 1917. The same year, the Gincburg family left Kiev for Równe in then Polish Volynia; it was in Równe that the future poet received a high-school education and wrote her first poetry in her chosen Polish language;[6] after graduation, she studied at Warsaw University. Ginczanka participated in the vibrant literary life of Warsaw, belonging to Witold Gombrowicz's circle of the Ziemiańska Café and quickly establishing her reputation as a poet. In 1936, she published her first and only volume of poetry, *O centaurach* (About Centaurs). Before the war, her poetry ranged from satirical and antifascist verses to sensuous expressions of her femininity. Her lyrical voice, which was just coming into its own during the prewar years, was overshadowed almost completely by her experience of the war.

Ginczanka's modest wartime output defies scholarship's division into the concentration camp and ghetto literature: the poet was never confined to either of these places. During the war, she went from Warsaw to Równe, only to wind up seeking shelter again, this time in Soviet-occupied Lwów, where she married an art historian, Michał Weinzieher, although she had a relationship with an artist named Janusz Woźniakowski. Hitler's invasion of the Soviet Union and its annexed Polish territory, including Lwów, changed the status of the Jewish population. For Ginczanka, the invasion marked a turning point in her biographical experience: from that moment on, she could never openly identify herself as Jewish and decided to live "on the surface" as a Polish gentile. In Lwów, she almost perished because of a neighbor's denouncement. Subsequently, helped by Woźniakowski and her friend Maria Güntner, she moved to Kraków, where she stayed with Weinzieher. He and Woźniakowski were arrested and murdered first. Ginczanka's arrest by the Gestapo had an additional tragic dimension: she was imprisoned for her connection to the underground communist movement, not for her Jewish origins.[7]

Ginczanka's poems most strikingly attest to the degree to which her life became a precarious exercise in survival. In one untitled poem, she refers to the event that nearly cost her her life when she was denounced to the *Schutzpolizei* by her neighbor Chominowa and Chominowa's son, a Nazi collaborator, both mentioned in the text. Ginczanka escaped because her roommate, a waiter, led her out through the building's other exit.[8] The manuscript survived and is now preserved in a protective folder in one of Warsaw's archives, contained but secure.[9] Consigned to this sadly collective and archival existence, it can only remotely hark back to its former proximity to the author's hand and, thus, to its former *precarium* status. Perceived as an object, the poem first reveals a tension between its ontological and epistemological nature. Its very existence, as both a textual Holocaust relic/trace and an archived poetic text capable of bearing witness, engages the dual status of survival and death characteristic of *precarium*.

After the war, this particle of Ginczanka's poetic legacy resurfaced in the hands of Lusia Stauber, the author's childhood friend, who submitted it for publication. Years later, Stauber could not recall how she came to possess this shred of a manuscript, wrinkled and written in pencil.[10] It seems likely that the circumstances surrounding both its writing and discovery will remain a matter of conjecture for the foreseeable future. Furthermore, the exact date of one of Ginczanka's last works, considered by the poet Anna Kamieńska to be one of the most beautiful Polish poems,[11] remains speculative. Contrary to the wartime custom, cultivated by some poets, of providing precise dates and even hours of composition, the manuscript indicates only that it was written in 1942. Thus the probabilistic terms *approximately* or *circa* frame the work's origins, predetermining its auratic quality and interpretative ambiguities. This absence of a more specific data contributes an additional layer of meaning to the lyric: aside from the drastic thematic core built around the projected death of its author and subsequent looting of her home, it can be read as an itinerant and lacunary Holocaust text.

Furthermore, the text bears no title, not a common practice for the poet. As a matter of fact, this is the only untitled lyric in her oeuvre. The necessity of identification compels critics, including myself, to employ the Horatian "Non omnis moriar" or "Testament mój" (literally "My Last Will"), a title borrowed from a canonical lyric by the Romantic poet Juliusz Słowacki.[12] Both titles identify and introduce the poem in a different manner through engagement with two different intertexts. Was it the poet's deliberate decision to engage an artistic interplay between the absence of the title and the text? Or was the lack of a title the inadvertent effect of an unfinished job?

It is my contention that Ginczanka's is an unfinished text, which by no means makes its artistic quality inferior.[13] One of its moments of incompletion is deliberate and is directly related to the poem's *precarium*. The sixth line of "My Last Will" contains a striking ellipsis inserted in the middle of a bitter imperative sentence—"Let then your hand ferret out the *J* things." The adjective "żydowskie,"[14] which specifies the provenance of the poet's possessions and, indirectly, her identity, is not spelled out in its entirety, but marked only with its initial letter *J* (ż). Although, elsewhere, Ginczanka thrives on dashes and, in general, uses rather idiosyncratic punctuation, she never employs ellipsis. The elliptical void in "My Last Will" interrupts the flow of the cadence and puzzles the reader. The act of elliptical a(void)ance generates a new, more open meaning and complicates the existing meaning. What under normal circumstances would be a pedantic preoccupation with this single letter, the solitary *J* in this case positions that letter on a thin line between life and death and aligns philology with a search for the poetic voice's identity. The deletion of the word *Jewish*, motivated by Ginczanka's self-preservation instinct hardened under the pressures of reality, is a particularly disturbing example of a self-imposed textual censorship. Had it been included in its entirety, this adjective could have betrayed the author's identity and granted a strong suicidal undercurrent.[15] Thus the poet seemed to ask, even command, the reader: "Read my poem, but do not decipher everything."

In the manuscript, this strategy of masking is visible on the poem's surface. I am puzzled, however, by the complexity of this denial: leaving the initial letter *J* undeleted is a gesture of both masking and unmasking and, even, unmasking the masked. It is as though Ginczanka wanted to indicate exactly the word she omitted.[16] The letter *J* stands out against the blank space, rendering the unpenned rest of the word all the more noticeable in its absentia. Since it is obvious which word matches the grapheme and the verse's lines, the attempt to mask the authorial identity cannot help but reveal its author. The erasure betrays the erasing hand. Therefore, the message hidden behind the letter *J* could be formulated otherwise: "Read and decipher this palimpsest, because its incompleteness demands completion."[17]

The poem's visceral quality derives also from the concrete beginnings of its pre-history. Beside a clearly justified form of self-censorship, the poet was not under the usual restrictions, which limited those who lived in ghettos.[18] Nonetheless, the Aryan side was also under strict Nazi control, and one had to be cautious and wary even, or, as her story indicates, especially of immediate neighbors. Those who lived there "na fałszywych papierach" (on false IDs) had to exercise utmost control over their actions and visibility, often to the point of modifying their physical appearances. In this situation, Ginczanka's decision to identify the ones who denounced her contradicts her desire to suppress her own Jewishness. As such, it indicates her threatened status. "Abandoned by the law," to use Giorgio Agamben's phrase, Ginczanka reveals an unusually strong, almost compulsive desire to accuse those who betrayed her. Seeking more than mere caution, she enforces the *letter of the moral law*, which is fused with her irresistible desire for vengeance and justice. Precisely on this ethical level, her determination to expose the Chomins takes on an undertone similar to the one found in the Oyneg Shabes archives. Here we find a systematic authorial condemnation for the depraved behavior they saw in the population at large. The incriminating message of Ginczanka's poem affected the precarious state of the manuscript, becoming a two-edged sword, since it directly implicated the poet.

Could we go, then, so far as to speculate that Ginczanka was tempted to conceive of the poem as a self-marking sign and self-denouncing *letter*?[19] It would not be difficult to corroborate its self-denouncing strategy on the basis of her identification of the perpetrators as those who sent Schutzpolizei to arrest her, as well as her decision to leave the letter *J* undeleted. Since a critical part of the lyric's semantic content rests on Ginczanka's Jewish identity, this single letter, which makes her ethnic identity *literal*, oscillates ambiguously between self-betrayal and self-preservation in both their poetic and real varieties.[20]

Throughout history, Jewish people have been characterized in many different ways and Jewishness as a life-threatening factor and a stigma was imposed on them. Long before World War II, Ginczanka confessed to her friend Maria Brandysowa that "She felt like a black" (Araszkiewicz 2001, 45) and was aware that her Semitic facial features were a marker which identified her externally as Jewish. This sophisticated and poised woman-poet felt that her features drew too much attention to her and labeled her according to the widespread stereotype of a very elegant Jewish woman.[21] Based on our knowledge of her, Ginczanka did not evade her identity before the war, although she did not identify with religious Judaism. As a poet, though, she wrote only in the Polish language; therefore, her inner sense of identity could have been bivalent. The Nazi occupation forced her to deny her Jewishness and live under a false identity on the so-called Aryan side of various Polish cities, with every change of address imposing a new strategy of survival and identification with her ascribed role of a Polish Catholic woman. The unwritten stipulation, that Ginczanka had to perform a constant disavowal of her Jewish identity in order to avoid arousing suspicion, carried over into the lyric itself.[22]

Due to the poetic word's concretely "material" quality, achieved in "My Last Will" through the presence of objects and the semantic burden of the letter *J*, the very letter attains a special material-like status. The materiality of this letter conjoins both the symbolic and the real. As such, it is a type of materiality which is without matter.[23] Contemporary linguistics rejects Jacques Lacan's conceptualization of the letter as material because the psychoanalyst understands letters as more than just (graphic) representations of sounds.[24] Lacan's concept of the letter as a physical phenomenon rooted in matter might be grounded in his intellectual affiliation with surrealism—a movement that experimented with the material and visual status of letters.[25] Yet the materiality of the letter without matter takes on utopian overtones in "My Last Will" due to the fact that it cannot be fully attained, but only approximated. Also, in my understanding of the letter *J*, I have to take into consideration the working of denial: the more the *J* repeats itself as a primary signifier of identity in Ginczanka's life, the more she insists on its renunciation. Thus, the *J* becomes poignant largely because it both negates and, simultaneously, reinforces her identity. The reverse disavowal is also true: the more she tries to deny her identity, the more insistent its awareness becomes. Thus, if there is a Jewess in this text, her fractured, elliptical presence is sanctioned not only by the alphabet.

A Woman as a Looted Dwelling

La femme est demeure pour elle-même.

—Anne Jouranville

Like many others using false identity papers, Ginczanka paid a steep price for her survival—the price of mounting depression. Afraid of leaving her apartment except at night because her attractive, yet marked, appearance might catch the attention of the police, she would stay inside, smoking cigarettes incessantly. As one of her visitors remembered, her rented room was in disarray, and scattered sheets of paper and loose cosmetic powder covered her furniture, creating the image of a distressed and melancholic person (Kiec 1994, 160). In lyrics written before "My Last Will," her authorial voice expressed, in sublimated form, the conflicting but delicately balanced desire to live and to succumb to her melancholic death-drive. Her precarious and traumatic existence in hiding is intensified in her "Last Will," one of her last surviving poems and one that brings her life to a symbolic conclusion.

Although Ginczanka's "Last Will" evidences certain similarities with other poetic texts *of* the Holocaust, it more explicitly articulates the physical potential of the word as it expresses the hazardous connection between the violated self and the objectual dynamic of the *Endlösung* (Final Solution). Here, I focus primarily on the representational dimension of Ginczanka's poetic testament.[26] Since objects figure so prominently in this poem, the reader may be inclined to a certain historical curiosity about their ultimate disposition. The poet's biographer offers some insight into the dynamics between the poem's context and its represented reality. According to Kiec, after fleeing from Warsaw to her hometown Równe, Ginczanka stayed with her grandmother, Klara Sandberg, the poet's only close relative remaining in Poland. Perhaps, in a moment of dark premonition, Sandberg outfitted her talented and sensitive granddaughter with various practical household items, including bedding, silverware, and china—the paraphernalia typically owned by a well-to-do bourgeois family.[27] Probably, she hoped that by so providing for her granddaughter she would ensure her survival on the Aryan side. This mournful dowry seems to be the prototype of the objects that make their appearance in "My Last Will," amid the chaos of the poet's violated microcosm. Like many Holocaust objects that outlived their owners, these items undoubtedly circulated after the poet's arrest, having changed hands frequently. One can imagine that, perhaps, some of them might still exist and even be in use, having been termed *rzeczy pożydowskie* (post-Jewish things) that, along with *poniemieckie* (post-German) things, indicate the provenance of the last war's material legacy.[28]

The looting of Jewish property and murder motivated by greed are often described in the most matter-of-fact way in Holocaust testimonies and fiction.[29] Ginczanka's text differs radically from the majority of such accounts; in its dramatic mediation and representation of reality, it adopts an intimate perspective that is noticeably devoid of self-pity. The poet speaks of her own blood and clothes, of her violated selfhood and her formerly intimate space, the latter of which has become the scene of murder. Both life and property would be taken directly and violently from the poet. Ginczanka's "proud estate" can be associated with favorite tropes in feminist criticism wherein the woman and her body are viewed in terms of the home. In this sense, Anne Jouranville is right: a woman represents a bodily possession in her own eyes, and her claim of ownership does not need to be proven.[30]

In such an extreme situation, the notion of the home changes, and the very idea of household equipment undergoes a transformation as well. Under normal circumstances, a home indicates the safety and privacy provided by its protective walls and proverbial roof. The idea of home as shelter from both enemies and the elements prevails over the notion of the abode as defined according to its contents, furnishing, or even the space of the everyday.[31] Ginczanka's poem radically revises this view. Her room is no longer a safe haven, but a hostile environment in which the poet is trapped. Likewise, the objects that fill this room do not help her survive, but actually expose her to peril because of the petty greed they engender. In a scenario of the simplified war economy of exchange, material possessions, once the concrete expression of an ephemeral self, become currency and serve to buy bread or to save a life. In Ginczanka's case, however, rather than reaffirming survival, the poet's assets contribute to her symbolic demise: the order of Jewish Otherness overlaps the order of the poet's material possessions as the other; this twofold logic justifies the act of looting—from the vantage point of the looters.[32]

For Ginczanka, her proud home is subjected to brutal dispossession. Such an image leaves nothing abstract or remote. In fact, in this context, the phrase *poetic vision* fails to fully encompass the lyric's semantics. The material and bodily substance of Ginczanka's text, enhanced by her vivid enumeration of objects, rapidly becomes so intense that the reader can feel it almost tangibly. "My Last Will" emphasizes its matter-less material world and, in doing so, substantiates the aesthetics of horror. The direct representation of the plundered domestic realm increases the poetic word's physicality: every object, from the perverted intimacy of the bed sheets to the poet's implied corpse, serves to reinforce the visceral mediacy of the word.

The offering of the body and the blood begs a reference to the semantics of the Shoah. Doctrinal purity aside, the blood, the body's essence, spilled and mixed with feathers, could bring also to mind another religious offering: the consubstantiation of bread and wine in the Eucharist. So visualized, the concept strikes us as foreign to the Jewish subject of the poem. And yet it is not. Ginczanka's entire education, her readings, and her circle of friends informed her as an assimilated person. This identity is reflected in her poetry, which indicates how eclectic her cultural background was. In fact, one could argue that in this respect her avoidance of references to the Jewish tradition and her cultural eclecticism are reminiscent of the approach employed by the most prominent Polish-Jewish poets of that era, most notably, Bolesław Leśmian and such members of the Skamander group as Julian Tuwim and Antoni Słonimski.[33]

As a counterpoint to the predators' ironically treated transfiguration, the self's prophesied nonexistence acquires a serious and even tragic tone. Beyond the theological implications of the rites of death that Ginczanka prescribes for herself, another equally daring aspect of this symbolism reverses the reading of the bloodshed's theological meaning. The blood, as essence of the bodily self, is spilled and mixed with the feathers scattered about. This brutalization of human material otherness connects the imagery of the poem with the iconography of the pogrom. The feathers scattered around the scene are indispensable props in photographic and other reports from the sites of pogroms; also, during the liquidation of the Warsaw Ghetto, its streets were covered with feathers. The poet draws on this pictorial tradition in her gruesome, sensual visualization of feathers mixed with blood, of the stark contrast between the red blood and white feathers as well as the intermingled red and white of the murderers' hands.

Through the lens of one of the most concrete poems written on the horror of death, the poet envisions her end as a murder committed in her own bedroom. The thirst for blood and spoils that her neighbors (whom she addresses sarcastically as her "dear ones") display make her solitude and vulnerability all the more tragic.[34] "My Last Will's" most ghastly aspect comes from the way it implies the looters' rapacious gaze at the risk of identifying with it, thereby augmenting the actual value of the poet's possessions. Clearly, in the poet's treatment, the plunderers' objectual desire transports them into a fantasy world. While they would celebrate their new trophies amid the crime scene, a parody of transfiguration would take place to transform the brutes into winged, "angelic" creatures.

The perpetrators' hands render the moment of ironic transfiguration tangible.[35] In this way, hands function both as search instruments and, smeared with blood, as tools of murder. In either role, they demonstrate a cruel dexterity and imply a callous physical contact with the victim's body and her material possessions. As is often the case in the Holocaust experience, Midas' touch and his uninhibited material desire prevail over Anteus' life-restoring touch. In "My Last Will," the derogatory semantics of touch also encompass the careless ease with which the looters destroy objects in their search for more precious, hidden spoils. The demolition of furniture and bedding implies two conflicting objectual approaches: the sarcastic knowing gaze of the poet and her fumbling hands in opposition to the sharp gaze of her neighbors and their destructive hands that perform a hasty search for valuables.

As a recurring trope in Holocaust literature, touch is inextricably bound up with narratives of human–objectual relation. Holocaust literature, to be sure, recuperates and violates both objects and the senses. That of touch embraces a whole range of negative emotions: threat, violation, and pain. The firmly established hierarchy of the senses and their epistemological aptness is reordered in the literature of the Holocaust; here, touch often is elevated to the master sense, distorting traditional Western ocularcentrism.[36] In doing so, it challenges us to reconsider this humanistic discourse in this particular light.

Directly related to the sense of touch is the Nazi practice of searching orifices of the body for precious valuables, evidenced in numerous literary and historical sources. The formation of the Sonderkommando was for the purpose of having a special unit to manage the processing of dead bodies and the retrieval of gold from their orifices. The Nazis believed that Jewish gold—for which the Jewish body served as mere packaging—would resolve economic problems on many levels. When Emanuel Ringelblum writes about searches, he has in mind slightly different types of searches; he means those of a political nature and those motivated by material greed, which were performed on living human beings: "The frequent and thorough searches that were actually carried out were aimed at something altogether different: finding foreign currency, gold, diamonds, valuables, merchandise and the like. Such searches have been going on during the entire three and a half years of war and continue to this day" (Ringelblum 1988, 471). Numerous Holocaust diaries also describe looting disguised as inspections. The search that one Polish-Jewish family experienced when two Gestapo men raided their apartment one autumn night in 1940 serves as a case in point. One of them "grabs a tiny little pillow stuffed with rugs, old stockings and various old clouts. Delighted to have ostensibly found this cleverly hidden treasure, he briskly and nervously pulls off the pillowcase with a murderous gaze and throws out the old rugs in an uncontrollable rage."[37] In this case, the Gestapo officer's objectual pleasure-seeking search turns out to be anticlimactic. This episode, like countless similar instances that occurred inside and outside the closed spheres of ghettos, refers to the type of *Dienlichkeit* that is redefined by the Holocaust's economy of looting and its attendant (il)logic of suspicion. According to this strategy, useful objects such as couches and pillows, insoles of boots, and cloths double as relatively worthless (by comparison with their contents) spaces in which to conceal jewelry or money. The Nazis projected a stereotypical linkage between Jewishness and material wealth onto nearly every Jew. This approach was informally acknowledged, and it was assumed that people who had some valuables would hide them, especially once they had been confined. Edgar Allan Poe's trick of the purloined letter would not work under those circumstances.

The supposedly misleading idea of keeping precious items inside inconspicuous containers or bodily orifices was based on a double denial. The victims were convinced that their oppressors did not know about their secrets, while the oppressors assumed that the victims did not know that they knew everything about their deception. Lacan, intrigued by this mechanism of deception, gave it an ancient Greek name of *agalma* (glory, ornament, treasure). For him, it represented a turning point in his early rethinking of the object of desire.[38] In his seminar of 1960–1961, he first conceived of the object of desire as the *objet petit a*. Then came a turning point, in which Lacan reversed the dynamics of the *objet petit a*: from being directed to the object of desire, he saw it as the very cause of desire, the object-cause of desire. He pointed out that one seeks the object of desire in the other in much the same manner as the ancient Greeks, who sought ornate figurines of gods within ordinary boxes. It would be difficult to find "ordinary boxes" in Plato's *Symposium*, where *to agalma, to agalmatos* refer not to them, but to statues of Silenus. In the *Symposium*, Alcibiades compares Socrates to the busts of ugly Silenus, "which are set up in the statuaries' shops, holding pipes and flutes in their mouths; and they are made to open in the middle, and have images of gods inside them."[39] Perceived as valuable objects, these ornamental artifacts, often statuettes of gods hidden within seemingly worthless containers, signified offerings pleasing to the gods. Insignificant containers, therefore, protected ornate figurines very much like the ugly and unkempt Socrates who was, nonetheless, a fount of wisdom. Inspired by the Lacanian concept of *agalma*, I wish to facilitate the argument that for the Nazis—or Ginczanka's neighbors for that matter—gold in pillows or uteruses triggered a special type of objectual desire focused on the core matter that demanded separation and retrieval from its surrounding waste matter.

Instances of agalmatic desire from both modern and ancient periods address the question of *jouissance*: a joyful, satisfying finale granted to the finder. However, in Ginczanka's inverted vocabulary, the moment of rejoicing does not belong to her potential killers. Instead, *jouissance* infuses the poet's diminishing presence. With her beautiful "light dresses," which engender her wardrobe while taking on "ghostly existence,"[40] Ginczanka endows her neighbors with something else: the gift of permanent guilt. Giving her personal belongings and, by extension, the fragmented self imprinted in her dresses to her neighbor/murderers, the poet secures an uncanny victory. This victory, permeated by vengeance, triggers yet another passing moment of *jouissance*: the remembrance of her actual selfhood that may linger for some time, stigmatized by murder, in her dresses and bedding, since these items were in such proximity to her body as to, perhaps, impart its faint scent.

Perceived as objects of cult, *agalmata* represent the polar opposite of elaborately ornamented caskets such as reliquaries, which contain teeth, bones, or other bodily relics of saints. Occasionally of dubious provenance and quite disappointing to nonbelievers, these relics participate in an intricate game of displaying and protecting. This, then, sets them apart from *agalmata*, which are constituted by their being entirely hidden and sheltered. My question here is whether the agalmatic desire, in the historic circumstances of death camps, so clearly devoid of religious connotations, also lacks a sexual drive. Employing a well-worn Freudian symbol, one could claim that the penetration of small, dark enclosed spaces by the perpetrators reinforces Lacan's formulation of the agalmatic nature of the object of desire. The desire for material possessions can represent the force as irresistible as the libidinal drive. Furthermore, greed and libido can be interchangeable.[41] But for the Holocaust scholar, contemplating the agalmatic model as a method of representing objectual needs and desires, an application by analogy with psychoanalytic theories would unnecessarily homogenize the discourse. While master–slave dialectics can possess an erotic undercurrent, the presence of objectual desires within this relationship requires a more nuanced hermeneutic approach and an acknowledgment that nonerotic types of agalmatic desire are not only possible, but can, indeed, prevail.[42] The distinction between an objectual Lacanian drive and its entirely sexual Freudian counterpart should be introduced in any reexamination of the material object world of the Holocaust. Only then can desired objects achieve agency of their own and be desired on the basis of their own materiality and value, instead of as a mere substitute for another aim.

On Legacy, Ironically

> . . . "Marching girls, Jewish,
> Expressed their only joy, of vengeance."
>
> —Czesław Miłosz

Ginczanka designs the end of her life as both a given and a gift. By listing the plethora of objects to be given and taken, she sarcastically frames the entire scene of exchange. She then further complicates the scenario by bequeathing what would be taken from her under any circumstances, proffering objects that are already the de facto (if not legal) property of the Generalgouvernement. As described in the introduction and reiterated here, the legal situation greatly facilitated the circulation of Jewish possessions, not just of the real estate but also of smaller scale objects, to which the poem attests. In giving her property to her persecutor and, narratively, to the addressee of the poem, Ginczanka adds, by means of this evidence, a prosecutorial value to her condemnation, thereby enhancing the poem's historical relevance. On the other hand, captured in the related acts of both looting and looking for hidden treasures, the hangmen demonstrate a debased materialistic outlook, a version of agalmatic want that goes hand-in-hand with their callous and greedy nature. In this sense, Ginczanka's reluctance to demonize them is consistent with her contempt for them: they are representatives of the mob.

Given that Ginczanka writes during a time of an ongoing violation of Jewish ownership, her act of giving becomes even more patently impossible. She does not, therefore, offer these gifts with the expectation of any future exchange—an action that, according to Derrida's idealistic notion of giving, would undermine her gift.[43] Her earthly possessions are in the flux of ontological transit: they are simultaneously bequeathed and destroyed; they are listed, but their concreteness is undermined by an employment of hyperbole; they are given, even while they are being looted. Although she defines her possessions as "Jewish things," she does not explain exactly why her light dresses are exclusively Jewish. After all, clothes, like the home interior and the body, are a type of rich cultural text, which propagates associations and tropes often exceeding cultural and ethnic delineations. What is it, then, that makes them—or any object—Jewish or, for that matter, non-Jewish?

Ginczanka lists only indispensable items—items with a direct use value. In doing so, she constantly negotiates between the rigor of enumerating and depicting them hyperbolically.[44] Her list does not include any paraphernalia with clear religious, cultural, or national designation. Therefore, the objects are Jewish because their owner is Jewish; or, more precisely, they are taken away from their owner because she Jewish. Accordingly, the redistribution of goods whose Jewishness is not inherent in them would quickly strip them of such a designation. In particular, greed and vulgar practicality can change an object's legal status and strip away its liquid identity, as if this was a mere projection.

Yet, it is not always so clear. When Michał Głowiński asks how it was possible that the Nazi could live amid furniture looted from Głowiński's own family without perceiving this as abject, he espouses a belief in the unchangeable essence of things.[45] His is the question of an essentialist. However, as Derrida paradoxically observed, the Jew has no essence, in that "his essence is the lack of it."[46] Likewise, the fluid identity status of material objects, whose abundance is reflected in "My Last Will," denies and erases the essence of objects because their direct use value prevails over their past, cultural associations, and sensuous perception such as smell: in one word, over their identity.

Besides her material legacy, Ginczanka had to deal with the poetic aspects of her inheritance. Despite her status as a victim, the poet betrays neither the Kierkegaardian fear of death nor any sort of fatalistic resignation. She sublimates her angst, transforming it into ironic *jouissance*.[47] This irony, which verges on bitter sarcasm, is not an intrinsic element of the poetic last will in its ancient Roman variation, which she refers to directly in the first line by quoting the most famous passage from Horace's ode. This ironic farewell to the world appears, however, for the first time in Western writings before Horace, in Plato's *Phaedo*. Socrates requests that a rooster be offered on his behalf to Asclepios, the god of healing; since he, himself, faced death, it is an imminently ironic gesture.

Ginczanka, however, reverses the thematic expectations inherent in the genre of the poetic testament, and, in particular, in Horace's ephemeral legacy through integrating François Villon's ironically treated objectual legacy into her poem. She draws on the tradition from Villon's *Le Petit Testament,* in which he bequeathed pawned items to clerks, a few coins to moneylenders, and his hair clippings to his barber. The predominant genre of Ginczanka's poem, the testament, is also inherently attuned to the materiality of her own body. She emphasizes this materiality by constructing the themes of the poem around her own murder and the plunder of her room.[48] Here, her symbolic murder is reminiscent of Villon's "Ballade des pendus." Sentenced to death for entirely different reasons than Ginczanka, he imagined his body hanged on the scaffold and rotting in the air, a sort of out-of-body experience that Ginczanka shares when she envisions her death as an ugly, unsublimated massacre that takes place in her room. The elaboration of this theme by Ginczanka can be pushed further. In contrast to the Polish-Jewish poet's solitude, her predecessors did not feel alienated from a poetic community. Ginczanka's confession—"I have left no heir here"—disrupts the continuity of a poetic lineage and negates any sense of her perceived impact on Polish poetry. The process of disowning the future generation of Polish poets with the full force of her derision shifts the emphasis to what she intends to give: her material legacy, her "Jewish things."

Although Ginczanka lived under constant threat of death, her poem is devoid of anxiety about the unknown. Instead, the poet takes a leap of certainty into her predictable—if not inevitable—end in order to write a poetic, yet clearly itemized, last will. The poetic word, pressed into the service of delimiting her artistic and material legacy, acquires physical qualities and becomes itself a bequeathed, fragmented object.[49] These qualities strongly suggest a continuation of the sensual imagery that Ginczanka developed in her prewar work. This time, however, the word is not employed to evoke the poet's erotic longing, but foreshadows Ginczanka's own symbolic nonexistence, which sits in opposition to the continuous existence of her belongings and, ultimately, to the survival of her incriminating poem. The word, however, did not become flesh; in real life, Ginczanka was not killed in her home, nor was she alone at the time of her death. In this respect, her last will, arguably, fails as a prophetic vision only because of the detailed circumstances it evokes. In this sense and only in this sense, it may not matter how Ginczanka died in real life, since what ultimately matters within the restricted written space of her poem is the directness and palpability of its testimonial account.

Codetta

Pitched against Szlengel's "Top Hat," Ginczanka's "My Last Will" engages a new space of identities in counterpoint to Szlengel's: in one case, Jewishness is problematized and erased by material abundance, while in the other, it is the lack of material objects that emphasizes Jewishness. Both poems inadvertently lack certain finishing touches; both are informed by intentional ellipses that emulate the process of planning one's nonexistence; of hesitating for the purpose of achieving the strongest effect on the other actor on stage; of intentionally leaving traces of a creative process to express the artistic pleasure of giving form. Both poems are also infused with a certain inconsistency, with regard to their punctuation and other aspects, that indicates that the poem's editing process was likely left incomplete. In sum, both lyrics emphasize the discontinuity of the Holocaust text and, moreover, of its very creation as something foreshadowing the poets' nonexistence. As such, these Holocaust texts sit in opposition to their own continuous circulation.

Text

Non omnis moriar—moje dumne włości,
Łąki moich obrusów, twierdze szaf niezłomnych,
Prześcieradła rozległe, drogocenna pościel
I suknie, jasne suknie pozostaną po mnie.
Nie zostawiłam tutaj żadnego dziedzica,
Niech więc rzeczy ż twoja dłoń wyszpera,
Chominowo, lwowianko, dzielna żono szpicla,
Donosicielko chyża, matko folskdojczera.
Tobie, twoim niech służą, bo po cóż by obcym.
Bliscy moi—nie lutnia to, nie puste imię.
Pamiętam o was, wyście, kiedy szli szupowcy,
Też pamiętali o mnie. Przypomnieli i mnie.
Niech przyjaciele moi siądą przy pucharze
I zapiją mój pogrzeb i własne bogactwo:
Kilimy i makaty, półmiski, lichtarze—
Niech piją noc całą, a o świcie brzasku
Niech zaczną szukać cennych kamieni i złota
W kanapach, materacach, kołdrach i dywanach.
O, jak będzie się palić w ręku im robota,
Kłęby włosia końskiego i morskiego siana,
Chmury rozprutych poduszek i obłoki pierzyn
Do rąk im przylgną, w skrzydła zmienią ręce obie;
To krew moja pakuły z puchem zlepi świeżym
I uskrzydlonych nagle w aniołów przemieni.

ON WASTE AND MATTER

CHAPTER THREE

Holocaust Soap and the Story of Its Production

I did not make up anything.

—Zofia Nałkowska on *Medallions*

In Nałkowska everything is a construction.

—Michał Głowiński (not on *Medallions*)

Soap, Ladies and Gentlemen, die Seife, die Seifenkugel, *you know, certainly*, what *it is*.

—Francis Ponge

OAP'S *TELOS* IS TO PURIFY, to clean and then to disappear completely. Its semantics should be in conflict with its impure origins, in the same manner as its cleansing effect clashes with dirty hands. Contrary to Francis Ponge's assessment in the inscription, which is concerned with soap's phenomenological "whatness," consumers have only a vague idea of the contents of the cosmetic (including its main ingredient, animal fat) or the chemical process required to transform that coarse material into a pleasantly scented, neatly molded, and packaged cosmetic.[1] Our everyday consumption of soap is one of the least complex, and thus most overlooked, occurrences. The narrative of soap's consumption is brief and takes place entirely on the body's surface, between the skin and the pleasantly disappearing product.[2] The gist of this narrative can be contained in one sentence: the soap, made from an animal's body, washes another body—in other words, the body washes the body.

Indicated by Freud to be a "yardstick" of civilization,[3] soap is later defined in nearly military terms of "a civilization's triumph over the forces of defilement and excrement."[4] But what, ladies and gentlemen, if a human body is washed by soap manufactured from the human body? Such an uncanny, and seemingly impossible, concept of the everyday artifact perverts the main trope of civilization to which the cosmetic traditionally belongs, since such soap dehumanizes one body in order to rehumanize another. As I will attempt to demonstrate, this kind of soap—its use, production, symbolization, and network of cultural associations in which it is entangled—represents one of the most complex cultural texts in that it embraces both the civilizational and anti-civilizational impulses. Therefore, the story of its actual manufacture overlaps with my reconstructing the story of its cultural production.

The utilization of cadavers for educational and medical purposes has a long history, one that is often intermingled with unethical practices regarding the provenance of these bodies. The Nazis who viewed the ideologically categorized body as fit for recycling obviously acted without obtaining consent as they used cadavers of those people whom they criminalized or considered racially "inferior." Today's ethical standards allow the harvesting of organs and body parts *pro publico bono* only with consent from the donor or his or her family. This understanding would render both present and historical practices of utilizing unclaimed bodies, as well as those of paupers and criminals, illegal, regardless of the purpose for which the bodies were used. This, however, was not the case, especially, when boiling, dissection, and display of bodily remnants coincided with the medieval Catholic cult of relics considered to be holy.

The implications of a human subject producing and using a cosmetic made from bodily matter retrieved and recycled from other human subjects without their consent draw us, then, into the sphere of ethics. In this case, however, the ethical proves to be entangled with less sublime questions—those of economics and the welfare of a society at war. Both aspects of the question prove to be conveniently intertwined with the promotion of economico-ethical happiness under the banner of utilitarianism. Since 1789, when Jeremy Bentham published his *An Introduction to the Principles of Morals and Legislation*, utilitarian philosophy has evolved into several distinct strands, including the codification of utilitarianism into a normative theory of ethics. The British philosopher's promotion of ethics, calling for the overall happiness of both the agent of an action and everyone affected by this action, privileges results over methods. Utilitarianism's teleological character, neatly opposed to deontological ethical theories concerned with moral duties and obligations instead of with goals and ends, eventually evolved into present-day consequentialism. We can trace the utilitarian underpinnings of a variety of twentieth-century developments in the realms of economics, social sciences, and, yes, politics. The misapplied utilitarian doctrine of motivation, privileging ends above means, would vindicate many dictators and their followers, including such Nazi scientists as Professor Rudolf Maria Spanner.

In that he used human corpses for the production of soap, Dr. Spanner's research represents one of most notorious cases of the recycling of the human body for utilitarian purposes. In reconstructing the story of this experimental, scientific production, I mainly rely on Zofia Nałkowska's "Professor Spanner," the opening reportage in her collection entitled *Medaliony* (Medallions). As far as I know, Nałkowska's reportage, although translated into more than twenty languages, has never existed as a strong point of reference in the Holocaust discourse outside of Poland. Nałkowska (1884–1954) was a distinguished writer, playwright, and essayist, best known for several of her prewar psychological novels.[5] She was also actively engaged in sociopolitical questions, and it was her work on behalf of political prisoners in Towarzystwo Opieki nad Więźniami (The Association of the Care of Prisoners), which resulted in a collection of reports entitled *Ściany świata* (The Walls of the World) (1931) that is directly related to *Medallions*. After World War II, Nałkowska remained active in a variety of official functions, most notably as a member of the Committee of Research on Hitlerite Crimes, collecting former Nazi victims' testimonies, taking field trips to death camps and other sites of the genocide such as Spanner's lab. *Medallions* recorded her continued engagement on behalf of the silenced victims.

The understated content of "Professor Spanner" is framed by historical facts: together with a crew of lab assistants, prep workers, and students in the forensic laboratory of the Danzig medical school, Dr. Spanner recycled human fat into soap. As the Soviet Army advanced, Dr. Spanner, avoiding his scientific, moral, and technical responsibility, fled to the western part of Germany.[6] Since he did not kill people in order to make soap and could have been prosecuted only for removing evidence, his *numéro savon*[7] turned out to be a classic case of the divide between juridical and ethical law, a divide that effectively enabled him to avoid punishment.[8]

During the Nuremberg trials, Soviet prosecutor L. N. Smirnov submitted a bar of soap allegedly made of human fat, understanding that this item demonstrated important legal evidence that the industrial production of human soap did take place, contrary to the fact that Spanner's manufacture was not able to mass produce the cosmetic. Subsequently, survivors,[9] activists of such stature as Simon Wiesenthal, as well as historians, maintained that the soap was made of human fat. Later on, the fact was dismissed as not based on reality. However, the investigation was reactivated under the aegis of the National Remembrance Institute in Poland.[10] When, thanks to the German prosecutors, an extant soap sample (considered lost) was discovered in the Hague archives, a series of tests was conducted. They confirmed that Spanner's soap *was* made of human fat and, ultimately, corroborated the facts reported by Nałkowska.[11]

From a historical distance of more than half a century, we see that one of the Holocaust's projects was to transform or negate the presence of cultural traces, archival materials, material remainders of massacres, vestiges of crematoria, and, in sum, to blot out all traces of life, death, and even traces themselves. Texts of the Holocaust, as testimonial traces, contained descriptions of transformational processes that questioned the durability and resistance to the recycling of both bodily matter and material objects. The question that comes to mind is that of how long a man remains a man, how long after death his body continues to be a vessel of human content. Nałkowska represented the stages of transformation of the body as a pseudoscientific and violent spectacle, juxtaposing the anonymity of fat to the bodily forms, often fragmented, but still bearing vestiges of human shapes.

The Holocaust subjugated both material objects and human corpses to the recycling process, whose first stage rendered them ontologically equal. Manufacturing soap from human fat represented an extreme example of the transformational model, according to which both the surface and the core of the individual body are metamorphosed and processed beyond recognition. Both human-made and organic matter were made vulnerable as never before and were destined to be completely recycled, without any residual remainder. In the trajectory relating the permanence and impermanence of matter, a defining path for the Holocaust transformational paradigm, the intent to erase vestiges of raw material became paramount. In order to achieve this goal, recycling occurred to various degrees.

Although at the beginning of Spanner's operation the corpses he processed were Jewish, toward the end of the war he used racially and ethnically diverse corpses for his experiments. In general, the processing of corpses speaks both of a perverted utilitarianism and of a certain shift in the Nazi approach to the Jewish body. The Nazi vision of the perfect society excluded the supposedly dangerous, effeminate, and diseased Jewish body. In order to create and substantiate this racist formulation, the Nazis drew on a mixture of medieval conceptions and aspects of modern philosophy that they buttressed with deviant scientific claims. Their central principle was the necessity of a complete removal of the Jewish body from society. But once the project of eliminating the revolting body was moved from the level of ideology into that of its practical realization, in particular after the Wannsee conference, another shift took place. During this stage, the Jewish corpse was endowed with a set of new, yet opposite, qualities. When death removed the threat and disgust that the body represented, new traits were inscribed on the corpse through its treatment. On the one hand, being a mere husk inside which was hidden sought-after Jewish gold, the body was useless. On the other, it became a locus of diverse resources, even a commodity in itself. With this radical change—characteristic of the transformational paradigm to which the dead body was subjugated—its previously pronounced and targeted racial, cultural, ethnic essence, was completely erased. In this way, the assumed uselessness of a corpse perceived only as an object was replaced by a redefined use-value. Such a permissive resourcefulness, part of the larger Nazi utilitarianism, could only be facilitated by an overarching totalitarian power.

Upon closer scrutiny, the story of Spanner's production (and first attempts at circulation) of his variety of soap demonstrated denial and repression, both of which were supported by any number of ideological rationalizations. The rationale given by one of the interrogated medical doctors (and his colleagues) revealed that it was "common knowledge that he was an obedient party member."[12] Moreover, as the other doctor indicated, "[a]t that time, Germans were experiencing a severe shortage of fat. Given Germany's economic state, he could have been tempted to do it for the good of the nation" (Nałkowska 2000, 10). Thus, Spanner's readiness was justified both by the Reich's economic demands and by his loyalty to the NSDAP.[13] These testimonies—dull expressions of false consciousness, delivered in front of the Committee—have a certain Conradian effect: the witnesses spoke of the antagonist Spanner in his absence and, in doing so, relativized the actual impact of his research. One articulated Spanner's utilitarian goal of improving the quality of life in the Third Reich, while the other defined him as a totalitarian subject. What was so extraordinary about the comment concerning his obedience to the party was the fact that it escaped the eye of another totalitarian subject—the Polish censor who accepted Nałkowska's *Medallions* for publication at the time when the Polish press was under communist control. Thus censorship, understood as a part of a larger discourse on traces and obfuscation, appeared on the fringes of her collection.

An erasure of what one may call historical documents was painfully familiar to Nałkowska, who, during the war, kept two diaries. In one, she wrote about everyday events, albeit deeply colored by the Nazi occupation: she describes her and her family's struggle for survival in Warsaw, her job in a small tobacco shop, and her writing and social life intertwined with sporadic visits to the countryside. The other diary was defined more strictly and kept completely secret, for she intended it to be an account of everything related to the persecution and extermination of the Jewish population. Since she likely knew and participated in conspiratorial rescue operations and underground cultural life, Nałkowska's knowledge about the unfolding extermination exceeded the vagueness of rumors that circulated in Warsaw and made the second diary particularly incriminating. The writer later burned these records in a stove when the Gestapo searched her apartment building, executing thusly the ultimate act of *precarium* on her own work. The auto-da-fé of her diary was yet another act of self-protection and self-censorship performed under the pressure of life-threatening circumstances, rather than an enactment of her inner desire. The destruction of her writings did not extend to her other wartime diaries, which contained scarcer, more coded notes about the plight of Jews, usually referred to periphrastically as "the people behind the wall." The same attentive empathy with the plight of Jews, so characteristic of Nałkowska's wartime writings, is also visible throughout *Medallions*.[14]

Vagaries of the Scientific Self

Utilitarian morals were fused with the ideological semantics of the Nazis by means of a much older tradition of dehumanization, which treated the body as nothing more than reified meat. Julia Kristeva would consider such an approach to cadavers as an argument in support of her concept of the abject corpse, which is neither subject nor object.[15] In the places of extermination and recycling, however, a corpse was only an object remotely reflecting its previous ontology. Spanner's lab served as a case in point, in its role as a part of a smoothly functioning war machine, whose executioners were eager to improve the mechanization of death. Following the installment of a guillotine in the Danzig prison, Spanner dealt with an abundance of "raw material" for his covert research. The recycling in Spanner's lab demonstrated this mechanized treatment in each of its steps. First, the cadavers were "halved, quartered, and skinned" (9); then, the bones were removed; and the so-called saponification concluded the process. The writer described its end result as "a whitish, rough soap" (Nałkowska 2000, 9) formed in metal molds. Strikingly similar, providing both a parallel and a precedent for this commodification of the body, is the fragmentation of the animal body that occurs in the slaughterhouse. There, animals are killed, skinned, disemboweled, cut into pieces, boiled, smoked, and packed, all in the name of producing food for humans. For Daniel Pick, a slaughterhouse became the metaphor for a war that emphasized the division of labor and the speed with which the carcasses were processed.[16] Each worker was responsible for a specific morsel of each carcass, such that the animal would never appear to the worker as a physical whole, but only in a multiplicity of identical parts from countless individual animals. The division of labor determined the slaughterhouse's similarity to an assembly line, where each worker played a small role in a precisely outlined process of assembly; instead of piecing together, the system employed in a slaughterhouse disconnected and undid what was an original bodily unity.

Division of labor governed the manufacture of soap in the Danzig institution and played an important role in the preservation of secrecy. According to Nałkowska, except for Spanner and two of his lab assistants, no one involved in manufacturing the soap observed or participated in the entire cycle, which began when the prisoners were led to the guillotine, followed by their execution and the collection and transportation of their bodies to the lab, where the eerie final artifact was produced. And yet this conceptualization does not account for the final stages of soap production, during which the fragmented body underwent a complete recycling and disappeared, so that nothing even remotely reminiscent of the initial human form and substance remained. These stages prompted one of the reportage's main questions as to how long after death and the processes of recycling the body continued to house human content and, moreover, was recognizable as human.

The uncanny connection between the war and meat production did not escape Nałkowska, who ruminated in her *Diary 1939–1944* about the link between the war machinery and those people who were caught in it, as though in a "meat grinding machine" (Nałkowska 1975–2000, 5: 305). While there is nothing particularly novel about this association,[17] it resonated differently for this writer in that, through it, she directly connected the concept of the self, anchored in the soma, with the meat that constituted her own diet—only to undermine it with disbelief:

> It's strange that this, which makes me happen, through which I participate in the world, through which I feel myself—is *meat* (the meat brought from "town" for dinner).[18] For thinking about man in chemical categories can be borne easily. The fact that life "borrows" free elements of a dead world, does not cause resistance, there is a quiet acceptance and understanding of it. But when viewed with the eye of "naïve realism," meat as an organ of life and consciousness, as the site where the sweetness and horror of life occur—what an arbitrariness, what a perfunctory concept. (Nałkowska 1975–2000, 5: 490)

Dialectical materialism, which Nałkowska embraced in her youth (although not in any orthodox manner), eventually took on a form of monism in her writings. She was convinced that, in a strictly biological sense, there was no ontological difference between nature and humanity. As she claimed in an interview in the 1930s, "Man is made more or less of the same material as the world; he is con-generic with it."[19] In a later response, the writer modified her biological monism somewhat by including another ideological element from her formative period: a belief in science. The fusion of dialectical materialism with a scientific approach to reality prompted her to proclaim, with what would seem now an inflated sense of optimism, a radical faith in the "Soviet experiment" and its limitless, scientific progress:

> Considered at this angle the future and durability of the Soviet experiment seems to me to depend on whether "matter," as a gnoseological category, will prove—so to speak—its developmental capacity, its capacity to adapt to the ever more stunning discoveries within hard science, blowing up the essence and quality of matter as the subject of physics.[20]

Inspired by scientific research in its Soviet instantiation, and as though intoxicated by the prospect of future technological advancement, Nałkowska displayed no foreboding about the effects of its deployment against mankind. This prewar ideology—of a materialist cognition without ethical safeguards— would return like a boomerang in her *Medallions*.

Curiously enough, in defining material unity, Nałkowska never engaged dialectical materialism in her own fiction. She also overlooked the idea of her characters' material/somatic foundation, focusing instead on a psychological dimension and their interactions with the world.[21] *Medallions*, however, is an obvious exception. Here, stories of cannibalism, torture, starvation, horrible wounds, and beatings bring the suffering body, in all its mortal materiality, into the narrative foreground. In this collection, Nałkowska revised not only the bio-ontological position of the human subject; she also modified the world, which framed these subjects in terms of a radical corpo-reality.

Nałkowska's voicing a futuristic trust in physics and its transformation of matter occurred several years before her carefully measured reportage from Spanner's lab. It almost overlapped in time with the monistic theses she articulated in her wartime diary. As such, these claims marked an important direction in her thinking about the limitations of human cognition. However, the writer did not connect them, perhaps leaving this aspect up to readers to decide. It was as if for her the ethical consequences of Spanner's activities made them incompatible with human cognition, in general, and scientific knowledge, in particular.

Had she consistently revised the concept of homogeneity of matter, would Nałkowska then adopt utilitarianism and, in its name, vindicate Spanner, who obviously chose not to distinguish between human and animal soma? Or would her position remain irresolvable on account of the apparent split in ethical, juridical, and scientific reasoning? Had she connected her prewar vision of the blown-up matter with the wartime construction and use of the atomic bomb, would she condemn one or the other? As far as we know, she did not find it necessary to revise her own scientific fetishes, including her concept of somatic homogeneity, which troubled her so much during wartime.[22] Nazi experimentation in human recycling, in which the separation of the somatic and the individual (human) became obsolete, was a direct challenge to Nałkowska's scientific ideology. She posed the questions and cannot be blamed for not finding an answer to this problem.

"Meat in the Pot"

Nałkowska's reportage was conceived of as a passage through the uncanny underground facility that constituted Spanner's lab. First, the narrator, already familiar with the premises, conveyed to the reader a confused sensation that something was fundamentally wrong with the place. Spanner's facility looked like an abandoned forensic lab with corpses lying in various configurations and shapes. Only later was the site's true function disclosed to the reader as the passage through the basement revealed the gradual dismantling of the corpses into parts: shaved heads in one place, flayed skin in another, a boiled torso further down. And, as the body was becoming more and more fragmented, the incriminating evidence of Spanner's research became insurmountable. This feeling coincided with the construction of the passage, from the ground level to the basement, as an archetypal descent to the underworld (*katabasis*); as a passage from the solemn to the abject, from the highest to the vulgarized, from the whole to the fragmented, from an aporia of the place to a recognition of its function. The site ultimately disclosed its dead corporeal reality—its corpo-reality.

Although Nałkowska's description of this site integrates several textual and visual traditions, the parallel with a slaughterhouse and meat-processing factory, as a workplace ruled by mechanized neutralization of ethics, becomes particularly apt. The uniformity of images of a mechanized, serialized death stunned the writer because each cadaver had a clean cut on the neck, signifying the violation of the body. For Nałkowska, this line was too perfect, too precise, to the extent that she perceived the preserved corpses as made of stone. Only later would the technological cause of that neatness become clear to her: it was the guillotine blade that made such a disquietingly neat cut.

Elias Canetti made the gruesome remark that seeing a heap of corpses is an ancient spectacle; he outlined the way in which such an event empowers the victorious and satisfies the powerful. However, that ancient sight was not what Nałkowska reported from Danzig. Not quite. Her experience there modified Canetti's observation, emphasizing the difference that existed between *any* dead body and a dead body that has been quartered and boiled. This distinction between the spectacles of dehumanization became obvious to them only when they came across a cauldron containing a dismembered and boiled human torso: "There, on the cooled hearth, stood a huge cauldron brimming with a dark liquid. Someone familiar with the premises poked under the lid and retrieved a boiled human torso, skinned and dripping with the liquid" (Nałkowska 2000, 4). This dark liquid—fat—was what interested Spanner most. Usually, fat connotes the interiority of the body; however, its exteriorized and liquefied state implied violence and the stage beyond which recycling would completely obliterate the shape of the body.

Everything in this episode—the lifting of the lid, the color of the liquid, the pulling out of a boiled and flayed body—was concerned with demonstrating the crucial stage in the recycling of the commodified and fragmented human body: the retrieval of fat from soma.[23] Almost indiscernibly, Nałkowska changed the status of what was collected and unseen to that which was displayed, to the spectacle of reification. Through the realization of the lab's true function, the space transmogrified from the forensic lab into a soap-manufacturing place. Therefore, her reportage was conceived as a carefully dosed distribution of knowledge, or rather of both the initial lack and the gradual acquisition of knowledge by the reader. Only the visitors investigating the basement understood the unfolding logic of the whole cycle—which is to say, when they knew—the dead participated unknowingly and passively in the spectacle of showing and recycling their own cadavers.

For the dead, the gesture of showing and, thus, "museuming" their cadavers took place without their knowledge. As they lay extended, they resembled the dead Psyche from Freud's last written note.[24] Like her, they were unaware of the ongoing panoptic spectacle. Having been shown, they were subsequently subjected to an aestheticizing strategy, in which Nałkowska elevated the status of the immobile body to that of a work of art, to a stone sculpture,[25] only to overshadow this visual impression by the images of a drastically chopped up and deformed human soma. One such heap of shaved heads lying chaotically, one on top of another—"like potatoes poured onto the ground" (Nałkowska 2000, 4)—made the spectacle grotesque and almost unreal, despite the comparison taken from the vocabulary of a naturalist.

Nałkowska's polarized representation of the human soma (portrayed either as sculpted stones or potatoes) might appear unwarranted to a critic seeking consistency in her narrative. This conflicting construction subjected the fragmented soma to two contradictory systems: that of modernist aestheticism and naturalist authenticity. In fact, this apparent confusion stemmed from the author's previously unresolved and intrinsically incoherent philosophy.[26] However, from my critical perspective, which does not privilege consistency in art, the rupture caused by her reliance on two different sets of imageries represented her scene more effectively, affected the representational dimension, and, thus, contributed to a greater dramatic tension within the narrative.

The uneven, oscillating pull of contradictory values and perspectives is best documented in the imagery of collective and individual deaths. For the writer, this must have been a formidable challenge, as she strove to find an adequate strategy to represent the morbid spectacle of recycling human soma. Demands of communicating the mass death called for the representation of a total distortion of unique bodily forms. Therefore, Nałkowska suspended the spectacle of erasing individual bodily forms, of turning them into anonymous piles of meat and cauldrons of fat, to expose to the readers' voyeuristic gaze two, complementing each other, bodily fragments that were still legible and were represented by the writer as inscriptions subjected to her decoding. One of them is the able-bodied and tattooed torso of a sailor, reduced to being *res extensa:*

> In one sarcophagus, the so-called headless "sailor" lay prostrate on a heap of cadavers. He was an impressive youth, as big as a gladiator. The silhouette of a ship was tattooed on his broad chest. Across the contour of the two masts hung the sign of vain faith: God is with us. (Nałkowska 2000, 3–4)

Despite its defacement, the headless torso still bore traces of its previous personhood, since one was able to follow the chain of signification that retained its individuality; the ship indicated the sailor's line of work, the body build spoke of his strength and height, and the tattooed skinscript was a confession of his faith.[27] In fact, this skinscript was longer and contained more information than was conveyed to the reader, since it also indicated that the wretched sailor had served since 1930 as a crewmember on the Polish destroyer, *Wicher* (The Gale). Nałkowska excluded this information from representation and reduced the already sparse data to a shred, only to question the effectiveness of the sailor's religious beliefs. Her verdict denied any agency to the sailor, rendering his faith and his corpse entirely powerless: he was decapitated, exposed, and denigrated, intended for consumption in the form of soap. Intended for a mystical consumption, Christ's *hic est enim corpus meum*, as an article of faith, had no power to redeem the sailor's defaced cadaver. Through this and similar narrative interventions present in her collection, Nałkowska negated any soteriological possibility, a maneuver in sync with her pronounced atheism that also constitutes one of her volume's most complete and coherent aspects.

In yet another glimpse, the writer used her descriptive skills to create a death mask. This time, the image of a singular death reversed the meaning and the form of the sailor's corpse: all that remained of the body was the head severed from the torso. In this coincidental manner, both corpses complemented each other:

> In the corner of one vat lay the small, cream-colored head of a boy who couldn't have been more than eighteen years old when he died. His dark, somewhat slanted eyes weren't closed, the eyelids were only slightly lowered. The full mouth, of the same color as the face, bore a patient, sad smile. The strong, straight brow was raised as though in disbelief. In this most odd and inconceivable position, he awaited the world's final verdict. (Nałkowska 2000, 4)

Again, Nałkowska excised the bodily shred from any theology of embodiment. Instead, the youth's decapitated head recalled the Cartesian dualism as a philosophical trope. It signified the location of the thought-producing brain, the thinking substance, the *res cogitans*. In approaching this death mask, Nałkowska focused on seeking a lasting meaning in the subtly detailed facial expression frozen by rigor mortis. In this instance, her mimetic precision demanded an unusual degree of insight, a means of getting, literally, under the skin—even at the risk of destabilizing her usual policy of nonintrusion.

Although throughout *Medallions* the authorial position is defined through this nonintrusive approach to the lives and narratives of Holocaust victims, in these two brief glimpses at individualized death Nałkowska deemed authorial intervention necessary perhaps because, first of all, these shreds of the human form could not speak for themselves, but also because of their particularly disturbing nature. The writer's usual gesture of self-decentering[28] would have proven ineffective in conveying her horrifying encounter with the dismembered youth. Therefore, she created space for a rather discrete evaluation in an otherwise factual description of the victim's age, smile, and raised eyebrows—as though to prevent herself from mimicking the mere mechanical listing of the "parts among parts."

Ewa Frąckowiak-Wiegandtowa remarked that after Nałkowska's authorial debut, the adjective *dziwny* (odd, strange) belonged to the author's entrenched lexical repertoire. She criticized, however, what she viewed as the writer's predilection for this adjective, maintaining that, in using it, Nałkowska tended to blur everything (Frąckowiak-Wiegandtowa 1975, 36).[29] The word, particularly popular in the Young Poland period, can easily obfuscate the meaning of its context and, indeed, even sound naïve. In the case of Nałkowska's Holocaust narration, though, we deal with a different, quite subtle, and relevant meaning of "most odd, perplexing" as a qualifier for her encounter with the dead youth. Balancing a difficult act between the tender and dispassionate, Nałkowska conveyed the individual death in terms of an extreme experience with which she empathized *against all odds* and, especially, against an overwhelming sense of loss and dehumanization.

This impossible gesture came with a price: the crisis of *Einfühlung* was enhanced by a universal awareness that another's experience of dying cannot be reconstructed. The boy's death mask suggested the lengths to which one could, or rather could not, go in an attempt to read someone else's passage to death. There was no easy way out of this cognitive conundrum, although the necessity of differentiating the movement toward death from death's finality was critical to the entire Holocaust experience, as it transcended the limits of universal accessibility.

Nałkowska ended her attempt at invoking individual death with a nod toward the inaccessible. Was it the brutality of his execution at such a young age that the victim himself could not conceive? Since it would be preposterous to use a prosopopeic voice and speak in his name, the unreachable was negotiated through the spectator's contradictory rhetoric of oddity and *Einfühlung*. The writer's reading the skinscripts on the sailor's headless body along with the mortuary traces left on his facial features pointed to an insurmountable distinction between the living spectators and the dead subjugated to ongoing scopic inquiry. It also pointed to the living spectator who participated in this process and inscribed on it the verdict of disbelief as an ethical response. This had to do with the dynamics of (un)knowing throughout the narrative, in which the living had access to different aspects of both knowledge and its lack, while the dead represented the unknowing. The final act of recycling the corpses into soap constituted their ultimate knowing (and the victims' unknowing) and reflected the entire trajectory from the single, recycled body to the cosmetic.

In her wartime diary, Nałkowska pondered the eerie and repetitious nature of the war experience, its uncanny resemblance to other wars and how it all always-already was. Her contemplation of the war pointed to the repetitious nature of its universal cruelty, as well as to its mimetic representation. If we follow the author's premise that "wszystko to już było" (it all always-already was), paradoxically, several new cognitive possibilities are open for interpretation, shifting the narrative from the historical referent to the author's artistic construal. Besides and beyond the accuracy of the parallel with the slaughterhouse, Nałkowska's narrative also engaged other contextual, religious, literary, and pictorial traditions. By retreating to her old vocabulary (and interpretative habit), which connoted a feeling of strangeness, oddity, and disbelief, Nałkowska enabled an evaluative mechanism, which referred as far back as Ezekiel's vision of the bodies of deportees from Jerusalem in a foreign city, described rather bluntly by the prophet as "the meat in the pot." While the prophet's better-known intimations of his people's rebirth and redemption from his second vision were hardly relevant to Nałkowska's non-soteriological conception, his rhetoric, combined with the pictorial concreteness characteristic of his first vision, anticipated not just the accumulation of fragmented corpses in Spanner's lab, but, to a certain extent, the nonredemptive twentieth-century artistic practices of fragmenting and, most notably, dissolving the body.

Furthermore, under the writer's pen, the modernist order of the slaughterhouse was intertwined with another form of imagery—the Shakespearean horror understood as violation of ethics, a sphere of the evil subjected to a taboo, hence associating such activity with witchcraft. The eerie witches, Macbeth's helpers, brew a potion out of morsels of animal bodies mixed with pieces of human corpses: "a liver of a blaspheming Jew," "Nose of Turk; and Tartar's lips / Finger of birth-strangl'd babe."[30] This concoction of anatomical fragments was based on a simple recipe: it consisted of everything that, in Shakespeare's time, represented the Other and, as such, became a candidate for sacrifice.[31]

Unlike the witches, who were not task-oriented, Spanner had a clearly defined utilitarian goal that prevailed over his antisemitism: to provide soap for Germany. Indeed, during the earlier stages of his operation, the corpses Spanner processed were Jewish, mainly from the Stutthof concentration camp. However, toward the end of the war, he used, in the mode of the Shakespearean witches, racially and ethnically diverse corpses in his experiments. Nałkowska's reportage uncovered the use of ethnically diverse bodies in Spanner's lab, since the vats contained a diversified human soma, diverse in terms of the victims' national and racial origin: the bodies of Soviet prisoners of war, of Jews from East Prussia and Pomerania, of patients from the psychiatric institute in Conradstein, as well as corpses of executed German officers, possibly victims of the escalating purge of the anti-Hitlerite opposition, sent from both the Danzig and Königsberg state prisons. Since the bodies were sent from the entire Pomerania region, one can safely surmise that there were more Polish cadavers than the corpse of the one sailor.

This defies the popular perception that the soap was made of "pure Jewish fat." Since, during the war, the abbreviation *R.I.F* (with no final period) was inscribed on bars of soap, these letters were mistranslated and misspelled as *Rein Idische Seif* (pure Jewish soap), when, in reality, the abbreviation stood for *Reichstelle fur Industrielle Fettvergsorgung* (State Center for Supply of Fats). We may consider this misperception a curious symptom of a purist and essentialist reading, or, at least, note that the tension between essentialism and utilitarianism reaches its peak in this misreading.

The Smell of Truth and Two Digressions

> "Don't economize on soap!"
> (Sign on the wall of the washroom in Auschwitz)
>
> —Primo Levi

Both the medical and the chemical processes taking place secretly in the Danzig forensic lab were based on the initial premise that the body could be completely transformed into a new and useful product. If the body, in the Nazi project, was to be transformed totally (into soap), it was presumed that its new utilitarian ontology would retain no vestiges or traces of its previous status—which is to say, nothing human. For Spanner, fulfilling the objective of such recycling meant eliminating the last remaining human trace: the soap's stubbornly persistent, peculiar odor. The interrogated lab worker confessed that this product "didn't smell very good. Professor Spanner tried hard to get rid of the smell. He wrote away to chemical factories for oils. But *you could always tell the soap was different*" (emphasis added, Nałkowska 2000, 9). Since the doctor could not erase the trace of the constituent bodies from the disgusting soap, his research thus emphasized the tension inherent in soap between its sanitary use and abjection. The appearance of the odor as a by-product of the fat recycling revealed the limits of scientific progress and, subsequently, of the transformational method that he used: even in its radically altered form, the soap continued in its abjection, exuding, in one of the unwilling consumers' own words, an "unpleasant" human odor.

In the lab's utilitarian microcosm, where everything was permitted, reaching a solution to the unappealing smell was only a matter of time. Yet the divide between the utilitarian approach to the body and the principle of absolute permissiveness did not necessarily inform a clash between them. In fact, Arendt pointed out in her *Origins of Totalitarianism*, the claim of absolute permissiveness was already a part of nineteenth-century utilitarian understanding of common sense (Arendt 1985, 440). If we follow her analysis of permissive utilitarianism as present within totalitarianism, one thing becomes quite clear. The enclosed realm of a concentration camp and a zone such as the one under Spanner's control share one characteristic: the totalitarian power that allowed the cruelest, craziest, and "most odd" (many of them nonutilitarian) concepts to be materialized. And it was permissiveness in its totalitarian version that facilitated Spanner's utilitarian inventiveness,[32] which for one of his lab workers spoke of the arcane knowledge of "how to make something—from nothing . . . " (Nałkowska 2000, 9).

The usage of soap was cleverly manipulated in Auschwitz in order to dispel a fear of death in the newly arrived prisoners. Primo Levi mentions that the signs encouraging a liberal use of soap were undermined by the poor quality of the product distributed to prisoners.[33] In the larger context of the genocide, an excursion into cosmetic supplies in wartime France seems a bit out of place, but, after all, the war was prompted, among others, by a grandiose project of social hygiene. The greatly simplified bodily hygiene and a corresponding shortage of cosmetic supplies was, so to speak, collateral damage incited by a war economy. Soap, usually taken for granted, became scarce even in France during the war. The provincial town of Roanne in central France and, later, the village of Coligny, north of Lyon, served as the wartime refuge of the French poet Francis Ponge and his family, who experienced war through "restrictions of all kinds, and soap, real soap, was particularly missed."[34] His complaint pertained to the same inferior quality of soap as that mentioned by Levi: "We had only the worst ersätze—which did not froth at all" (Ponge 1969, 11). The inferior quality of soap, predicated on widespread shortages, motivated the poet to focus his post-phenomenological gaze on other aspects of the cosmetic. He observed its hard substance: "a sort of stone" (14), "Magic stone!" (21), "Slobbering stone . . . " (28). In short, Ponge invented soap anew and construed its naturalness as stone.

Even during postwar years, by which time conditions had improved, Ponge perceived soap as an illusive product. Whenever he tried to touch its pebble-like form, the soap would foam and slide easily from his hands. Gazing thus at its absence, he reflected on its slippery and almost deceitful, yet tangible, concreteness. For him too, soap's teleology was to disappear—either in water or in the war.[35] Like a stone, Ponge's soap had weight, but its flowery aroma was beyond his olfactory expectations, for "it was a little more strongly scented" (1969, 63).[36] I do not suggest that he became a bit indifferent to the odor of history; rather, in all probability, the stench of decomposing corpses—*that* horrible stench mentioned by Tadeusz Borowski, Janet Flanner, and W. G. Sebald among others—never reached Roanne and Coligny. Pleasant or not, for Ponge, the smell transcended the questions of matter and its markers to enter the domain of olfacometry and subjective responses to odors.

Arguably, no modernist inquiry into the sense of smell can match Patrick Süskind's novel *Perfume*, which made a compelling equation between the soul and the individual's essence as constituted in a bodily smell.[37] Thus this odor, if captured and retained (as the protagonist-perfumist desired to do), would preserve the core of an individual soul. But the perfumer had to kill in order to extract a unique essence. Was the German writer speculating about the (im)permanence of the soul and matter in the manner that I struggled to dispel on these pages? Hardly. Rather, he focused on the social repercussions of the perfect perfume in a manner that allowed an allegorization of the political. In "Professor Spanner," on the other hand, the persisting odor of the soap suggested that between the intimate and somatic traverses something that can be qualified as an irreducible phenomenon, indivisible and invisible, the most intimate and little known bond between the physiological and the spiritual.

While Süskind's "alchemist" set for himself the goal of both discovery and preservation, perhaps even respect, of the individual bodily essence, Spanner intended to obliterate the bodily core entirely from his final product. The symbolic concept of (un)recyclability did not exist in his mortuary science prior to recycling. Spanner's *savon* did not yield itself to pleasant consumption, for it remained abject from beginning to end and, thus, he furtively searched for an effective recipe to dispel human vestige—in the ethereal form of smell—in order to manufacture the better quality soap worthy of every German bathroom.

This odor—the invisible remainder/reminder of the soap's true origin—signaled a particular glitch in Nazi recycling. The trace of the human agent, if you will, worked against the total reduction of the reified body into nothing. Thus the human agent destabilized, albeit temporarily, the unvoiced ideological assumption concerning the utilitarian and biopolitical status of the human soma as easily recyclable. The undesirable smell of the extract spoke of the spectral Derridian trace, of the illusive core that continued to remind its consumers of their own bio-ontology. Only a complete obfuscation of the human agent could make the process successful. Instead, the somatic object of scientific desire, which was sought only that it might be destroyed and never again desired, resisted the complete transformation. It became a spectral remainder/reminder of a seemingly neutralized truth, its working parallel to that of memory. Of all the types of Holocaust recycling, this one failed.

CHAPTER FOUR

The Guilty Afterlife of the Soma

And who among you, the living,
Has seen death without feeling guilty?

—Tadeusz Borowski

O NE OF THE PARTICULARLY intensive periods of hermeneutic and artistic preoccupation with apocalypticism, intermingled with forebodings of the looming historical catastrophe, occurred in the 1930s, when diverse forms of cultural and historical pessimism came to the fore across various disciplines. In 1930, D. H. Lawrence wrote his last book, *Apocalypse* (published posthumously in 1931), which underscored St. John's desire for revenge and power in his *Revelation*. Albert Schweitzer's study, *Die Mystik des Apostels Paulus* (The Mysticism of Paul the Apostle, 1930), triggered a new interest in apocalyptic eschatology. Also in the 1930s in Poland, Bruno Schulz worked on his only novel, *Mesjasz* (The Messiah), while Szymon Aszkenazy, a prominent professor of Polish history, made strikingly accurate prophecies of World War II's destruction.[1] In those years, Walter Benjamin pondered over his messianic–materialist theses for what became known as "Über den Begriff der Geschichte" (On the Concept of History), a text he completed in the early months of 1940. These simultaneous but unrelated, independently conceived ideas within theology, literature, and philosophy of history, which expressed more than mere apprehensions born from *Zeitgeist*, came to an end, at least in Eastern Europe, in 1939. By then, the future had become the present.

In the 1930s, the sense of looming catastrophe also became a major concern for the young poet, Czesław Miłosz (1911–2004), and his colleagues from the poetic group Żagary in Wilno.[2] When the German army invaded and occupied Poland, it was as if this scenario of annihilation were unfolding according to the apocalyptic vision imagined in both Miłosz's *Poemat o czasie zastygłym* (The Poem on Frozen Time)[3] and other poems written before the war. Miłosz, who spent most of the war years in Warsaw, did not join the underground army; he nonetheless remained active in both the underground publishing scene and in organizing and participating in cultural events.[4] This in no way implies that he was spared the trials and tribulations of the city's civil population during the war. In 1944, as the Warsaw uprising was taking place,[5] Miłosz and his family left the city.

To Touch the Poem

A steady stream of poetry volumes, essays, novels, correspondence, and interviews marked Miłosz's laborious life. In one such volume of interviews, entitled *Rozmowy polskie 1979–1998* (Polish Conversations 1979–1998), he reminisced about leaving Warsaw during the uprising. Besides the fact that it engaged yet another variation on the theme of manuscripts' *precarium*, his tale about exit from Warsaw is worth noting here. It bears the classic characteristics of a war tale triggered by a chance development, and is permeated by the lasting shock of an unknown. Miłosz (2006, 782) recalls as follows:

> The uprising caught us unaware not at home, but in the streets. Everything was being shelled. We went not far away from the apartment house on Kielecka Street, where we lived and, during one of the pauses in the shelling my wife Janka went to the house for her mother who lived with us. She returned with her mother and brought the manuscripts of my poems. We exited only with what we had on us.[6]

The peculiarity of this understated narrative of the exodus of the extended Miłosz family has to do with its unsung heroine, the poet's wife. The story raises questions destined to remain unanswered. Why didn't the couple go together to pick up his mother-in-law and his manuscripts? Why did the poet entrust this mission to his wife? Among the manuscripts that Janina Miłosz took from their flat were some of the best lyrics the poet ever wrote: his wartime artistic contribution, including his poetic commentary on the annihilation of Jews. Later on, Miłosz recalled that he kept all his poems in a briefcase; undoubtedly among them were such implicating poems as "Campo dei Fiori" and "A Poor Christian Looks at the Ghetto." Thus, during the family's departure, the manuscripts were always with him, exposing him to huge personal risk.[7]

The poet's return to Warsaw in the spring of 1945 forced him to confront the totality of the city's destruction.[8] Miłosz himself had not experienced this, although he did witness fighting in the ghetto and its demolition. Upon his return, he was exposed to the void that had replaced the city in which he had once lived:

> It was April. I went to the site where the house, in which we lived, stood. Nothing remained, that is, the house was there, but the apartment that we inhabited, had simply disappeared—the house was hit by the artillery shell

and the apartment fell down to the cellar. I found something else there, a copy of *Trzy zimy* pierced throughout by shrapnel.[9] Some scraps of paper were scattered in debris. (Miłosz 2006, 782)

The experience of finding a damaged volume of *Trzy zimy* (Three Winters), metonymically shot through, as if instead of its own creator, and scattered about among ruins, indicated the omnipresence of *precarium* as it relates to the material foundation of a literary text. Following the thread of his poems' materiality to the Miłosz archive in the Beinecke Rare Books Collection at Yale University, I found that this thread ended in a void. Then, in 1994, the archive contained no handwritten manuscripts of his wartime poetry, but only typed copies. Neatly organized in cardboard boxes were sheets of paper, all in the same format, and the paper had yellowed considerably. Seldom does one come across such legible archival manuscripts; presumably, they were typed in preparation for publication in the underground press, for on the typed pages were no inscribed traces of the drama of history other than that about which the poems themselves speak. Miłosz's characteristic habit of literally blackening his manuscript pages with doodles, covering them with little drawings and geometric figures, filling the pages with the convoluted traces of his revisions and of his truly Benedictine work—the whole rich and unique scene of writing one finds in his postwar manuscripts—was missing. One cannot touch his wartime poems in their creative beginning, at the moment the poet translated his dark vision into the word.

This lack becomes all the more important in the case of one of his better-known poems, "Campo dei Fiori" (1943). Miłosz was haunted by a keen awareness of the disjuncture between the Holocaust word and the factuality of death in this poem, which built a humanistic parallel between the execution of the Italian humanist and astronomer, Giordano Bruno, and the death of the Warsaw Jews in the uprising of April 1943. The common term of comparison—between Giordano Bruno, who was burned at the stake, and the burning of both the ghetto and its denizens—was a singular silence and striking loneliness in death.[10] The silencing and killing of those innocent people who were confined within the walls of the ghetto corresponded to the silencing and burning alive of the philosopher and astronomer who believed in the infinity of the universe and the multiplicity of worlds.

The prescient poet included in his fifth strophe two possible ways of reading the parallel that encompassed the future reader's indifference toward death and suffering of the Other, oblivion as well as transience.

> Someone will read as moral
> that the people of Rome or Warsaw
> haggle, laugh, make love

as they pass by martyrs' pyres.
Someone else will read
of the passing of things human,
of the oblivion
born before the flames have died. ("Campo dei Fiori"; Miłosz 2001a, 34)

Miłosz juxtaposed these two scenes of reading with his own understanding of
an unjust and lonely death as inexpressible in language with barbarism,
whether that of the Holy Inquisition or of Nazism. For him, the insufficiency
of language to capture the essence of murder delineated the limits of representation. To speak of the death of the wronged Other meant to give an inadequate name to an unnamable horror, to provide an articulation of that which
cannot speak directly of the ultimate terror of death. Miłosz eliminated pros-
opopeia from his poetic vocabulary; the victims he described could not express their suffering and, thus, the possibility of communication was negated.[11]
This devoicing of victims also operated beyond historical and quantitative lo-
calities: Miłosz confronted both mass genocide and the murder of one individual either by means of silence or the muted word. Thus a hermeneutic
operation encountered the ineffable: the region of the Real that did not have
the adequate symbolization because the victims were not heard, but were silenced and mute. Miłosz's "Campo dei Fiori" belongs to a handful of texts
written by non-Jewish writers during the ghetto uprising (or the Holocaust, for
that matter)[12] that, to my knowledge, make the first attempt at textualizing the
ineffability of the Holocaust which is not caused by the linguistic and aesthetic limitations inherent in the poetic word as it confronts the Holocaust,
but stems from the simple historical facts such as the muting of victims.

Regardless of Miłosz' poetic witnessing of devoiced victims, questions of negative aesthetics and the inadequacy of linguistic means were seldom articulated
during the war. Even if these questions had been raised at that time, they would
not have stopped those writing during the war nor weakened their inscriptions.[13]
An intuitive sense of the word's irrelevance remained peripheral; if it motivated
literary reflection about the reality of the uncanny, this happened primarily
through a gradual shift toward more ascetic and austere forms of expression.
This transition also incorporated the grammar of objects. In general, the Ur-po-
ets of the Holocaust insisted on the inflammatory, testimonial, or material value
of the word above that of its poetic expressivity. This occurred mostly due to their
language and craft having been developed during the interwar years. When
confronted with the unprecedented monstrosity of the war, their "attitude to the
language [was] altered," as Miłosz noted in his essay "Ruins and Poetry."[14] Going
beyond a mere linguistic diagnosis, the poet maintained that—during the war—
language's calling was to "recover its simplest function" and purpose in describ-

ing a reality that was "massive, tangible, and terrifying in its concreteness" (1983, 80). Indeed, only a few poets and writers were aware of the inadequacy of language in the face of the Holocaust. Even fewer felt a need to revise their prewar vocabulary; within Polish literature, Miłosz was such a notable case. Since then, critical and poetic confrontations of the insufficiency of language have formed the thrust of the discourse, thanks to poetic insights that hark back to Miłosz and Paul Celan, as well as the critical writings of George Steiner and Susan Horowitz, among others. In a way, the crisis involved in any literary representation of the ghetto/camp-universe reflects a humbling awareness of the insufficiency of scholarly inquiry into the Holocaust.

Despite his awareness of this fundamental disjuncture, Miłosz remained prolific as a poet during the Nazi occupation of Poland. The volume *Ocalenie* (Rescue), published right after the war, strongly supports this claim. Two poetic cycles in this oeuvre are noteworthy—not in the least because they stand a world apart: "Głosy biednych ludzi" (Voices of Poor People) and "Świat. Poema naiwne" (The World. Naïve Poems). In the first cycle, Miłosz attempts to name the immediate reality of the war, while the second exemplifies a poetic universe that bears no similarity to the concrete horror of the time. Within these two cycles, Miłosz, ever the dualistic poet, juxtaposes some of the lyrics, achieving greater contrast and creating conflicting propositions. The impact of T. S. Eliot's poetry—in particular his *Waste Land*, which Miłosz translated into Polish during the war—was critical in Miłosz's forging of a new and more concise poetic style and vision. This emerging style can be seen especially in "Voices of Poor People," and is considered to be the sign of a new variety of poetry based on increased political awareness.[15] Included in "Voices of Poor People," Miłosz's poem, "Biedny chrześcijanin patrzy na getto" (A Poor Christian Looks at the Ghetto, 1943) masterfully interweaves two disparate dimensions: an uncanny, palpable vision of the afterlife and an account of ongoing horrific destruction. The poem provides an unusual perspective on the genocide, for it is entirely focused on present death juxtaposed with a vision of eternity, with the material and the messianic melted into the now.

"Under Erasure"

It is curious that the destruction of the Warsaw Ghetto, grasped in a few separate poetic shots, entirely erases human agency from the annihilation, as though there had been no military action involved and no human tools of destruction employed during the process of its demolition. What is at work here is a pure—unnamed but enormous—force that negates all forms of the universe. Therefore, to say that the poem is precise or journalistic in its reportage of historical events is to undermine its deliberately nebulous representation.[16] The poet relegates to the poem's paratexts[17] the role of defining historical parameters for the text as a whole. This identification is channeled through the poem's title, with date and place given as well, so as to dispel any doubt about which events are invoked in the main body of the text: its current moment, its *Jetzzeit*, reflects the ongoing pacification of the uprising in the Warsaw Ghetto and the annihilation of its inhabitants.[18] The poem's unspoken premise is that Jews function here as centuries-old scapegoats, terrorized and targeted for annihilation. Meanwhile, unlike the indifferent populace of Warsaw portrayed in "Campo dei Fiori," the Pole in "A Poor Christian" watches the fighting in the ghetto as if it were some sort of a macabre theater. This places him on the representational axis as a slave who is overpowered, brutalized, and because of this, forced into inaction. Written during the Holocaust, the poem anticipates the problems of both bearing direct witness and the moral implications of doing so; these would be debated still further in the post-Holocaust stage.

In evoking, in all its overwhelming scale, the complete erasure of (in)animate life, the poet replaced a Hegelian movement of history with a very different rhythm, one that equated the Spirit of History with the Spirit of Destruction. Although this method coincided with Walter Benjamin's concept, Miłosz was not a follower of Benjamin. Indeed, in "A Poor Christian," a poem so keen on showing both the catastrophic fragmentation of matter and the lingering life of the pneuma, Miłosz could not be seen as any sort of materialist, even one as complex as Benjamin. In Benjamin's vision, catastrophes punctuated historical temporality, while for Miłosz, refuting in the spring of 1943 the broadly Hegelian conceptualization of history, there was only one such absolute occurrence: the annihilation of the Jewish population. In his poetic *hic et nunc*, Miłosz took off the attire of a prophet and spoke of a fulfilled apocalypse, of the irrevocably destroyed world, writing of Warsaw Jewry. To achieve this goal, he engaged the totalizing grammar of chaos and annihilation.

This restricted point of view is analogous to Leonardo da Vinci's *The Deluge*, the images of which I find illuminating. In his case, a material occurrence of apocalyptic proportions preoccupied the artist in his later years, between 1511 and 1514. Prior to this stage (c. 1498), he made a rather peculiar drawing, a harbinger of his later preoccupation, representing a number of objects—spectacles, musical instruments, gardening implements—raining down from the skies. The painter inscribed the ground below the falling tools with a moralistic caption. According to this—certainly not novel—apocalyptic scenario, humankind is punished and destroyed by its own uninhibited desire. Later on, however, da Vinci moved from the apocalyptic surplus of objects falling on the greedy mass of mankind to develop a contrasting, nonobjective pictorial vision of the end of the world. In a stunning series of ten black-chalk drawings, known as *The Deluge*, he depicted the destruction of the world by the power of water. Not a thing remained unscathed by this elemental destructive force. Again and again, Leonardo envisioned the blank and nonobjective walls of rain, the apocalypse to which this time he did not append any moral judgment.

Contrary to his familiar pictorial tradition, these drawings do not depict minute details of destruction. Instead, they invoke sweeping waves of total annihilation. Although Leonardo's objective was not to represent abstract images, the manner in which he painted the destruction had an inadvertent effect, akin to nonobjective reality. It took the artist years to shift his perspective on the apocalypse from the showering plethora of objects to their erasure. This shift was accompanied by a transition from a moralizing approach to a mute appreciation of images of destruction. The length of time between these two opposite visions arguably explains his far-reaching transformation of vision from objectual to nearly nonobjectual. Leonardo's testing of apocalyptic waters is instructive in more ways than this one. First of all, his proto-abstract gesture of erasing entirely the world of objects engaged only one element as an instrument of destruction; by clinging to this single element, the artist enhanced the expressivity of his vision.[19] Furthermore, in producing two opposing scenarios, with completely different pictorial representations of destruction, Leonardo demonstrated his consideration for both the ethically grounded concept of the end of the world and the ontological one.

Arguably more conditioned by historical events than was Leonardo, Miłosz envisioned fire as the main force of the unfolding spectacle of destruction, burning down everything with the might of an unleashed nuclear explosion. Yet, there exists a basic difference between the imagery and reality of flood and fire, since fire is not *un univers immediate*, as it demands the presence of durable matter more than water does.[20] Fire's negative energy is unstoppable only if there is something to be devoured, only as it feeds on creation turning it into ashes. Flames that cause this transformation are absent in ashes; their lack constitutes ashes' essence.[21] In this respect, "A Poor Christian" gives an account of the devastation according to several major categories. Gone are the concrete, everyday things that constitute reality and, with them, the coherent shapes of the cityscape. The scale of destruction is rendered almost tangible through his listing of erased raw metals (copper, silver, nickel) and fabrics (silk, linen). Rudimentary geometric forms, such as balls and crystals, usually subjected to an abstract rigor and not necessarily grounded in materiality, cannot escape the ongoing erasure, suggesting that the conceptual destruction is as far-fetched as that of the material world. A whole range of man-made products (flax, glass, linen, wire, paper, cellulose), along with fractured artifacts (violin strings, trumpets, foam of gypsum) marks the transition to nothingness. Yet the inventory of material substance subjugated to complete annihilation is not exhaustive. Among the major missing elements is the human body, evoked in its already extremely fragmented form. Only such vestiges as hair and bones, included in one of the poetic inventories, signal the otherwise unlisted and, thus, nonexisting body. Standing metonymically for the excluded body, these particles reveal the fractured and fragmented body in all its deadness. As both human and animal features, hair and bones fuse these two categories. At this juncture, we encounter the mechanism whereby bio-ontological diversity is reduced to the level of organic matter. This justifies the absence of either perpetrators or victims reminiscent of Leonardo's rigorous representational logic.

Cataclysms, either natural or historical, trigger far-reaching transformational developments. While natural disasters participate in the series of changes capable of bringing about new forms of biological life, Miłosz's vision of the ongoing fragmentation and deletion of the visible world—its surfaces, cores, and forms—does not go in this direction. Neither does he lapse into lamentation, as he does in some of his postwar elegies. His deceitfully dispassionate listing of the overwhelming disaster leads directly into the void, a negative aesthetic that recalls T. S. Eliot's "The Waste Land," concluding as it does with an image of bare earth and a single tree trunk. The drastic reduction of the animate and inanimate content of *Jetzzeit* to "ground zero" is necessitated by the poem's shift to eschatology: there are no obvious reasons for matter to appear in its unchanged earthly forms in the hereafter that follows the apocalypse.

What conjoins the two distinct spheres—cataclysm and the afterlife—is the reappearance of organic matter during its decomposition. While the devastation gains full momentum, the recycling of the body, unlisted till now, has already begun. On the ground above, small diligent insects are busy reprocessing the dead soma. This disintegration, which claims the decomposing and fragmented body as a part of nature, is not portrayed as business as usual, nor is there a trace of the Baroque fascination with the humiliating finality of bodily splendor. If there is a connection to the Baroque sensitivity, it is local and related to Father Baka—the poetic authority on funerary matters in Polish literary tradition. This link is rather discreet, noticeable only in the poem's dynamic images of death. Here death is described in short words and brief verses that echo Baka's style.[22] Miłosz rearticulates these close-ups of disintegrating corporeality and restates them in order to instill a better sense of the process in all its unsightly particularity. Each revision affects a higher level of an objectual and chromatic concision: the open, fragmented body undergoes a transformation and its progression is marked by the differing colors of bodily parts. At the same time, every reiteration injects a new tone of violence and death into the poem. White and black bones along with red flesh disintegrate first into a colored vestige, then into ashes, and, finally, into nothing.

Last Things

Assisting in this breakdown of decaying bodily fragments are insects, frequently entering the final stages of imagined apocalyptic catastrophes. In fact,
some insects prove to be resilient to certain methods of annihilation, including
nuclear power; hence, they make frequent appearances in late modernist apocalyptic scenarios. Ants, obviously, belong to the domain of decomposition, a preoccupation that makes them carnivorous, but the sight of bees assigned this role
may raise the reader's eyebrow, for, usually, the latter do not busy themselves
with decomposing cadavers or with organic material of any kind.[23] The occluded
meaning of the image, and its subsequent variations, involves more than the recycling to which these invertebrates were assigned. The poet also invokes a more
positive semantic of their labor: as a building process in miniature, it slightly
undermines the massive scale of annihilation. Although viewed as destructive
agents of nature, these insects are simultaneously building something unspecified around bones—"*Mrówki obudowują białą kość.*"[24] The Polish "obudować,
okryć lub okolić murem" signifies the constructing of a surface structure; hence,
the phrase "to build around" creates a visual effect of the swarming insects covering exteriorities of decaying bodily fragments. A standard symbolization of the
two insects refers to them as proverbial master builders, capable of an intricately
detailed workmanship that is coded in their genes. In the poem, however, they
are engaged in the final project of breaking down decaying bodily fragments,
from which there is seemingly no return. They are, paradoxically, building the
void. As agents of both destruction and construction—of recycling the dead
soma by transforming its still formed matter into ashes—the insects link the
Spirit of Destruction to the Spirit of Earth. And the earth is claimed by the poet
as the vestigial domain of ashes—of "undead" bodily matter (Czarnecka and
Fiut 1987, 132).[25] Thus, the underworld is defined as a place of ontological in-betweenness, in which one encounters the indeterminacy of matter instead of its
finality. Let us follow this lead.

To begin with, Miłosz puts a mole at work in this underworld. Asked by
Czarnecka about this uncanny creature, the poet offered a circumventing answer, which preserved the hermetic aspect of his eschatology "undisturbed"
by an interpretative inquiry: "I don't know who the guardian mole is. . . . [O]
ne can imagine a subterranean space where something alive is moving. If
that's how it moves, it must be a mole. What other creatures move through the
ground?" (Czarnecka and Fiut 1987, 133). When an avowed naturalist (but no
great lover of nature) like Miłosz, who knew more than a thing or two about
flora and fauna, claimed that only moles live underground, he again deliberately risked the reader's smile. And so the guardian mole, the only living creature in the huge depository of ashes, continues to intrigue other critics. Leonard

Nathan and Arthur Quinn maintain in their monograph that "[t]he interpretive temptation the poem leaves us with is to determine the identity of the strange 'guardian mole.'"[26] Despite espousing this desire, they do not manage to establish its identity; in fact, they follow the poet's equivocal—if not reluctant—commentary. In Miłosz studies, this is an established type of reading, which considers, and often faithfully follows, the extensive corpus of his critical commentaries to his writings. Indeed, these viewpoints are important because they were made by the poet himself; often they contain priceless bits of information, as his copious interviews, essays, and notes to *Utwory zebrane* (Collected Works) demonstrate. In this particular instance, however, the lack of any authorial feedback becomes a reverse strategy, perhaps suggestive of his protection of the poem. One senses here a certain discomfort on the poet's part that persisted many years after the lyric was written. Let us contemplate the presence of the laborious mole who guards the afterlife and see to what extent the creature indeed resists interpretation.

Mysterious and hybrid beings and events abound in apocalyptic texts. Hybridity plays an important role in any eschatological imagery, as it destabilizes known categories or violates them.[27] The mole created by Miłosz is one of them, a hybrid being, whose appearance undermines everyday logic. The mole's hybridity is construed by adding the additional features to those of his own; its natural blindness is counterbalanced by its vision additionally enhanced by the lamp on its forehead to invoke contradiction. Although moles are blind, this uncanny creature whose scrutinizing gaze causes the soul to shiver with fear can see from under its "swollen eyelid" without an eye. Furthermore, for the blind mole that sees, the soul is not invisible.[28] One of the souls, the poetic persona, is also granted the capacity of vision. The persona is, therefore, both gazed at and gazing, aware of the mole's gaze and returning this awareness. In the poem, the traditionally invisible underworld is constituted visually, as a wholly specular concept. The Polish poet's general insistence on the visual and spatial character of the world to come links his imagined subterranean universe to Rainer Maria Rilke's location of Hades in a mine. One finds an instructive object lesson, comparable to Miłosz's account of the underworld, in Rilke's poem "Orpheus, Euridice, and Hermes."[29] It is a mine, an underground site of hard labor, yet devoid of any images of labor. Rilke imagines this mine within the old tradition of the sublimation of afterlife and, thus, it represents the locus of transparent and disembodied spirits. Nonetheless, Rilke's poem functions here as one of Miłosz's primary intertexts.[30] What situates Rilke's symbolist vision of the afterlife as a mine so close to Miłosz's Holocaust poem is the illusive and ominous appearance of the guardian mole. If the underworld can be imagined as a mine, a mole can be a miner, which explains why the creature is equipped with a lamp on its forehead. Another feature of the guardian mole who mines souls underground complicates this simple decoding. The mole's swollen eyelids turn him not only into just any patriarch but, more specifically, into one from the Judaic tradition. If so, its lamp becomes a reflection of the tefillin attached to the foreheads of praying Jews. Thus, the bizarre equipment on the mole's head speaks of its higher, supernatural capacities to distinguish ashes from ashes, soul from soul. These capacities are especially important in making him a clairvoyant, since turning the body into ashes transforms its previous visually defined form into its lack, into formlessness.

The formlessness of ashes is overcome not only through the mole's gaze, but also because bodily vestiges, turned into creaturely ones,[31] remain the site of the seeing, thinking, and trembling self who inhabits ashes. In this sense, Derrida is right when he suggests that "ashes are the house of being" (1987b, 25). One must ask, then, how the following crucial discrimination can be attempted—how the individual self (or immortal soul) is preserved and distinguished from the other selves in an underground full of ashes. In this instance, the answer lies in an intense visualization of the underworld, which performs the individual through light and color.[32] The ashes are illuminated by the soul, and each soul emanates a different spectrum of colorful light to which the uncanny mole's higher and terrifying capacity of the gaze (which exists somewhere beyond his dysfunctional physical eye) is very sensitive:

> He distinguishes human ashes by their luminous vapor,[33]
> The ashes of each man by a different part of the spectrum.
> ("A Poor Christian Looks at the Ghetto"; Miłosz 2001a, 63)

This insertion of the theosophic idea, the identification of an individual human being with a particular spectrum of light emanating from his ashes, most likely derives from Rudolf Steiner's occultism. In Steiner's theosophy, the reading of an individual in the afterlife begins with grasping of her or his inner life projected as a definite chromatic appearance, which overcomes the ashes' duality:

> In accordance with theosophical teaching, thought is not the abstraction it is commonly considered to be, but is built up of definite forms, the shape of which depends on the quality of the thought. It also causes definite vibrations, which are seen as colors. Hence, clairvoyants may tell the state of a man's development from the appearance of his astral body.[34]

Steiner specifies how the visual reading of the chromatic body is intimately related to another valuation—that of ethical worthiness (in Steiner's lexicon, "development") of each individual. Thus the scenario of the Day of Judgment is inscribed within the process of recognition; indeed, the atonement begins then:

For example, some suggest that a nebulous appearance indicates imperfect development, while an ovoid appearance betokens a more perfect develop-ment. As the colors are indicative of the kind of thought, the variety of these in the astral body indicates the possessor's character. Inferior thoughts pro-duce loud colors, so that rage, for instance, will be recognized by the red appearance of the astral body. Higher thoughts will be recognizable by the presence of delicate colors; religious thought, for instance, will cause a blue color. ("Knowledge of the State"; Steiner)

Disturbingly, however, the afterlife—traditionally the sphere of God the Omnivoyeur and his All-Seeing Eye—is also governed by the mole's voyeuris-tic scrutiny of the *anatomical* details of genitals. To employ the mole's know-ing gaze in the search for anatomical distinctions ultimately makes this blind creature a voyeur employed by God; he is His extension in the same way as angels extend God in more traditional theologies. On His behalf, the mole sees, counts, and discriminates.

The afterlife as a repository of undead ashes,[35] through which one laborious messenger digs, is therefore a place of ontological in-betweenness in appear-ances only. In the poem, this site becomes something more, namely, the specta-cle of individuation on the level of the soma. Instead of matter's finality and indeterminacy caused by the fusion of various ashes, one encounters the strictly defined spectral order of the underworld: the mole separates undistinguished ashes into individual beings. His ultimate goal is to sort out the saved souls from the condemned ones. This rigid eschatological discrimination is based on the absence (or presence) of the religious mark on the body and can be translated only as the circumcision effect. Within the historical temporality of the Holo-caust, circumcision meant death, while its absence delineated the zone of rela-tive safety. In the post-historical temporality of the Last Judgment, the logic is reversed, as circumcision ceases to mark identity in a negative or punitive way. The order of voyeuristic sadism in the Holocaust is inverted here, so that escha-tological justice can be done: a mohel's cut that renewed the Covenant allows the mole to differentiate the uncircumcised/condemned from the circumcised/ saved. Those who were condemned to death during the war would be saved; those who were saved would be condemned in the world to come. In other words, within the post-historical logic, unmarked bodies are perceived as marked. In this radical inversion, the (un)marked poetic self—the Jew of the New Testament— confesses his fear and guilt.

Full of forebodings, the poetic "I" gazes at the ghetto engulfed by flames and speaks in the language of biblical prophets, with their dark imagery, nebu-lous wording, and passionate vengeance in relating the fulfilled apocalypse. Amid historical events that would be named the Holocaust only much later, the frantic poetic self articulates eschatological ethics akin, by virtue of its severity, to that of the Last Judgment. When Marian Stala, a prominent Miłosz scholar, claims that Miłosz's poetry invokes no sense of self-pity, that there is no frightened poetic persona in the poet's oeuvre, he does not consider the figure of the "poor Christian," the culpable yet terrified, empathic gentile spectator who gives active witness to the atrocities committed on Jews.[36]

The poem's uncanny imagery and unrelenting judgment makes another critic, Jan Błoński, on a different occasion, call the poem both "terrifying" and "full of fear."[37] The poem may indeed give the reader shivers. The poetic narrator/self speaks from the perspective of eternity and points to the traces of blood from his absent body (the "red trace" and "the place left after his body" in its third stanza), which imply his violent end. The drastic glimpse at the voided entirety of the body and the somatic absence translated into a vestige contradict the reappearance of the "broken" (*rozbite*) body in the fifth stanza. The lack of the *corpus delicti* in this out-of-the-body experience and the unsightly death scene correspond to other scenarios prescribed by poets for their violent demise, here augmented by the horror of looking at the burning ghetto intermingled with the nearly palpable awe of the Last Judgment. Full of dread in uttering the prophetic word, the overburdened poetic persona seems to be molded after the image of the Emperor Hadrian's *animula blandula vagula*, and trembles, imprisoned in glowing ashes as he awaits his final verdict from the guardian of the underworld.

How relentless the poet is to himself! Throughout this poem, Miłosz has already given his poetic testimony to the genocide and, thus, has signed a moral contract based on compassion; his guilt should be remarkably diminished. His may be only a guilt of impassivity, but the act of giving witness undermines his noninvolvement and his passive spectatorship; the latter is destabilized furthermore because he identifies, in a gesture that was suicidal at that time, with the Jews. To my knowledge, no non-Jewish author who lived under the terror of the Nazi rule would have signed an audacious poetic document of this caliber. The fact that Miłosz kept his poem close to him, in a suitcase, demonstrates an incredibly high level of both self-awareness and ethical conscience fused with a sense of responsibility. Such ethical "action" during the Holocaust when, let me repeat, even symbolic identification with Jews was possible only at great personal risk, makes Miłosz's position truly singular. It must be emphasized that Miłosz does not, however, formulate any moral imperative according to which the rest of Nazi occupied Europe should follow his ethical gesture. In discussing Miłosz's war poems, Donald Davie emphasizes that "shame and guilt [are] peculiar to Miłosz himself" (Davie 1986, 62) in that the poet reserves these absolute moral standards of responsibility and involvement only for himself. This judgment was his personal matter, voiced in the most daring of his poems. Perhaps this was one of the reasons the poet was not willing to engage in the hermenutics of "A Poor Christian."

The final shift within the field of the visualized underworld poses further interpretive problems. Miłosz does not construe the realm of the hereafter in terms
of an ethereal existence of dead spirits. Even in the sphere of the afterlife, the
pneuma is closely bound up with matter and, indeed, remains incarnated in
ashes. The earth, seen from this perspective, discloses its material substance
composed of ashes, of the decomposed soma. In terms of transformational logic,
the earth as an enormous underground cemetery symbolizes a regression to *ma-
teria prima* as a theologically motivated phenomenon. Ashes—as organic and
formless substances that are not quite objectual—are subjected to a hypostasis
that raises questions as to how the pneumatic traverses the somatic, precisely
because the poet has eclipsed from representation the intimate bond between
the soma and the pneuma. Desacralized in an ongoing process of secularization
and, in particular, by the Holocaust's burning of bodies and disrespectful dis-
posal of the remains, ashes are re-sacralized by Miłosz's ethical revision of the
radical theological opposition between flesh and soul.[38] Nonetheless, Miłosz, as
the poet of the Holocaust, gives differing answers as to whether a recycling of
soma is a sacrilegious and irrevocable process, particularly if he approaches the
issue from within theologies of embodiment. His perspective is not comparable
with any other solution of that time, partly because of his uncanny combination
of somatic and ethical perspectives with eschatological ones.

Since ashes preserve the individual incarnation and markings, their un-
deadness and in-betweenness are understated, to say the least. Ashes are not
the substance in which life still lingers, but the agency from which individual
life resurrects itself in an unorthodox way. The closure of the poem informs
another aspect of Miłosz's daring and syncretic ideas: the re-presentation of
the fragmented soma through which life and the pneumatic traverse visually
in the form of a unique shade of light. This heterogeneous concept, derived
from occultism, Judaism, and Christianity, juxtaposes the apocalyptic imagery of matter's total destruction to the post-apocalyptic theology of pneumatic
continuity within the (un)marked soma. In doing so, the poet creates a new
solution for the Holocaust's soteriology, whose very uniqueness has a shocking
effect on account of its sadistically voyeuristic character.

Remarkably, Miłosz's articulation of the future post-Holocaust judgment as
well as the soteriological justice have lost none of its relevance today. This may
be one of the reasons Miłosz avoided extensive commentary on the poem, either in interviews or in authorial notes and autobiographical essays. An attempt at positioning the poem and its implications regarding Polish–Jewish
coexistence was already made by Błoński. In this study on the material world
in the literature of the Holocaust, there is no room to follow Błoński's direction. Miłosz wrote the poem, letting it speak for itself. This chapter shows how
it spoke to me.

The grammar of vestiges, engaged in the transformational mechanism to which the soma is subjugated, determines the representation of the poetic persona's own fate. Permeated by the personal guilt of impassivity, will the soul return from ashes to a wholesome resurrected body? Is Ezekiel's vision of dried bones returning to life, a sort of counter-recycling poignant in this context, a solution for the Holocaust poet? Yes and no, if one apprehends the total eschatological project in Miłosz's wartime poetry. The poet's eschatology, imagined during the war, cannot be reduced to its one variant represented in "A Poor Christian," but may only be appreciated/viewed within the constellation of other poems. One of them, "Café," appears before "A Poor Christian" for the purpose of deliberately enhancing their opposing concepts of the afterlife. In both poems, soteriological expectations stem, rather predictably, from the region of the soma, from weighing its deadness against the possibility of its resurrection. "Café" negates any such theological hope:

> The same winter fog on the window,
> but nobody will enter.
> The handful of ashes,
> the stain of rotting flesh covered with lime
> will not take a hat off, say joyfully:
> Let's have vodka.[39]

Here, as in most of Miłosz's poetry, an autobiographical thread is present. This postapocalyptic elegy is framed by a recollection of the past culture of cafés and cabarets so essential to the interwar artistic and literary life in Poland's capital city. Within this unsentimentalized frame, he mourns his friends, the young poets of Warsaw who perished during World War II. Miłosz's grief finds no consolation, as he declares the impossibility of a return to life and enjoyment. His dead colleagues' somatic vestiges, reduced to mere waste, are so powerless that they can no longer give testimony, even of a forensic sort. "The stain of rotting flesh" replaces the fragmented body in "A Poor Christian" and negates the individual soul's continued existence in the afterlife.

To reiterate, Czesław Miłosz considers both ends of eschatology, so to speak. His convictions and beliefs are tested one against another for their better attainment. In "Café," his reaction to death tends toward the materialist premise that the after-death processes encompass only decaying matter. This negativity is counterbalanced in "A Poor Christian Looks at the Ghetto." The poems oscillate between two extremes: the skeptical and the hopeful assumptions about the posthumous future. The soma's recycling in "A Poor Christian" revises the concept of its counter-recycling in "Café." In the poet's arguing pro and contra, nothing resonates more persuasively than his engagement with the inescapable testimony of the body and, by extension, the material world.

Texts

"Campo di Fiori"

W Rzymie na Campo di Fiori
Kosze oliwek i cytryn,
Bruk opryskany winem
I odłamkami kwiatów.
Różowe owoce morza
Sypią na stoły przekupnie,
Naręcza ciemnych winogron
Padają na puch brzoskwini.

Tu, na tym właśnie placu
Spalono Giordana Bruna,
Kat płomień stosu zażegnął
W kole ciekawej gawiedzi.
A ledwo płomień przygasnął,
Znów pełne były tawerny,
Kosze oliwek i cytryn
Nieśli przekupnie na głowach.

Wspomniałem Campo di Fiori
W Warszawie przy karuzeli,
W pogodny wieczór wiosenny,
Przy dźwiękach skocznej muzyki.
Salwy za murem getta
Głuszyła skoczna melodia
I wzlatywały pary
Wysoko w pogodne niebo.

Czasem wiatr z domów płonących
Przynosił czarne latawce,
Łapali skrawki w powietrzu
Jadący na karuzeli.
Rozwiewał suknie dziewczynom
Ten wiatr od murów płonących,
Śmiały się tłumy wesołe
W czas pięknej warszawskiej niedzieli.

Morał ktoś może wyczyta,
Że lud warszawski czy rzymski
Handluje, bawi się, kocha
Mijając męczeńskie stosy.
Inny ktoś morał wyczyta
O rzeczy ludzkich mijaniu,
O zapomnieniu, co rośnie,
Nim jeszcze płomień przygasnął.

Ja jednak wtedy myślałem
O samotności ginących.
O tym, że kiedy Giordano
Wstępował na rusztowanie,
Nie znalazł w ludzkim języku
Ani jednego wyrazu,
Aby nim ludzkość pożegnać,
Tę ludzkość, która zostaje.

Już biegli wychylać wino,
Sprzedawać białe rozgwiazdy,
Kosze oliwek i cytryn
Nieśli w wesołym gwarze.
I był już od nich odległy,
Jakby minęły wieki,
A oni chwilę czekali
Na jego odlot w pożarze.

I ci ginący, samotni,
Już zapomniani od świata,
Język nasz stał się im obcy
Jak język dawnej planety.
Aż wszystko będzie legendą
I wtedy po wielu latach
Na nowym Campo di Fiori
Bunt wznieci słowo poety.
Warszawa-Wielkanoc, 1943

"CAMPO DEI FIORI"

In Rome on the Campo dei Fiori
baskets of olives and lemons,
cobbles spattered with wine

and the wreckage of flowers.
Vendors cover the trestles
with rose-pink fish;
armfuls of dark grapes
heaped on peach-down.

On this same square
they burned Giordano Bruno.
Henchmen kindled the pyre
close-pressed by the mob.
Before the flames had died
the taverns were full again,
baskets of olives and lemons
again on the vendors' shoulders.

I thought of the Campo dei Fiori
in Warsaw by the sky-carousel
one clear spring evening
to the strains of a carnival tune.
The bright melody drowned
the salvos from the ghetto wall,
and couples were flying
high in the cloudless sky.

At times wind from the burning
would drift dark kites along
and riders on the carousel
caught petals in midair.
That same hot wind
blew open the skirts of the girls
and the crowds were laughing
on that beautiful Warsaw Sunday.

Someone will read as moral
that the people of Rome or Warsaw
haggle, laugh, make love
as they pass by martyrs' pyres.
Someone else will read
of the passing of things human,
of the oblivion
born before the flames have died.

But that day I thought only
of the loneliness of the dying,

of how, when Giordano
climbed to his burning
he could not find
in any human tongue
words for mankind,
mankind who live on.

Already they were back at their wine
or peddled their white starfish,
baskets of olives and lemons
they had shouldered to the fair,
and he already distanced
as if centuries had passed
while they paused just a moment
For his flying in the fire.

Those dying here, the lonely
forgotten by the world,
our tongue becomes for them
the language of an ancient planet.
Until, when all is legend
and many years have passed,
on a new Campo dei Fiori
rage will kindle at a poet's word.

"BIEDNY CHRZEŚCIJANIN PATRZY NA GETTO"

Pszczoły obudowują czerwoną wątrobę,
Mrówki obudowują czarną kość,
Rozpoczyna się rozdzieranie, deptanie jedwabi,
Rozpoczyna się tłuczenie szkła, drzewa, miedzi, niklu, srebra, pian
Gipsowych, blach, strun, trąbek, liści, kul, kryształów—
Pyk! Fosforyczny ogień z żółtych ścian
Pochłania ludzkie i zwierzęce włosie.

Pszczoły obudowują plaster płuc,
Mrówki obudowują białą kość,
Rozdzierany jest papier, kauczuk, płótno, skóra, len,
Włókna, materie, celuloza, włos, wężowa łuska, druty,
Wali się w ogniu dach, ściana i żar ogarnia fundament.
Jest już tylko piaszczysta, zdeptana, z jednym z drzewem bez liści
Ziemia.

Powoli, drążąc tunel, posuwa się strażnik-kret
Z małą czerwoną latarką przypiętą na czole.
Dotyka ciał pogrzebanych, liczy, przedziera się dalej,
Rozróżnia ludzki popiół po tęczującym oparze,
Popiół każdego człowieka po innej barwie tęczy.
Pszczoły obudowują czerwony ślad,
Mrówki obudowują miejsce po moim ciele.

Boję się, tak się boję strażnika-kreta.
Jego obrzmiała powieka jak u patriarchy,
Który siadywał dużo w blasku świec
Czytając wielką księgę gatunku.

Cóż powiem mu, ja, Żyd Nowego Testamentu,
Czekający od dwóch tysięcy lat na powrót Jezusa?
Moje rozbite ciało wyda mnie jego spojrzeniu
I policzy mnie między pomocników śmierci:
Nieobrzezanych.

"A Poor Christian Looks at the Ghetto"

Bees build around red liver,
Ants build around black bone.
It has begun: the trampling on silks,
It has begun: the breaking of glass, wood, copper, nickel, silver, foam
Of gypsum, iron sheets, violin strings, trumpets, leaves, balls, crystals.
Poof! Phosphorescent fire from yellow walls
Engulfs animal and human hair.

Bees build around the honeycomb of lungs,
Ants build around white bone.
Torn is paper, rubber, linen, leather, flax,
Fiber, fabrics, cellulose, snakeskin, wire.
The roof and the wall collapse in flame and heat seizes the
foundations.
Now there is only the earth: sandy, trodden down,
With one leafless tree.

Slowly, boring a tunnel, a guardian mole makes his way
With a small red lamp fastened to his forehead.
He touches buried bodies, counts them, pushes on,
He distinguishes human ashes by their luminous vapor,
The ashes of each man by a different part of the spectrum.

Bees build around a red trace.
Ants build around the place left by my body.

I am afraid, so afraid of the guardian mole,
He has swollen eyelids, like a Patriarch
Who has sat much in the light of candles
Reading the great book of the species.

What will I tell him, I, a Jew of the New Testament,
Waiting two thousand years for the second coming of Jesus?
My broken body will deliver me to his sight
And he will count me among the helpers of death:
The uncircumcised.

Warsaw, 1943

ON CONTACT

CHAPTER FIVE

The Manuscript Lost in Warsaw

I<small>T HAS BECOME</small> a cultural ritual of sorts that prominent artists give or sell their archives, sometimes their only asset, to libraries and other institutions to make sure that their legacy exists in the public domain instead of as a burden to relatives. This gesture sacrifices the intimacy of connection that one develops with his own artistic oeuvre and its material, tangible form; it is a vestige of one's labor, creation made tangible. Irreducible to mere material possession or intellectual property, an archive speaks of creative legacy, property, and much more, mainly because it implicates identity. Bentham defines the relationship between property and identity, already invoked here, in terms of an emotional incorporation of the material by the self: "our property becomes a part of our being, and cannot be torn from us without rending us to the quick" (Bentham 1814, 115). This understanding of the strong emotional bond between humans and their belongings engages the relationship between the author and his or her manuscripts.

My case in point is Jerzy Andrzejewski (1909–1983), a prominent writer, critic, and political activist whose work and ideological affinities underwent several shifts. His first novel, *Ład serca* (A Heart's Order) (1938), which brought him immediate recognition, determined his earliest image as a Catholic moralist writer. For the first two years of the war, the young writer was engaged in underground resistance activities and efforts to rescue Jews, displaying a great deal of courage and neglecting his writing.[1] When his plans for two novels failed, he shifted to other genres and wrote several short stories that reflected the ongoing conflicts among Poles caused by the war. The issue of clashing subjectivities brought about by the German occupation represented for him a far more compelling sphere than either the representation of the war itself or the Polish underground's military confrontations with the Nazis. Within this framework, Andrzejewski took on the risky and thorny subject of a seemingly eternal Polish–Jewish antinomy in his *Wielki Tydzień* (Holy Week), which is more a novella or a compact novel than a short story.

Set in Warsaw during Holy Week of 1943, *Wielki Tydzień* (Holy Week) details how, in one part of the city, Poles are preparing for the Easter holidays, while the other part, namely the ghetto, in which the uprising is going on, is burning. The work, first read by the author in a private gathering, was not well received.[2] The most severe judgment of it was passed by prominent poet and writer, Jarosław Iwaszkiewicz, who accused Andrzejewski of exploiting the Jewish tragedy much too quickly, as if only belated use of the topic was permissible.[3] The gravity of this attack was extraordinary in that Iwaszkiewicz entirely overlooked not only Andrzejewski's active compassion towards the Jewish plight, but also the author's readiness to take the personal risk inevitably connected with undertaking such issues during wartime.

We do not know much about the first version of the novella, written as the events of the ghetto uprising were unfolding. Years after the war the original manuscript was lost, despite Andrzejewski's almost obsessive habit of preserving the meticulous order of his archives. In the writer's archive there still is a file labeled *Wielki Tydzień—wersja I i II* (Holy Week—versions 1 and 2).[4] Strangely, not a trace of the first version remains there. What is known, however, is Andrzejewski's decision to rewrite *Holy Week* according to his new ideological ideas, as part of his "road to realism."[5] Given the fact that the original disappeared, Andrzejewski's postwar inscription made on the erased version bears all the quality of a palimpsest.

Since the manuscript of *Holy Week* was *not* lost during the war, nothing seems to indicate at first glance that the original version was subjugated to *precarium*. But it was, and Andrzejewski had to negotiate its continued existence against *precarium*. Unlike Miłosz, Andrzejewski was not able to smuggle his archive out of Warsaw during the 1944 mass exodus of the civilian population. Attempting to save it, he resorted to a much more expedient—and perhaps safer—method, since in his archive was his 1943 version of *Holy Week*, a text that contained material incriminating the occupiers. Since he lived with his family in Bielany, a distant and relatively quiet outskirt of Warsaw, it was possible to protect both his familial and artistic archives in a simple and reliable way. As Andrzejewski recalled, "a lot of things, which we could not take, we buried in the ground. . . . [A]ll my manuscripts and notes, the various mementos, the photographs, the letters—many years of the past went to the ground."[6] They were dug out after the war, apparently undamaged, because the writer never complained of even their partial damage.

In the story of the writer's archives there appears, however, one intriguing episode of his deliberate fabrication of the *precarium* status of a portion of his archive. The story began in prewar times, when Andrzejewski gave his entire juvenile production to a close friend, Józef Chudek (Synoradzka 1997, 13). Later on, the writer claimed that this part of his oeuvre had been irrevocably lost during the war. That he could believe right after the war that his juvenile writings were irrevocably lost is quite understandable. He made this claim in his 1945 memoir, *Jak zostałem pisarzem* (How I Became a Writer), published in *Odrodzenie*. When Chudek sent a letter to *Odrodzenie* the following year, explaining that the manuscripts were intact and, in fact, still in his possession, Andrzejewski responded, inexplicably, with shock rather than gratitude, straining his friendship with Chudek. Furthermore, the author repeated his story of the apparent wartime loss in his *Notatki do autobiografii* (Notes to the Autobiography), which was published in 1980 (thirty-four years after Chudek's letter!). It seems that Andrzejewski, a perfectionist par excellence, felt compelled to make the symbolic sacrifice of his weakest writings, using as a pretext the usual fate of manuscripts during wartime. It would be presumptuous to suppose that he merely wanted to participate in a widespread postwar counting of losses, since he in fact had lost his own mother in the Ravensbrück concentration camp during the war and suffered greatly following her death.[7] The loss of a few manuscripts would have been only a minor setback, and would not have set him apart from other Polish literati, who had almost invariably suffered similar losses.[8]

The second version of *Holy Week*—that is, the hypertext "overwritten" on the original just after the war—depicts the variety of reactions in Polish society toward the Jewish population and the armed Jewish resistance. In the novella, Alpha-Andrzejewski,[9] the committed moralist, puts all of society on trial. His shift from the psychological framework of the novella's earlier version to an emotionally charged, but nevertheless more realistic, framework of the newer version coincided with his planned ideological reinscribing of the novella. Most likely, as Synoradzka, the writer's biographer, claims, the palimpsestic revision resulted from Andrzejewski's discovery of several antisemitic events that occurred in various Polish cities during the spring and summer of 1945.[10] To a lesser extent, it was also motivated by Andrzejewski's experience of systemic changes in postwar Polish politics, although eventually he became a proponent of both socialist realism and the communist governement.[11] Andrzejewski was pressured by the leftist critics who dominated the Polish literary scene at the time, especially by the prominent and highly intelligent Jan Kott, who praised the novella's hypertext. Because of Kott's access to the original wartime version, he was the only one in a position to make such a comparative evaluation.[12] Both motivational plans were oriented to achieve different goals; in fact, they bifurcated. Andrzejewski's reaction against antisemitism embodied a corrective, humanistic impulse and engaged a wider discourse on Polish–Jewish coexistence; it had a cultural resonance intertwined strongly with the recent history. The second motivation, which adjusted the text to the new politics and aesthetics propagated in Poland, anticipated a response within a narrower group of readers and was decidedly a compromise.

The (Un)making of Warsaw

The reinscription of the novella resulted in an altered genre and its descriptive emphasis: from a psychological to a more realistic depiction of Polish society at the time of the genocide. This shift required that Andrzejewski make use of a different representational strategy. In order to distinguish between the differing predicaments of Poles and Jews, while simultaneously maintaining his perspective on the peril and unpredictability of human nature deemed universal and not necessarily conditioned by wartime, Andrzejewski chose for his new version public and private space: the streets and homes of Warsaw. In the restaged version of *Holy Week*, the entire drama took place on the "Aryan side." The ghetto side, engulfed in flames, remained persistently in the background. This juxtaposition revealed the peripheral significance the Jewish uprising bore for the majority of Warsaw's non-Jewish population. The other part of Warsaw seemed quieter and less crowded, filled with rickshaws and poorly dressed pedestrians minding their own business, it was nonetheless scarred by the occupation. Even on this other side of Warsaw, the population was subjected to mass arrests and death visible to everyone. Landau (1962) mentions that beginning with the 1939 invasion and bombardments, "on nearly every plaza, infrequently on streets and even in courtyards are arranged temporary cemeteries containing those killed during bombardments" (1: 34). Another decisive factor, which changed the grammar of the streets of Warsaw, was determined by the Nazi occupational law based on the racist criterion of the German nation's superiority made visible by the warning sign *Nur für Deutsche* (for Germans only), which was placed nearly everywhere, in parks, on benches, in restaurants, in tramways.

The Warsaw Ghetto, along with many other ghettos created during World War II, was not of the type exemplified by historical Jewish neighborhoods and shtetls prior to the war, such as Kazimierz in Kraków. Instead of merely existing as enclosed urban spaces with permeable borders, as they had previously, the ghettos of the 1940s became specific spatial enclaves entirely extricated from the surrounding public sphere. Walled completely on November 26, 1940, the Warsaw Ghetto became, within a year, a tightly sealed zone defined by labyrinthine and frequently revised borders. The spatial division separated Polish citizens into two groups: Polish and Jewish, regardless of their individual sense of belonging, identity, or language. This topographic division of the city by the walls of the ghetto, which Joanna Rostropowicz Clark aptly described as absolute, reflected other much deeper differences.[13] For example, by the infamous governor Fischer's order, each unjustified exit from the "Jewish district" was punished by death. Urban spatiality so rigidly delimited according to the rule of race, control, and fear of contamination thereby led to a zone of exclusion.[14] The Warsaw Ghetto, one of the largest Nazi projects of its kind, was produced as a space of exception: a depository of undesirable human bodies doomed to be erased. Probably the most telling indicator of the division and its impact on the population and public space was the fact that civilian deaths became common occurrences on the streets of the ghetto. The process of erasing human life became a public event; according to some witnesses, as early as winter 1941/42, frozen and often naked cadavers of children and the elderly lying on sidewalks were registered as a typical event.[15] Mary Berg writes that the passersby became accustomed to the horror of this view,[16] and yet this frequent sight must have been painful not only because of the blatant disregard for humanity it displayed, but also because of an obvious disrespect for the strict burial rituals established in Judaism.

The dehumanizing impact of the German occupation was manifold and included transmogrifications of public space. For example, the Nazi propagandistic predilection for huge pseudo-classical buildings and grand-scale military parades was a well-known aspect that co-produced this ambiguity. In the occupied territories across Europe, no imposing pseudo-Doric style edifices were built, since these countries were treated as a part of a wider economic exploitation. To control the occupied peoples, the Nazis resorted to other means of propaganda, which were employed on a different and more modest, but nonetheless effective, level: such means of inducing terror as deportations and mass public executions, police and military presence, radio announcements, posters. I have already mentioned, in chapter 4, one example of the propagandistic manipulation of the public space: *karuzela* (a roundabout)[17] installed by the German occupiers on the Krasiński Plaza in the "Aryan" part of Warsaw.[18] The decision to place the structure by the walls of the ghetto seemed not to be calculated solely to provide entertainment for the masses. Very likely, its secondary motive was to lower the morale of the people *behind* the wall, who could see those on the other side enjoying themselves and freely moving about on the streets.[19] One assumes that not only were old resentments deepened by this perfidious manipulation, but that new wounds were added and the roundabout—a shrewdly divisive factor—intensified a collective sense on the part of ghetto inhabitants that they were dying in solitude. In Andrzejewski's account, which differs somewhat from that of Miłosz, the roundabout is under construction and serves German soldiers as cover from the bullets of the insurgents.[20] The crowd of Varsovians observing this fight entertains itself; their total contempt for the troops is enhanced by their admiration for the insurgents who, at that moment, were still resisting the "krauts." In invoking the reaction of the crowd, Andrzejewski did not spare his people, but described their negative reaction as well.[21]

These events occurred against a backdrop of the city under erasure. Never a writer to relish the sumptuous descriptions of edifices and interiors considered de rigueur in realistic novels, Andrzejewski used buildings, their façades and interiors, detritus, or solitary objects to build backgrounds for the more abstract dramas of human emotions. Consequently, he did not elevate inanimate things to the role of protagonists in any of his narratives. This does not mean that Andrzejewski employed large or small objects in an incidental manner. Instead, he would connect even the most trivial ones to his characters, making them participants in the sphere of psychological action and in a larger social context. This measure of the writer's representational control is most obvious when the material world and its props are employed both skillfully and economically in an important episode.

The abrupt political events caused by the war left their mark of discontinuity on the social, mental, and economic make-up of life. As reflected in Andrzejewski's realistic strategy for his hypertext, these changes had implications for his construction of war interiors. While I am not concerned here with the history of interior design as construed in literature, some relevant guideposts should be erected. To begin with, Andrzejewski's postwar sense of interior is indicative of Balzac's realistic tradition, which first drew a strict correlation between owner and abode. The signs Balzac inscribed into furniture and other accoutrements portrayed their owner's social class, interests, and even inner state with mirror-like perfection. Balzac tolerated no accidental objects in his rigid unison of significa-tion: a miniature of a young girl placed on a dresser signified the dweller's ardor; old and ugly furniture, lacking in comfort, spoke of the impoverishment of the pensioners in *Pére Goriot* (Old Goriot); an elegant and luxurious Parisian drawing room depicted Goriot's daughters' snobbery and upper-class social standing. Nonetheless, Balzac could afford certain nuances and a degree of individualiza-tion within this framework of correspondence. So a nouveau-riche's drawing room would usually differ from a parlor of an impoverished aristocrat whose taste would, according to Balzac's conservative hierarchy, always remain superior. An understanding of the material object-world in Balzac's fiction, as an epic text evocative of the entire history of the French nation, becomes crucial for any un-derstanding of authorial delight in the descriptive and detailed language of furni-ture, luxurious fabrics and wallpapers, and precious knick-knacks.[22]

Likewise, Andrzejewski construed a parallel between inhabitant and interior similar to the neo-Platonic framework, according to which the visible exterior re-vealed the hidden interior. He somewhat modified this symmetry in *Holy Week*, taking into account the fact that some of his novella's characters dwelled in flats disturbed by the war and, thus, only a few homes in his representation remained intact. In order to describe more precisely Andrzejewski's sense of interior, the whole concept should be posited contextually within the larger Polish tradition of writing the interior. During the interwar period that constituted Andrzejewski's formative and debut years, one novel occupied a special place in Polish literature, largely due to a changing sense of the private interior. Maria Kuncewiczowa's novel, *Cudzoziemka* (The Strange Woman), published in 1935, dramatized the intergenerational clash through a portrayal of the shift in attitudes toward household objects and the symbolic value attributed to family heirlooms. Kuncewiczowa captured the shift from a symbolic interior based on historical and national values—where furniture and family heirlooms represent patriotism and where patriarchal tradition stands as a part of familial memory—to a more functionalist and cosmopolitan conception of interior, in which objects already emancipated from the cohesive, symbolic order attain new functionality. Baudrillard in his *The System of Objects* analyzes the transformation of auratic and symbolic systems of interior through the functionalist paradigm and, finally, into the consumerist approach to domestic space and objects. [23]

Clearly applicable to Kuncewiczowa's novel, Baudrillard's concept of the symbolic does not agree with Balzac's parallelism. In a nutshell, the difference on Balzac's part lies in his advancing the concept of a domestic interior that is already disrupted during the tumultuous nineteenth century in France. For Baudrillard, by contrast, the domestic sphere remains an unchangeable and essentially patriarchal project until the symbolic network of objects is liberated, for the sake of their pure function, from the sentiments of the past. This change could occur on a larger scale only after World War I. The functionalist approach does not recognize family myths as embodied in furniture, portraits, or mementos. Instead, it disposes of these narratives of identity by subordinating and fragmenting them; within this model, a dweller with a long, rich familial history chooses not to display its mementos, preferring rather to be surrounded by abstract paintings, for example. Although she or he has no personal or historical connection with this art, she or he values it for reasons other than the familial. Let us take a look at the evidence of the transition *Holy Week* makes in this direction.

Wartime Dwellings

Entering Andrzejewski's wartime interiors, one sees both symbolic and functionalist types of interiors. Unlike in Kuncewiczowa's novel, no transition between the two is captured. While Andrzejewski's interiors demonstrate that he already absorbed Kuncewiczowa's object lesson, they do not display a clash of generations, but exist simultaneously. Indeed, some of them represent the his-torical Balzac-like paradigm, while others reproduce a functionalist one. Since Malecki is a young architect, the apartment he rents aptly illustrates this new functionalist mode.[24] Andrzejewski draws a parallel between the inhabitant and his space, in this case to reflect Malecki's profession. The character lives in a rela-tively new apartment building located in an almost pastoral setting on the out-skirts of the city.[25] Filled with the sunshine and fresh air that penetrates the residence through its French doors and windows, the flat has all the commodi-ties required by functionalism's attention to design, hygiene, and simplicity. There is a bathroom and a balcony; the rooms appear not to be overcrowded with knick-knacks and the clutter condemned, above all, by functionalism's te-nets. It is sparsely furnished with only necessary items: a drawing table, a rattan crib, and a couch appear in brief glimpses, lit discreetly by electric lamps. The objects are subordinated to the dwellers' needs in the strikingly colorless envi-ronment required by the modernist credo that was, nonetheless, cozy.

The overarching simplicity and practicality of Malecki's interior is not alto-gether remarkable for, after all, architects are renowned for living in particu-larly sophisticated and practically conceived abodes. As this space is the architect's home, it reflects his taste and professional background rather than merely the scarcity of goods that afflicted the wartime populace. Malecki's clean-cut interior gains contrast and vividness only when viewed as an em-bodiment of functionalism and is compared with other Polish homes evoked in the novella. His is clearly a modernist interior that mimics prewar trends in the Polish school of architecture,[26] in particular, the functionalist approach championed from 1926 by the periodical *Praesens* and its circle of editors fasci-nated by the avant-garde revolution.[27] The group had little opportunity to im-plement their ideas and it is almost ironic that it was Andrzejewski who realized, textually, their ideals in the Malecki place.[28] The building's entire structure is liberated from ornaments and decorations, its size far from osten-tatious and its primary concerns those of hygiene, fresh air, and adequate light. In the simple, practical design of this apartment, color becomes present only in its absence, in the necessary white walls. In short, it echoes Le Corbusier's notion of a decent living space produced for wide consumption.[29]

The enclave of the Malecki home, permeated by a cozy atmosphere and shown in glimpses, embodies the family's dreams, a sense of privacy,[30] and a modicum of stability. It is an interior that ought to mobilize ethical values, but its inhabitant's wartime narrative is less uplifting than one would expect/wish. An-drzejewski's is a tale of a single-minded man who works, falls in love with a Pol-ish-Catholic woman, and marries her. In this way, Malecki maintains the normalcy of his existence or, at least, nourishes hopes for such a future. When he encounters his prewar Polish Jewish friend Irena Lilien, he hesitates to help her because of the risk her very presence could pose to the lifestyle he has created for himself and his wife. Irena's unexpected reappearance in his life becomes the litmus test of his opportunism and egoism. His inability to help either Irena—or, for that matter, her father and his former mentor, Professor Lilien—incriminate Malecki as a textbook opportunist. During the growing persecution of Jews, he seems perpetually to have one reason or another to stay away from the Liliens, although there is no mention of conspiratorial activities or any other serious motive that would justify his tardiness.

The reader, with *post factum* knowledge, enters the novella's world with the feeling that it is on the edge of destruction. For even in this seemingly peaceful neighborhood at the edge of Warsaw, one can hear gunshots and patrols searching neighboring houses, and one sees searchlights in the night sky and flames over the ghetto. These echoes of war, intensified by the ghetto uprising, encroach upon the private space, turning it into an enclave decreasingly separated from public affairs. Andrzejewski caricatures a wartime "stability" achieved by the middle-class man who is not ready to sacrifice his everyday existence for any higher form of active engagement. In the author's moralistic idiom, Malecki's relatively safe microcosm, where even the number of rooms in his flat indicates a convenient and practical lifestyle, cannot avoid judgment. His very impassivity demands punishment.

Andrzejewski's ideologically conceived project attains its fully socio-ideological dimension only when yet another door, this time that of the landlord Zamoyski's luxurious abode, opens before the reader's scrutinizing eye. Even though Zamoyski is not a typical capitalist exploiter, his lifestyle, embodied by his domestic servant's livery, sets him apart. Predictably, his elegant and comfortable apartment conforms to stereotypical notions regarding an upper-class dweller who can afford a servant. The way in which Andrzejewski evokes this interior is fairly typical of his general method: one quick glance at the plush rugs and the encyclopedic collection of Polish dictionaries suffices to indicate the kind of person who lives there. The walls, decorated with old family portraits, connote symbolic values carried through generations. Zamoyski does not inhabit his dwelling alone, but shares it with the familial spirits. This interior, whose antiques, in their very *historicalness*, tell the embellished narrative of their owner's origins, thus (over)determines his identity. At first glance, the inhabitant's aristocratic last name seems to serve a similar function.[31]

The place, however, does more than generate empowering familial memories, for it offers a pleasant retreat from the gloomy reality of the Nazi occupation. The curtains lend privacy and safety to the study, and the room is defined by its inhabitant's cultural preoccupations with its most ritualistic and formalized variation: "It was a large room with an immense carpet and a heavy desk in the center, surrounded by massive bookshelves. On the walls, in opulently

gilded frames, hung old-fashioned portraits. The curtains draping the windows and the deep club chairs created an atmosphere of calm and quiet."[32]
Zamoyski's deliberately escapist project—circumscribed by a nostalgic and
conservative sense of Polishness—verges, largely because of its ceremonial
character, on a caricature of national ideals. To this end, Zamoyski's leisure
time, devoted to reading the national epic, Adam Mickiewicz's *Pan Tadeusz*,
enhances the sense of the interior as an alternate reality based on a mythic,
and even utopian, Polish past. In this myth-like reality, the utter realization of
a mimetic paradigm—indeed, a direct quotation from nineteenth-century
Polish novels—Zamoyski denies the fact that both he and his lovely refuge are,
in fact, surrounded by death and destruction.

Instead of a manifestation of Polish cultural ideals, Zamoyski's home is a
study in the art of simulation. Surrounded by Polish antiques, which generate
a false myth of origin, the landlord is not the Polish *pan* he pretends to be.
Having studied the manners and lifestyle of the archetypal Polish patriot and
aristocrat with great care, he has tediously copied them. In his otherwise perfect simulation, there is only one thing lacking: a sense of the auratic understood as a genuine expression of historicality. The erasure of the auratic in
Zamoyski's copy-home is not only facilitated by the dweller's exercises in simulation, but also by the war's immediate danger and the ongoing conflagration
of the distant ghetto (which Zamoyski tries to ignore, despite persistent and
disturbing signals in the background). Thus, without exception, his dwelling
is already devoid of a truly symbolic presence.

Zamoyski's overly correct Polish pronunciation becomes a salient feature in
his larger desire to camouflage himself as a nobleman with a family tradition
that incorporates the gentry lifestyle of the past. This camouflage does not fool
the eye, for the landlord has pronounced Semitic features.[33] From the perspective of its performer, this mimicry signals nothing but a type of denial that com-
prises the source of his deep apprehension and a looming void. Zamoyski/
Zamojski himself knows that he is an assimilated Polish Jew, a frightened man
trying to hide his true identity.

It is the hazardous, if denied, immediacy of the extermination that changes
the meaning of his mimicry game from pretentious to desperate, as his simulation, most likely carried on for years, has become a compromising means of
survival. In this sense, almost everyone who seeks survival is ultimately compromised in the novella. The landlord is not the only person who lives in denial; some of his tenants pretend to live normal lives, carrying out all their
prewar rituals, including attending religious ceremonies, fixing elaborate
meals, and cleaning.[34] The symbolic content of these activities is obliterated
and the mimicking surface conceals the real that functions in terms of "a
simulation of the third order."[35]

To seek a normal home in the novella would be an exercise in futility. Domestic normalcy is replaced in *Holy Week* by the typicality and conformity of life under the occupier's law and is informed by Andrzejewski's postwar ideology. In order to achieve this end, the *kamienica* was used. This type of concept-driven apartment building mirrors the dominant social hierarchy and constitutes a well-established topos in the Polish literary tradition, which harks back to Bolesław Prus's masterful nineteenth-century novel, *Lalka* (The Doll). According to Prus's realist vision, apartment buildings interiorized the class structure: the ground floor was for those with less than moderate incomes; the second floor, as in the palatial *piano nobile*, was inhabited by the rich; the higher floors were for families with modest income; and attics were occupied by students and artists. For writers, the social ladder embodied in urban architecture represented a convenient locus of class differences and conflicts. Andrzejewski reached for this Ur-model and used it for various purposes. The model of *kamienica* had to be somewhat modified in his work, for its representation of the cross-section of Polish society and the locus of a tragic conflict was too limited.

It is precisely Zamoyski's Bielany *kamienica* that portrays this slight variation from the realistic scheme. From the ground floor up, the building's inhabitants encompass almost all social strata: one lower-middle class family, two middle-class families, as well as the affluent landlord himself. The only missing stratum in this arrangement is a Polish proletarian family, which would typically inhabit the basement apartment or *suterena*. The proletarian lack indicates that Bielany, although not a fancy neighborhood, was a newer residential area. The working class lived primarily in the densely populated city center built in the nineteenth century. Since it was a type of dwelling indispensable to Andrzejewski's sketch of the differing destinies of the Warsaw population in *Holy Week*, the writer inserted a *suterena* in the novella's series of interiors and thus killed two birds with one stone, so to speak. Inhabited by a family struck by wartime tragedy and with one son recently released from Auschwitz, Andrzejewski used this subterranean site to discretely inject a Marxist conception of class divisions adapted to the year 1943. In this way, he projected yet another ideological demand on his representation. The outcome of this episodic scene invoked a meaningful parallel between the misery of this working-class family and the extreme living conditions in the ghetto. Andrzejewski's strategy implied that although they suffered less than the Jews, Poles did, in fact, suffer:

> Malecki descended after her and stopped at the door. The odor of poverty struck him immediately. In the basement was a kitchen nook, low-ceilinged, darkened with soot, and saturated with dampness. There was hardly any furniture. On a wooden bed next to the wall lay an old and emaciated man, covered with the remnants of a once-red quilt. (Andrzejewski 2006, 16)

While it remains unclear whether this object lesson—offered for the sake of Malecki's nemesis, Irena Lilien, who was unable to see beyond her own people's suffering—was at all effective, one general conclusion is in place. To imply yet another difference between the ghetto and the other side of Warsaw, Andrzejewski located the chain of wartime dwellings, despite the class difference that they reflected, in wholesome apartment buildings. This was the case until the 1944 uprising, when the city was leveled by bombardments and shelling.

In *Holy Week*, the symmetry between habitat and inhabitant is complicated by the numerous social mechanisms mobilized by the war and the Holocaust, especially by traditional Polish–Jewish antinomies and resentments that reached their climax during this time. *Holy Week* opens with a long overture that would be more at home, to make a pun, in a multivolume family saga or Balzac's *Comedie Humaine*. Harking back to the story of the nineteenth-century Lilien family as it does, the beginning of Andrzejewski's novella tells the story of acculturation and growing prosperity. In a truly Balzacian manner, the narrative of Irena's illustrious ancestors is intertwined with the generational accrual of family wealth, which allows the intellectually prominent twentieth-century Liliens their adequately elegant and comfortable lifestyle. At the center of their material possessions are lovely and spacious houses, hospitably open to their many friends. Jewelry, usually a prominent factor in the intrigues of affluent families, does not enter the picture until later and for reasons unrelated to *Holy Week*'s generic determinants. The reader is allowed to see how much *stuff* figures in the Lilien family's life and to what extent, prior to the war, this *stuff* is taken for granted. Andrzejewski's epic zeal reflects the true extent of the dispossession to which European Jewry was subjected by their sovereigns; this forms one aspect of the novel's material texture, the history of which Andrzejewski is in a position to sketch mimetically.

The story quickly unfolds when Malecki, the novella's protagonist, runs into his former girlfriend, the beautiful and embittered Irena, who lives in hiding on the "Aryan side" of town. This fateful encounter triggers a series of fatal incidents and unwanted consequences that threaten to destroy Malecki's world and, eventually, do so. But for now he is married with a baby on the way; Irena, like many Jews, is on the run, an outcast without shelter. When, after some hesitation, Malecki offers to help her, the time it takes him to reach the decision demonstrates to her that his was neither a spontaneous nor pure impulse, but a forced Samaritan act verging on suicide.[36]

When Irena Lilien comes to stay for a while in the Maleckis' apartment, her presence and unavoidable interaction with his neighbors, all of them Catholic Poles, becomes the focal point of the narrative. Her good looks attract too many admiring or suspicious looks. Irena's character belongs to the type of dark-haired, dark-eyed, and beautiful Jewish female characters whose presence in Polish literature was rekindled in Szczypiorski's novel *The Beautiful Mrs. Seidenman*.[37]

As a type, she and her literary predecessors derive from the legendary Esterka, supposed mistress of Kazimierz Wielki, a Polish king.[38] The patriarchal construal of these characters is twofold; while they form ardent liaisons with non-Jews, theirs can never be legalized relationships.[39] Such marital status also evaded the gorgeous Irena, forsaken by Malecki during the war. What role her Jewish origin played in this aborted love story is not difficult to ascertain. In addition, it is easy to imagine the (im)moral choices Malecki made in order to avoid easing her predicament. During their chance meeting, which spurs a tragic end for all involved, Irena harbors no illusions: love, friendship and basic human decency have all withered in front of her eyes through years of fear, humiliation, and loss. Her Jewish haute-bourgeoisie background, which used to provide her with not only a sense of stability and privilege, but also an exquisite tradition, becomes, for her, only a memory and the reason for her persecution.[40] These were the years that separated her from Malecki.

Holy Week is the author's first text in which he cannot identify with his characters and his people (Walas 1972, 39). Nonetheless, it would be difficult to reach the conclusion that Irena, like all characters in the novella, is an unpleasant character, even though she appears both blunt and disillusioned, embittered by her wartime experience.[41] Irena's tale, of which Malecki is unaware, is remarkably different from the wartime narratives of the impoverished Jewish masses, for it is that of a privileged Polish-Jewish woman during the Holocaust. The gradual liquidation of the family assets that Irena took for granted, as the truly privileged often do, helped her to survive on the "Aryan side" until 1943. At this point, she is the only living member of the Lilien family.

The novella sketches a convincing psychological portrait of a woman who has been wronged and, in the process, turned harsh. Completely alienated from those around her, Lilien becomes thoroughly burned-out, detached even from the material objects that facilitated her survival. Her material possessions, reduced to one suitcase, resurface again in the novella. After revealing to Irena that her non-Jewish friends have been arrested by the Gestapo for hiding her, Malecki adds that the suitcase with all her belongings has also been lost. Irena's reaction—"Oh that's silly! Isn't it only things?" (Andrzejewski 2006, 171)—displays her increased imperviousness to material possession, as it demonstrates her still very much intact integrity.[42] Besides a well-tailored, prewar suit, Irena carries mostly immaterial things—memories of her dead relatives, of the lost family home, and the heavy burden of persecution. In this sense, she herself becomes a repository for familial memories because even the scant handful of photographs of her parents were lost. Irena thus embodies the ancient wisdom: *omnia mea mecum porto*.[43] Contrary to Bentham's interpretation of one's emotional connection with property, she is liberated from it and, by implication, from the pain of loss.

With one exception. An antique ring is the last remnant—a vestigial sign par excellence—that connects her with the past. The reciprocal relationship between Irena and this ring is built on physical proximity, for it always bejewels her finger, remaining in direct contact with her skin. Her ring, besides symbolizing her familial bond and her wartime bondage as *homo sacer*, stands for her identity. That she remains close to it means that she is open to its symbolic value. The ring substantiates the notion of identity that stems from both emotional and spatial proximity between the human and the material. Bentham's notion of leaning toward the material-object world and informing a strong interconnection comes once again to mind. Applied to Irena and her antique ring, the symbolic depth of their bond gestures toward the link with her people and her growing awareness of the Jewish tragedy. Irena's chance for survival, if measured by the fiscal value of one old ring, remains minimal. But it is the more discrete signification of the ring that adds a coda to the Lilien family history. The ring itself comes to symbolize the concept of a return. At the end of the novella, as a result of an abrupt unfolding of chance events, Irena decides to go to the burning ghetto to accept the communal destiny of her people that she has so desperately managed to evade. Like several other assimilated Polish-Jewish characters portrayed in Polish literature, for example, Lilien's own father, the title character in Adolf Rudnicki's "Wielki Stefan Konecki" (The Great Stefan Konecki) and the old Jewish proprietress from Tadeusz Borowski's short story "Pożegnanie z Marią" (Farewell to Maria), Irena confronts and accepts her people's fate as her own. The seemingly irrational threads of voluntary return conclude the narrative.

Point Counterpoint

In 1943, when the plot of *Holy Week* begins, the Jews of Warsaw owned practically nothing. Their lives, although not yet dispossessed, were reduced to the most basic of necessities. Only a marginal part of Warsaw's population offered help and shelter to those who escaped the worst, either the ghetto or the concentration camp. Yet, in the novella, a beautiful and elegantly dressed woman is helped by a homely looking and plainly dressed one. Their differing appearances quickly become the referent of their fundamental incompatibility that, despite some mutual understanding—facilitated and defined by their womanhood—stands between Anna Malecka and Irena Lilien. Welcoming the Other becomes an intermingling of the feminine and hospitality. That they are a world apart quickly becomes obvious in the story, which emphasizes Irena's toughness and Anna's sensitivity and goodness. The strongest Jewish–Polish point-counterpoint dynamic in the novella is informed in one scene, which engages the mediation of objects in an interaction between Lilien and Malecka.

That such a scene occurs in a bedroom, whose primary function is the conjugal place of rest and intimacy, may be an awkward choice of an interior on Andrzejewski's part. But the inner sanctum actually belongs more to Anna than to her husband. It is her emotional territory, symbolically marked by her family snapshots and made cozy because of the crib. As the space with which Anna identifies, it is flanked by two experiential poles: that of her expecting a child and that of her mourning the loss of her brothers and father, whose pictures are displayed there. In her work of mourning, she can cling to the symbolic and material objects representing her family that she has archived, an emotional luxury of which Irena is deprived. And yet Anna's family photographs do not function as visual records but refer to something more primordial; as the *imagines* of her late relatives, they engage the hermeneutics of mourning in a manner akin to the death masks collected and displayed in ancient Roman homes. The spirits of the dead protect Malecka and her inner sanctum. Staged in-between, visualized by two objectual worlds that oppose each other within the space of her bedroom, permeated both by images of death and the hope for recovery, the entirely domesticated Anna fills her days with domestic chores. Her labor of love, making clothes for her baby, preempts another labor, the delivery of her child.

Anna's preoccupation is largely forced by the ersatz war economy that does not allow for any waste. Mending old clothes, darning socks, and reusing old men's coats to make woman's suits resulted in *moda okupacyjna* (the fashion of occupation), which for Szarota (1973, 247) was nothing else but "the standardization of poverty." Recycled from the couple's old shirts and pajamas, each article of baby clothing represented a palimpsestic work of art in miniature, since new layers were interwoven with the previous ones. These items made the ingenuous mother proud of their inconspicuous origin, of the old and the discarded reconstituted anew. The minute intricacy of things like baby clothes required a patient attention to detail on the part of their creator. A list of the products of her needle squeezed in a drawer came to stand for freshness and innocence extricated from the old:

> Here were tiny shirts, sleepers, bibs, sweaters, blankets, towels, diapers, and the most merry, silly and various sorts of trifles, all carefully and evenly folded and put away. (*Holy Week*; Andrzejewski 2006, 64)

The disarming contents of this drawer allowed the women to forget momentarily the threatening war. The language of maternal instinct, which found its voice in the clothes that previously had set Irena and Anna apart, now sutured their separation, bringing them closer to each other. Protected by the walls of Anna's home, by the cozy interiority of the bedroom, they shared yet another, smaller interior—the drawer that could be exploited for sexual associations, but instead released a therapeutic energy unrelated to Eros. Through this act, redolent with hope, they seemed to wish, jointly, to liberate from the enclosed, safe space the friendly domestic spirits, the *lara* and *penata* of the Polish home.

The bedroom manifests an uncanny dimension that emerges out of the checks and balances of both women's losses. It is only by coincidence that a pile of baby clothes taken from the chest of drawers provides a sole moment of relief and affords an unexpected *jouissance* to Irena who "greatly livened up and began to rummage through the soft flannels and cottons, lifting up the tiny blue sleepers to see them better under the light, and laughing as she saw how small they were" (Andrzejewski 2006, 65). They are delicate, soft, and welcoming to Irena's eager and playful touch; engaging with them, it is almost as if she were already playing with the Maleckis' baby. Her senses revive her undead, previous self through the symbolic promise of new life that proves irresistible. Likewise, through the restorative power of touch, seldom engaged in Holocaust writings, that which circumstance has rendered improbable—Irena's own motherhood and desire to become mother—become for her possible. For according to the old patriarchal premise, only motherhood would give her the self-fulfillment that each woman should desire.

Irena has been dispossessed of everything to the point that both she and her life have become, literally, bare. The loss of her relatives is followed by yet another loss: her family photographs are gone as well; there is no longer any symbolic imagery capable of supporting her memory. She presumes that such a total loss does not apply to Polish families, until her hostess, Anna, gives her a précis of each of her family losses: the family pictures displayed in the bedroom are her dead relatives, casualties of the ongoing war. Since Anna has suffered as many losses as Irena among her close family, a bond of mutual understanding is formed. The novelist endows the objects that, on the one hand, Poles possess and, on the other, Polish Jews are deprived of but can still relate to, with a remarkable individualized expressivity, for he catches the moment when one's material needs define the most intimate workings of the self. Because of this, the earlier claim that Irena is a burned-out person becomes one that relates to her inner state as projected onto objects.

In Polish, there is a colloquial expression *siłą rzeczy* (by the force of things), which does not denote their agency, but rather their gravity in propelling facts or determining fate. This "power of things" enacts the fleeting moment of real contact between them and Irena, as well as her connection with Anna. However, since *Holy Week* is not a messianic tale of destruction and restoration, but a realistic novella with strong psychological undercurrents, the signals of this transformation are proportionally weak in the narrative. The characters' awkward interactions, contrasted with their smooth relations with objects, are captured as misunderstandings arising from other errors. The self-enclosed subjectivities of characters *forced* to make moral choices create a background against which Anna stands alone, capable of sacrifice and uncalculated moral decisions.

Holy Week is not a work of accidental errors, but a hunting game during which each move (of the prey) must be calculated. Yet each of its planned moves is contradicted by inadvertent forces. It would be wrong to surmise that this is a universe of radical undecidability, for it is staged in a totalitarian state about to bring to conclusion its systematic plan of *Endlösung*. Therefore, one's death, usually the least predictable aspect of the future, can be actualized at any time. Simultaneously, the narrative is predetermined only in this sense, for there is no reason that could give meaning to a humiliating and painful demise. Andrzejewski demonstrates how heroic rescue efforts turn into disasters on account of the debasing moral chaos in which his characters exist; this chaos is unleashed by war and through, not entirely paradoxically, the very systematicity of the genocide machine in action. Since Andrzejewski continues in *Holy Week* his most obsessive preoccupations—his pondering over the human condition, fate, chance, despair, and loneliness—the layers of his older project shine through and inhabit the ideologically revised hypertext.

CHAPTER SIX

Things, Touch, and Detachment in Auschwitz

> . . . we fancy we can touch objects; nothing coming in between
> us and them.
>
> —Aristotle

T HE IMAGE OF A HOMELESS MAN carrying his earthly belongings in a bundle is a common feature of our urban experience. No one pays much attention to the fact that such bundles consist of damaged items that can no longer be put to use. If broken objects are not given to consumption, if their Heideggerian equipmentality is denied, what sort of connection still makes them essential for their owners? Why, in one of Tadeusz Borowski's short stories on Auschwitz, does a prisoner on his way to the gas chamber not want to give away either a parcel of food or his boots, his only remaining possessions? What is the nature of people's attachment to objects in a bare bio-political life?

In Search of the Law

Following Elie Wiesel's wisdom, I am not looking for definite answers to these questions, but rather for their more complex articulation in Tadeusz Borowski's writings.[1] Borowski (1922–1951), as a young poet whose two volumes of poetry were published underground during World War II, spent more than two years in Auschwitz and Dachau, separated by barbed-wire fences and guards from his Polish-Jewish fiancée; both survived and were married. He managed to stay in touch with her via correspondence, smuggled by other inmates. Throughout those years in the camps, despite the dangers of *precarium*, he managed to compose and preserve his poetry in a variety of conduits: as published,[2] written down, memorized,[3] performed orally, and circulated, first, within the circle of a few trusted inmates and, later, within a wider audience of Auschwitz prisoners, among whom he gained considerable name recognition as a poet and story teller. Borowski risked composing his poetry everywhere, usually keeping the manuscripts under the mattress of his bunk bed and resisting *precarium* under the worst circumstances imaginable. For example, "Do towarzysza więźnia" (To the Comrade Inmate) was written in the notorious Pawiak prison in Warsaw.[4] *Precarium* conditioned the ultimate fate of his poems written prior to his imprisonment, since his entire unpublished archive was burned during the Warsaw uprising. In 2001, these trials and tribulations took an unexpectedly positive turn, when more than one hundred poems were found, among which thirty-two had not been previously known.[5]

After the war, Borowski shifted gradually to prose.[6] His spectacular reappearance in the postwar Polish literary stage, his alliance and subsequent disenchantment with communist ideology, and his complicated personal life were cut short on July 1, 1951, when Borowski reached the point of no return on his own terms and gassed himself using the kitchen stove.

His camp output resembles a nonfictional narrative and is remarkably uncensored. Unlike the majority of postwar testimonies, it delivers a disturbingly honest message. On account of this candidness, he caused a debate among indignant Polish critics and survivors, who accused him of immoral and nihilistic leanings. Even today, an interpretative attempt to demonstrate Borowski's less "cynical" side is, from the outset, entangled in this longstanding critical controversy, in which his writings are considered offensive and scandalous.[7] Indeed, Borowski refused to identify himself with the martyrdom stamp imprinted onto numerous camp memoirs published after the war that represent a sentimental, heroic and, in a word, more digestible version of survival in Auschwitz. The possibility of distilling a value system already confounds the standard account of Borowski's Holocaust writings. For this reason, such a reading does not tolerate scholars interested in retrieving uncomplicated moral lessons. I invoke the ethical dimension of Borowski's vision here, mainly because it informs an intrinsic part of the writer's construction of objects, which in turn is directly related to the process of constitution by and of an Auschwitz prisoner's identity.

In the traditional vein of Borowski studies, as codified by the Polish scholars Tadeusz Drewnowski and Andrzej Werner, the discourse of dehumanization and reification figures so prominently that it effectively subordinates all other possible interpretations. According to these critics, Borowski's moral mission is founded upon his telling the uncomfortable and unadorned truth about how the inmates' need to survive at all costs resulted in their adherence to a simplified, social Darwinian code in which only the strongest survived. Paradoxically, this was what cemented their negative community, a community marked by radical separation and a detachment of its members from each other.[8] However, "the minimum of values whose traces are not quite visibly drawn, which makes us suspect that [Borowski's] Auschwitz short stories are not a nihilistic charge, is contained already in the author's decision to describe this 'world chiseled in stone.'"[9] In taking this position, intermingled with and conditioned by his survival guilt, the writer creates a sense of moral responsibility that is by and large absent from the mimetic surface of his short stories and is drawn from his prose's nondiegetic sources.

Borowski's writings seem predominantly to indicate that in order to survive at Auschwitz, prisoners were forced to forget everything they had learned and believed during their lives prior to imprisonment. Terror, hunger, labor, and the absolute reification of the individual constituted *la condition humaine* of all Auschwitz prisoners, whose status became that of living objects existing in a world devoid of spontaneity and spirituality even in the most basic forms (Werner 1971, 81). In fact, Werner reiterates that the Auschwitz prisoners represented a "community of objects."[10] As dehumanized objects, prisoners lived their undead lives, reduced solely to their bodily functions. They were forcibly "taught" to accept the rules of a grossly debased exchange economy. Since the illegal trading of goods never sufficiently provided for life's necessities, prisoners resorted to scavenging food and other items.[11]

The camp's logic stipulated that the juxtaposition between looted goods stored in nearby barracks and the bare life of prisoners should not be articulated in terms of a radical gap. On the contrary, uniformly ontologized by Borowski, the material world and the world of reified prisoners were parallel, subjugated to the same representational patterns. The rich and disturbing quality of Borowski's writings stems from the fact that he engages and transcends all existing models for the representation of the Holocaust object. This manifold signification often occurs in one sweeping episode or in a highly graphic image. Consider, for example, the following passage from "U nas w Auschwitzu" (Auschwitz, Our Home):

> If you get sick, everything is taken away from you: your clothes, your cap, your "organized" scarf, your handkerchief. If you die—your golden teeth, already recorded in the camp inventory, are extracted. Your body is burned and your ashes are used to fertilize the fields or fill in the ponds. Although in fact so much fat and bone is wasted in burning, so much flesh! so much heat! But elsewhere they make soap out of people, and lampshades out of human skin, and jewelry out of the bones.[12] (Borowski 1967, 131)

It is a mimetic illustration of the transformational paradigm: a violation of a prisoner's ownership precedes the violation of his or her body, concluded by the utilization of the corpse.

Borowski also retreats to the metonymic objectual paradigm, according to which belongings brought to the camp narrate their owners' identities and link them to their pre-camp lives and individual backgrounds; even the most trivial things are endowed with emotional value and, therefore, must be taken away. Other objects engaged in this pattern are acquired or manufactured in the camp and, while conditioning survival, participate in the process of constituting their owners' status as camp prisoners.[13]

Among the object relationships frequently and graphically depicted, yet never fully understood, are samples of the agalmatic pattern, which has been discussed in detail earlier in my work, in chapter 2. As one of the major mechanisms ordering the Holocaust material object world, it refers to the period's economy of looting.[14] The informal notion of this violent manner of dispossession, despite being particularly disturbing, was akin to a game of hide and seek. Borowski succinctly describes this process in the short story "Proszę państwa do gazu" (This Way for the Gas, Ladies and Gentlemen):

> They do not know that now in just a few moments they will die, that the gold, money, and diamonds which they have so prudently hidden in their clothing and on their bodies are now useless to them. Experienced professionals will probe into every recess of their flesh, will pull the gold from under the tongue and the diamonds from the uterus and the colon. They will rip out gold teeth. In tightly sealed crates they will ship them to Berlin. (Borowski 1967, 48–49)

This gruesome vision of the final destinies of the prisoners engages both the mimetic and the agalmatic representational paradigms, which overlap in the listing of what one could call the main 'material events' of a camp. The retrieval of gold or diamonds, hidden in the most guarded bodily parts (anus, uterus, mouth), reflects the exteriorization of that which is both intimate and interior, but also of the process whereby things traditionally hidden are exposed and made public. Arendt notes that the division between private and public "equals the distinction between things that should be shown and things that should be hidden."[15] If we follow her observation, it is not so much that the logic of agalmatic dispossession fuses the public and the private; rather, it totally destroys the sphere of the intimate and private, while substantially weakening the already transmogrified public sphere of the camp's communal life.[16]

From this viewpoint, corpses were treated as if they had a dual nature, that of both commodity and waste. It is critical to emphasize again that the irrational practice of concealing precious items inside body cavities was equivalent to hiding them in inconspicuous-looking containers and locations: the human/ somatic and objectual dimensions of dispossession were reduced, for this single purpose, to the same status of brutal reification. The agalmatic method, crucial in destroying any remaining vestiges of a private-public distinction that might have existed in the camp, necessarily repositions the body and corpse, shifting them, ultimately, to the sphere of recycling. Regardless of their status, the body and corpse belong to the domain controlled by a ruthlessness of both gaze and touch.[17] Within the agalmatic paradigm, touch—located at the threshold between internal and external worlds—comes to denote complete detachment.

In the context of Holocaust literature, as I have already mentioned, the firmly established hierarchy of the senses is challenged because touch, elevated to compete with gaze, replaces the unspoken word. Borowski frames the chain of signification—in which tactile ability becomes the passively touched (as in prisoners' dispossession)—with two opposing emotional gestures: a caress and a blow. The latter, usually understood as touch degenerated into aggressive disconnection, was mediated by weapons and whips, and was oft-symbolized by the leather gloves that protected the perpetrator's hands from direct contact with the "abject" prisoner's body. The hand, directed toward diverse sites of concealment, would first penetrate them and then both expose and retrieve hidden goods. This was complemented by the motion of the victim's hand, directed toward a different type of material good altogether, usually food.

Stressing the indispensability of touch for survival, Aristotle claims that no other sense can function without touch; in fact, he emphasizes the hierarchy of the senses as they contribute to the welfare of the animal or human being. Aristotle observes that all animals are endowed with this sense, whose loss results in death. In this way, he eliminates any horizontal interdependence of the senses.[18] The Aristotelian understanding of touch as a primordial sense competed with the Platonic elevation of sight to the noblest of senses; moreover, the bare life of the Holocaust demanded a revision of the Platonic order of senses. In this vein, Derrida, commenting on Aristotle's claim, retains touch's centrality, claiming, in short, that "touching, then, is a question of life and death" (Derrida 2005, 25). One can imagine that in the Darwinian jungle of Auschwitz, a prisoner deprived of the sense of touch, which enables certainty and guidance, would not survive.

At the Threshold

The loss of the sense of touch prefigures the death of Becker, an older Polish-Jewish prisoner infamous for "killing his own people" (Borowski 1967, 53) and even his own son in Borowski's "Dzień na Harmenzach" (A Day at Harmenz). Becker's ominously "murderous" stare changes into a guiltily blinking one after he is "selected for the chimney," to use the parlance of Auschwitz. Despite an obvious tension between him and Tadek, the story's narrator, Becker approaches Tadek, asking for food: "Tadek, I have been hungry for such a long time. Give me something to eat. Just this last time" (80). It is Tadek's neighbor, Kazik, who gives in to this solicitation, while Tadek observes the scene in a manner more akin to a psychological test than a token of pity. Kazik grants the condemned man his last meal, even though this privilege refers to the normal world outside of Auschwitz. Inviting Becker to have his meal on the upper bunk, Kazik then looks at the "fallen power" broker who has been downgraded to the lowest echelon of prisoners, and who, with half-closed eyes, almost like a blind man, is "vainly groping with his hand for the board to pull himself on to the bunk" (81). The narration of "A Day at Harmenz" concludes with this image, preventing the reader from knowing whether Becker was able to pull himself onto the bunk for his last meal.

One could certainly read this story as an Aristotelian parable about the primacy and indispensability of touch adapted to the "jungle" of Auschwitz. However, the narrative's inconclusive end is interconnected with a somewhat confusing interplay between Becker's searching hand and his apparent, if temporary, blindness.[19] Manual dexterity (and the lack thereof) becomes the key with which to unlock the meaning of this man's last visual imprint in the story. Becker's vital senses are not acting in concert; his fingers, despite touching the wood of the bunk, are not collecting tactile data and sending this information to his inner eye. Why did Borowski decide to represent Becker as a doubly blind man, as someone so completely detached that he could neither see, nor operate on a tactile level?

Our use of the hand's touch has turned this member of the human body into a particularly sensitive instrument of perception, which serves many important functions. Standing in for the lost vision of the blind is only one of them. The touch of a hand—a veritable tactile language—translates objectual worlds for those who cannot see with their eyes. The cognitive concordance that occurs between touch and inner vision has long been recognized by sculptors. Michelangelo, for example, believed that haptic faculties were necessary for a full aesthetic experience of sculpture, in which a hand touching its diverse surfaces would function as an exquisitely sensitive organ of sight, sending impulses to the eye itself.

Becker's hand and touch cannot participate in this type of sensuous communication. The cognitive (guiding) faculty of touch given to Becker must have simply withered, as did his coordination and the reciprocity between his touch and gaze. In diagnosing the prisoner's gaze–touch malfunction, Borowski represents Becker as a man losing both his struggle for survival and his grip on reality. His confusion signifies—for the reader—an indirect, double moral judgment, according to which Becker's alienation from the humanistic tradition of a "seeing" hand implies his total detachment from the world.

The governing power of the visible destabilizes the gaze–touch axis to privilege perpetrators; indeed, vision is usually located on their side.[20] In Borowski's lexicon, touch participates in an extensive interplay between things, the senses, and moral values in the camp. Touch marks every moment of the prisoner's experience, structuring it from the moment of arrival to the departure for gassing. Its ambiguous semantics includes both the brotherly embrace and the brutal blow, both of which are bestowed upon Tadek during his time in Auschwitz. Serving to inflict pain and enforce separation, the hand's contact is never associated with the magical healing touch, nor is it aligned with eroticism. The reason for this is clear: a caress would articulate the birth of a rudimentary attachment, which in turn would reveal a residue of intimacy and connection.

On the Connection

In order to invoke a positive relational bond, albeit one that is constantly undermined by the camp's power system, one needed a few objects—indeed, the fewer the better. In the form of a seemingly one-dimensional perspective, Borowski in fact smuggles a more complex notion of the interrelationship of prisoners with their exterior world into his narrative, through the language of objects and the senses. Unexpectedly, in his brutal concentration camp testimony, Borowski's matter-of-fact account describes fleeting moments of kinship between Auschwitz prisoners and their things, enhanced in the pandemonium that occurs when people are being led to death. This type of bond, in which a hand projects on the touched object the identity of its maker or user, is usually broken or absent in the camp, although a hand touching an object, unlike a hand touching another hand, can enact a meaningful connection with the objectual other. My case in point is a Polish-Jewish character who silently appears in Borowski's short story, "Człowiek z paczką" (The Man with the Package). The man is called the *Schreiber* because he has attained the privileged position of a scribe in one of the Auschwitz hospitals. His physically undemanding job, "the object of everybody's envy" (Borowski 1967, 147), requires him to fulfill certain clerical duties, selecting Jews for gassing and then taking them to the showers. When he himself becomes ill, he has to follow, step by step, the ghastly routine through which he led others; the surgically precise irony deployed to describe this twist of fate does not escape the reader.

The preparations he makes for his own death are rather unusual, as the *Schreiber* concentrates on packing his meager belongings as though preparing for a transfer from one camp to another. The objects he packs signify only the identity he has acquired as a concentration camp prisoner: no item in the parcel discloses anything about his life prior to the camp or has any sentimental value. "Our *Schreiber* . . . was carefully tying a string around a cardboard box in which he kept his Czech boots, laced to the knee, a spoon, a knife and a pencil, as well as some bacon, a few rolls and fruit" (Borowski 1967, 148). This inventory lists the objects critical for survival and unnecessary for a journey to the netherworld. The apparent (il)logic of his behavior makes the narrator shrug, for he is unable to understand why the *Schreiber* refutes the laws of the camp: "'He knows perfectly well—an old timer like him— . . . that within an hour or two he will go the gas chamber, naked, without a shirt, and without his package" (150). At the same time, the narrator fails to notice that no one utters a word of comfort to the departing man, who leaves alone, engulfed by a void filled only by his package. Later on, when one of the inmates pats him on the shoulder, one can read in this gesture pity mixed with contempt for the loser. Understanding the *Schreiber*'s reaction in terms of a fetishistic disavowal—the man knows very well he is going to die, but refuses to accept the truth—is a tempting, but inapplicable, approach. For the *Schreiber*'s entrance into the order of the Real takes the objectual world in all its seriousness, without considering his possessions conditionally or in a manner that would suture the gap between e(x)ternal reality and his inner self.

The "mysterious" agency of the *Schreiber*'s parcel is highlighted by the desperate manner in which its owner clings to it, refusing to be separated from it even when he is stripped naked and is on his way to the showers. Sarcastically depicted as "an extraordinary attachment to the last bit of property" (Borowski 1967, 150), the silent *Schreiber*'s disdain for camp rules nonetheless gives the narrator pause. In an apparent reversal of Gabriel Marcel's existentialist critique of the verb "to have" as an inadequate substitute for "to be," the narrator's point of view rests on the equation that to be, to stay alive, means to have.

The narrator's cynical reasoning and his harsh disapproval of the *Schreiber*'s enactment of his own rite of death is challenged by another observer, an old German-Jewish doctor: "I think that even if I was led to the oven, I would still believe that something would surely happen along the way. Holding a package would be a little like holding somebody's hand, you see" (Borowski 1967, 150). Not only does the doctor not employ the tool of his trade, the knowledge of symptoms, but he also retreats from this positivist understanding of the "case" to probe underneath the behavioral and the visual. What he finds there is his own humanist construal of the situation. For the doctor, the sensuous and ensuring experience of touch must be endowed with some therapeutic qualities (not, however, on the level delimited by his profession) able to ease, like a pair of crutches, a wounded subjectivity. His decidedly humanistic commentary, although reminding us of the metonymical function objects can play in Auschwitz's detached community, does not succeed in transforming the short story into a parable wherein objects stand in proxy for other humans to fulfill the need for brotherly touch.

These two commentators thus effectively articulate two opposing views on the role of the ordinary objects one holds onto at the moment of solitary death. Both perspectives are ideologically tainted. One is veiled by the pretenses of crude rational behavior as purported by the camp's utilitarian and totalitarian structure, while the other is sentimentally humanistic. One reduces the package to mere use-value, which does not amount to much on death row; the other elevates the package to the level of a metonymic carrier of brotherly support. The two interiorities, the doctor and Tadek, observing the exteriority of the man departing the worst of all possible worlds, offer opposing viewpoints and thus exercise only their own subjectivities, which in turn they project onto the condemned man. Looking at the *Schreiber* through a window, both men remain ironically windowless—with no channel of inner perception to reach and reveal the interiority of the man with his parcel—they epitomize, more than anything else, a rupture in the human bond. The camp's pragmatic appropriation of the visual appearance transfers the Leibnizian monadism of the prisoner into the realm of ideology understood, in the short story, as multiple truth.[21]

The semi-dialogic space informed by both prisoners creates narrative ambiguity, as often occurs in Borowski's prose. Indeed, the last sentence of the story, framed by the double negative "I do not know why . . . nobody could understand" (Borowski 1967, 151), overtly confirms this claim. The unknowing and not understanding become misunderstanding, suggesting a deliberate strategy reflective of the narrator's view. The behavior of the *Schreiber* selecting others for the gas chamber is entirely transparent, but the same man, seen in a last glimpse (holding a parcel after showering and, next, being driven to the gas chamber) remains, for the narrator, opaque and barely noticed.[22]

The third standpoint, present but not privileged by the narrative, is more intriguing. This view takes the *Schreiber's* stubborn refusal to give up his package as a way of depicting an overcoming of the traditional object–subject split. From the perspective of thing-discourse, the man's hand touching the surface of the package and feeling its texture, weight, and concreteness, regardless of the irrelevance of its content, gives him the gift of constancy and the proximity of material presence, the only presence of which he (by his own determination) is not deprived. The fact that the use-value of the objects in the package is totally negated by the onlooker serves to underscore the *Schreiber's* conscious spurning of the ruthless world of Auschwitz. The substantial materiality of the package he is carrying fulfills his desperate need for attachment, so he is not, if you will excuse the pun, out of touch with reality. His bond, however, is with the objects and not, as the doctor suggests, with mankind *through* the objects.

I argue that the materiality of the *Schreiber's* objects emerges with a forceful agency of its own, akin to that of talismans worn during dangerous pilgrimages, and that this force alone diminishes the pragmatic aspect of the contents of the package, even as it increases their unreadability. The things' force derives entirely from their own energy, not from their role as substitutes for human presence. In the absence of human bonds, and against the background of the detritus accumulated in the camp's storage rooms, one parcel alone becomes a stable material buttress with which the threatened self can face the immensity of omnipresent death. The *Schreiber's* instinctive ritualization of his own passage to death exemplifies perhaps the most daring defiance of the rules of the camp, including those that order its anonymous, dehumanizing death. In this light, it would not be difficult to see behind the behavior of "the man with a parcel" as a reenactment of one of the oldest funerary practices: the collection of tools, clothing, weapons, and vessels with which the burial places of ancient civilizations, most notably the Egyptian, were equipped (Levinas 1969, 191).[23]

This is more than an ethical moment and action. Levinas explains that, in forming a meaningful and sensuous relationship with objects, one also constructs and implies other, multiple interrelationships: "By the hand the object is in the end comprehended, touched, taken, borne and *referred* to other objects, clothed with a signification, *by reference* to other objects" (1969, 191). Partly in contrast to the doctor's elucidation, although in a certain agreement with his awareness of other forces resisting reification, this story is about a sensuous, physical, and intimate attachment to objects invoked by touch. The *Schreiber's* attachment to his modest possessions negates their use-value for the sake of their proximity. This proximity recreates a level of identity in which a human subject, looking at objects and being aware of their silent presence, touching and holding them in one's hand, even protecting and naming them, grants a meaningful spiritual contact. Consequently, I would situate the *Schreiber's* gesture, his holding the neatly packed burial equipment, closer to Benjamin's understanding of touch as an intimacy-restoring relation with objects.[24] The *Schreiber's* intimate and instinctual ritualization of his passage to death connotes, in the context of the camp, a strangely inverted relationship: his hand's touch understood as an intimate act mediating between the self and the material world, when there is seemingly nothing—not even space—between them. Ultimately, the *Schreiber's* behavior implies a collapse of boundaries between the subject and the object (purported by Descartes to be incommensurable), a sort of a secular consubstantiation, resulting in their momentary unity, their near-perfect proximity.

On Dispossession

The traumatic initiation rites of the camp were deliberately designed to destroy the newcomers' memories. Inmates were deprived of both their relatives and their belongings. Their identities were replaced with numbers tattooed on their arms. A shockingly different material object-world engulfed the prisoners, demanding that they develop a new vocabulary with which to confront it. One of the most effective means of depicting those things occurred on the level of terminology. In the slang of Auschwitz prisoners, recorded in Borowski's richly mimetic short stories, the vocabulary denoting tools comes first and usually accompanies words that designate space and the labor functions of the rank-and-file inmates and their guards. One does not need to argue the importance of terms such as *buksa* (bunk bed), *efekty* (effects), *klamoty* (junk), *rollwaga* (roller-wagon), or *traga* (handbarrow), all of which derive from German.[25] The other words in the list, such as *pasiaki* (stripes), which do not derive from German, indicate the commonality of imprisonment. What made "stripes," the standard-issue uniforms given to the prisoners, distinctive at Auschwitz was their blue and gray color. Though he was not certain about this fact, Borowski believed they were made out of nettles. "Well-cut and well-fit stripes signaled the owner's well-being, his function and self-respect" (Borowski et al. 2000, 194), Borowski comments ironically, indicating the inclination of Auschwitz inmates to embrace prison fads.[26]

Detritus in the camp was referred to, in camp lingo, as either *klamoty* or *efekty*. The former, *klamoty*, would not raise any eyebrows because it is still used in contemporary Polish. *Efekty*, however, would. Borowski gives some historical background for the changing usage of the word *efekty*. Initially, the word designated only the storage rooms for prisoners' private belongings, but later came to designate "a whole separate unit of the camp, in whose blocks riches taken from transports going to the crematorium lay—and disappear" (Borowski et al. 2000, 190). This everyday lexicon indicates to what extent the environment of a concentration camp represents a topsy-turvy world, where banal and ordinary routines (for example, surviving one more day) reappear as extraordinary accomplishments, while extraordinary events, such as terror and, in particular, the death of thousands of people, become common and unremarkable. According to this perverse logic, mundane objects in the Auschwitz (extra)ordinary-everyday, where survival verges on the miraculous, are endowed with metonymical functions. They appear as bearers of meaning and as loci of identity and memory. However, their ordinariness, defined by their use-value, assumes in extreme situations a different significance in relation to their users/owners, if we can speak of a *sensu stricto* objectual ownership among Auschwitz prisoners.

At the moment of arrival, repeatedly invoked in camp testimonies, the unloading of humans and objects fluctuates and, eventually, dissolves into a single stream of undifferentiated action and ontology. It does not matter who or what is carried out: luggage or "squashed" babies, since the infants' corpses are dealt with "like chicken, . . . several in each hand" ("This Way for the Gas, Ladies and Gentlemen"; Borowski 1967, 39), without marking any difference between them. People are "inhumanly crammed, buried under incredible heaps of luggage, suitcases, trunks, packages, crates, bundles of every description (everything that had been their past and was to start their future)" (37). It is impossible to compare various acts of dispossession and disrobing to the violent separation from relatives, children and, ultimately, life itself. Ethically and ontologically, they should constitute two distinctly different types of forced separation. Instead, they overlap and produce an even greater traumatic effect.

Borowski deals on two different levels with the question of how to adequately represent the process of disembarking and segregating people and their possessions. His depiction must simultaneously have a nearly palpable, sensuous concreteness and yet reach through to something rhetorically inexpressible. The most obvious tool to accomplish the task becomes the list. Lists of amassed objects turned to be especially efficient descriptive vehicles in the routine operations at Auschwitz: diverse lists of material and human worlds were produced by the perpetrators on a daily basis in order to control the mass murder taking place in the death camp and, thus, bureaucratically, to operate the concentration camp.[27] Unlike the lists made by the SS men, Borowski's listings are not very orderly:

> Suitcases, bundles, blankets, coats, handbags that open as they fall, spilling coins, gold, watches; mountains of bread pile up at the exits, heaps of marmalade, jams, masses of meat, sausages; sugar spills on the gravel. ("This Way for the Gas, Ladies and Gentlemen"; Borowski 1967, 38)

Such an act of listing denarrativizes his account. Detritus appears to be chaotic and excessive; the narrator mentions only a few objects in their singularity, underscoring the abundance of other goods to be taken away from the newly arrived.

Disembarking at Auschwitz represents a curiously inconsistent experience. On the one hand, we have the juxtaposition of the detached SS men and the despairing crowd; on the other, the notorious congestion of the "inhuman" crowd parallels the jumbled mass of belongings piled up "incredibly" and qualified by rhetorical cliché.[28] These dehumanizing events indicate the way in which the surplus of people and the accretion of their things convey the material world's sudden failure to exist as a stabilizing presence. From the point of view of an anxious newcomer, one's "stuff" (although dragged to the camp with considerable effort) becomes detritus: one quickly learns that it is less painful to give it up and yield to the rules that govern the place. Observing those who were unwilling to learn this lesson and the way in which they were treated by the perpetrators proved sufficient warning for the rest of the camp's inhabitants. I refer here to another scene of insubordination, in which the narrator describes a woman still uninitiated to Auschwitz: "A woman reaches down quickly to pick up her handbag. The whip flies, the woman screams, stumbles, and falls under the feet of the (surging) crowd" ("This Way for the Gas, Ladies and Gentlemen"; Borowski 1967, 38). Her disobedient gesture differs radically from that of the defeated *Schreiber*, who does not oppose his destiny, but strives to ritualize his passage to death. While she miscalculates in panic, he regains his singularity.

Holzhof or an Ethical Excursion on the *Muselmann*

Borowski never downplays the economy of exploitation in the camp-universe: "We work beneath the earth and above it, under a roof and in the rain, with the spade, the pickaxe and the crow-bar. We carry huge sacks of cement, lay bricks, put down rails, spread gravel, trample the earth" ("Auschwitz, Our Home"; Borowski 1967, 131). Furthermore, he emphasizes the impact of power and exploitation as the main driving factor in a society outside the camp. To this end, he negatively appraises Western civilization and its past empires, which he compares to the Third Reich in terms of the mechanism of power and slave labor employed by all of them. Condemning ancient civilizations—the cradle of Western civilization—he writes:

> We are laying the foundation for some new, monstrous civilization. Only now do I realize what price was paid for building the ancient civilizations. The Egyptian pyramids, the temples, and Greek statues—what a hideous crime they were! How much blood must have poured on to the Roman roads, the bulwarks, and the city walls. (131; emphasis added)

In Borowski's account, the gigantic machine of labor and exploitation organized by the Nazis corresponds to that of antiquity's slave labor system. Slave labor constitutes the *meta-reality* of the camp that ultimately transcends its economic and political functions, as well as their historical differences, and does not differ much from Hannah Arendt's analysis of the concepts of *zoe* and *homo sacer*, as she advances them in *The Origins of Totalitarianism* (1985, 297). It is within the ambiguous zone, whose existence was indicated by Giorgio Agamben, where the Nazi juridical foundation causes the collapse of differences—among them, between the objectual and the human—that the bio-politically bare form of life appears (1995, 159). One could argue that Arendt's concept of the slave in ancient societies "as worse than death" and as "akin to a tame animal" (1958, 84) adds a new meta-discursive weight to historical experiences such as Borowski's. I contend, therefore, that the concept of a camp as the *telos* of Western civilization was first formulated by this better-known Auschwitz prisoner, years before Agamben confronted the same subject in both his *Means without End* and *Homo Sacer: Sovereign Power and Bare Life*.

Besides the explicit construction of camp teleology offered in both "Auschwitz, Our Home," a hybrid narrative verging on a treatise on radical evil, and "The People Who Walked On," Borowski also employs a fulcrum of discreet moral impulses, which contradict the immoral law of Auschwitz and coincide in a sense with Agamben's theorization of a *Muselmann*. For the Polish writer, the bio-political life of a camp prisoner is infrequently a site of displaced ethics. Despite the camp's totalitarian laws and rules, suppressed or displaced ethical reactions reappear within the somatic foundation of the self. If emotional responses are shifted to the human soma, they must be limited to this site's specific language and expressed accordingly, that is, in a nonverbal and nondiscursive manner. Borowski therefore speaks of "biological emotions" (*odczucia biologiczne*) present in reified prisoners[29] and of the disparity between the brutalized, reified self and the revolting soma:

I stared into the night, numb, speechless, frozen with horror. My entire body trembled, and rebelled, somehow even without my participation. I no longer controlled my body, although I could feel its every tremor. My mind was completely calm, only the body seemed to revolt. ("The People Who Walked On"; Borowski 1967, 85)

It is not coincidental that Borowski's feeling of horror bears the qualities of the sublime.[30] As a bodily entity able to protest against the camp's brutality, this Auschwitz prisoner is entirely Borowski's own paradoxical construct of the un-ethical/ethical. When the prisoner's numbed mind ceases to serve as the locus of either consciousness or moral faculties, he utters no word of protest to the horror he observes and in which he participates. On a few occasions, the narrator is completely detached, but his incapacity to react is followed by his overwhelming sense of exhaustion, trembling, or nausea that signal the revolt of his uncontrol-lable body.[31] The human is retained not only in the human form, but reemerges in the form of deeply buried somatic reaction—primordial, "biological feelings"— of protest. The horror of mass killing is interiorized by the lonely prisoner posited against the heavens (lit not by the stars, but by the flames from the crematorium) in a situation that redefines the Kantian "moral law" and coincides with LaCapra's insight about the camp sublime (2003, 282).

Borowski conceived of his concept of an Auschwitz victim as a somatic en-tity with "biological emotions" in contrast to the reified figure of a *Muselmann* and a reductive dismantling of the latter. It took him one more experiential stage to learn and forge his own version of the *Muselmann* as the category of a dehumanized prisoner whose emotional and mental life had been shut down to the extent that it was closer to that of an animal, if not to an object (Borowski et al. 2000, 17). Borowski writes that the *Muselmann*,

literally, Muslim—[was] a physically and mentally totally depleted human being who no longer had the strength or the will to fight for his life. Usually suffering from Durchfall, phlegm or scabies [he was] more than ripe for the chimney. (192)

In this last stage, the destruction is total, and the prisoner inhabits a horrifying in-between sphere, as he is marked by an inability either to live or to die.

It is remarkable that Borowski speaks against the contempt of the camp community toward those who had reached this extreme (192); instead, he iden-tifies with them. The *Muselmann* is object-like, devoid of desire to live, stripped of dignity, and made inhuman in his still-lingering humanity.[32] Even the name of the place where those wretched prisoners lived is symbolic in its contempt—*Holzhof*, literally, a lumber yard or wood deposit (191). Unlike Imre Kertesz,[33] Borowski does not foreground the inner experience of Muselmannization, but treats the impact of the emotional on the somatic (and vice versa) as one aspect of the experience.

The writer's candid admission that just before the liberation of the Dachau concentration camp,[34] he became a member of the "walking dead," the lowest creature in camp hierarchy, bears the same conscious ethical weight as his identification with Tadek, his narrative persona who follows the camp's Darwinian code of survival, which always happened at the expense of the weakest. The general contempt toward the undead man-object must have continued in the postwar years, since Borowski observed that none of the camp memoirs he read confessed such a first-hand experience. One could counter-argue that the absence of this type of experiential somatic memory in survivors' memoirs resulted not so much from self-censorship and shame, but from the simple fact that so few *Muselmänner* survived to bear witness.

Borowski's focus on contempt makes space, paradoxically, for a reconceptualization of camp ethics along the axis of dignity and reified, inhuman life: the axis where indignity reaches dignity. While Borowski's identification with the figure of the undead is an ethical gesture, he makes no further claims regarding this experience. Namely, his confession does not go beyond the account of being reduced to a sick and emaciated body. He returned to life not to mystify his experience, but to tell its true and unembellished story. Indeed, for him there is no mystery about what constitutes the *Muselmann*. The underscoring of the inhuman, object-like life of a *Muselmann* is purported by Bruno Bettelheim[35] and, later, accepted by Werner, who also reads the unheard and unseen figures of *Muselmänner* through a paradigm of reification.[36] They are objects that cannot serve their perpetrators any longer, as they are broken, unusable, isolated, and "ripe for the chimney." Herein lies one of the camp's fundamental rules, which treats amassed objects in good condition as useless, and prisoners as wretched things, exploited to the extent that they become like broken objects to be disposed of. Yet the complexity of *Muselmänner* goes beyond this paradigm.

Taking into consideration Borowski's own experience of *Muselmannization* and his testimony's understated demystifying tone, we should consider his account in the context of the current discourse on the subject, which is mainly shaped by Agamben. In a nutshell, the philosopher makes a claim that has to do with his understanding of this extreme experience as representing the point of no return. Secondly, Agamben views the *Muselmann* as a witness to the impossible, as the bio-political, yet somewhat enigmatic, paradigm of modernity. In his interpretation, therefore, the prisoner with a broken body and spirit undergoes a complete reversal of status, since he—the victimized thing-man— is elevated to the level of bearing witness, promoted to the status of a solemn representative of the camp. Among Agamben's ideas on mass genocide, the *Muselmann* is the one that has caused the most controversy.

One cannot help but note that Agamben's conceptualization of the living-dead prisoner succumbs to the tendency to create a new secular myth about the tragic situation of mankind trapped behind the invisible bars of the camp called civilization. If the tragic position is marked by an impossibility to make choices, the living-dead inmate is precisely the anthropological figure Agamben seeks in order to develop a paradigmatic myth of modernity as camp. The experience of the impossible, therefore, must be the logical step toward reaching the point of no return. This bears the residue of other paradigmatic extreme experiences and, especially, directs us to ancient myths, a sphere of the impossible with which Agamben is very familiar. In the universe of ancient myths, a hero pays the ultimate price for his cognitive forays; he cannot fly toward the sun and return safely from such a daring cognitive exploration, neither can he look directly into the face of Gorgon without suffering terrifying consequences. In keeping with the large majority of mythic figures facing their points of no return, Agamben's *Muselmann*, the silenced somatic figure pushed to the edge of transparency and bare life, is awarded no hope of recovery. And yet, Agamben insists that this inhuman *homo sacer* does bear witness after reaching the point of no return, but offers a contradictory reading of how it is possible for the one who is neither dead nor alive to accomplish this. The entry into the zone of no return is precisely what, according to Agamben, gives the *Muselmann* the possibility to yield himself to symbolization, in which his impossible possibility opens a space for testimony.[37]

There is no doubt that Agamben, despite the mass of books on the subject of the Holocaust, is well acquainted with the discourse he has profoundly impacted. The writings of several survivors, including David Rousset, constitute the core of his direct sources. The philosopher's foremost informant, indeed, the pillar of his thought on the camp, is Levi. As an observer of other inmates' *Muselmanniza-tion*, Levi did not consider himself a true witness, ascribing this role to the undead who lived in the *Holzhof*.[38] For Agamben, however, Levi serves as "a perfect example of the complete witness" (1999, 16) insofar as he delivers his written testimony. In doing so, Agamben seems to be unaware of other witnesses who went through the experience. Therefore, I wish to suggest here two other cases—Borowski and Kertesz—who fulfilled both requirements of being both the Musselmänner and witnesses-cum-writers. Borowski, like the Hungarian writer after him, penned an account of his own becoming a *Muselmann* in "A True Story":

> I felt certain I was going to die. I lay on a bare straw mattress under a blanket that stank of the dried-up excrement and pus of my predecessors. I was so weak I could not even scratch myself or chase away the fleas. Enormous bedsores covered my hips, buttocks and shoulders. My skin, stretched tightly over the bones, felt red and hot, as from fresh sunburn. . . . At times I thought I would suffocate from thirst. (Borowski 1967, 157)

Shouldn't we also consider Borowski—and Kertesz, for that matter—a complete witness? Doesn't the Polish writer's identification with an Auschwitz prisoner as a *muzułman* in terms of a bio-political and reified entity qualify him for this role? His survival destabilizes Agamben's rather lofty, if complex, theoretization, since the writer's experience as a *Muselmann* imprinted itself on the somatic level of his entity and, within this zone, retained its potential for articulation. The Polish author proved through his own bodily experience that one *could* survive being a *Muselmann*, albeit at great expense. Thus, his own *Muselmanization* can be located midway between Bettelheim's "walking corpse" (1960, 157) and Agamben's conceptualizations of the *Muselmann* as an inhabitant of the zone where such notions as dignity and humanity cease to be relevant. The knowledge Borowski shares with us questions what remains most problematic in Agamben's theory, mainly because the former, granted the opportunity to return, proves the *possibility* of some recuperation from the *Muselmann's* state. Borowski's testimony does not insist on the authenticity of his experience (this is obvious and not worthy of further justification), but on its fully detailed historical record and its unique profile—the very aspects that LaCapra finds lacking in Agamben's universalized notion of a *Muselmann*. We could speak of the impossible made possible in Borowski's partial (or temporary) recuperation, if it weren't for the fact that Borowski—like Paul Celan, Jerzy Kosinski, Jean Amery, and Primo Levi—committed suicide. It is his suicide that demonstrates the real cost of his surviving Auschwitz. And this is Borowski's final message.

Coda: The Post-Holocaust Object

I don't walk, I step on . . .

—Jerzy Ficowski

Y AND LARGE, the material world of the Holocaust lay in ruins when it was first encountered by the liberating forces of the Allies and the Red Army. Looting of the camps' infrastructure, incited by legends that spread about apparent riches buried in the grounds, led to further destruction which was facilitated by the inferior quality of construction materials used to build barracks and other utilities. The need to protect sites of former concentration camps from further disintegration and looting became pressing even while the war was still going on. However, the Polish communist government, predictably preoccupied as it was with establishing a new political order in the largely anticommunist country, failed to take immediate action. It was only a group of conscientious citizens, most notably the writers Helena Boguszewska and her husband Jerzy Kornacki, who were committed to saving whatever the withdrawing Nazi troops did not manage to destroy. They launched a grass-roots organization with a mission to document survivors' stories and preserve the sites from even further destruction and pillaging through legal action and archivization. As early as July 1944, they approached the newly formed pro-Soviet Polish government in Lublin for funds to implement protective measures immediately in Majdanek, where at that time Zyklon B was still stored alongside other material evidence of mass genocide. In his unpublished manuscript, entitled *Kamieniołomy* (Quarries), Kornacki gives a detailed account of the complete lack of interest on the part of the new authorities. Not only did the couple and their collaborators struggle to get the attention of the new regime, but they often encountered conflicts with the Soviets (who were busy taking the more valuable archives to the Soviet Union). Despite these obstacles and lacking both the consent of the authorities and any legal provision for their work, they continued to collect documents from the camps and to interview survivors. Thus, taking personal risk, the group managed to initiate the process of creating commemorative museums in all camps built by the German occupiers on Polish territory. In September 1944, the group succeeded in launching the Institute for National Memory; later on, the Committee of Research on Hitlerite Crimes was founded.[1]

The following story illustrates how, after survivors' needs were addressed, another aspect of the situation in the camps called for immediate attention. Shortly after the war, a visitor to the Chełmno death camp noticed that a white, rough substance composed of small, sharp particles was spread all over the camp. Only later came the shocking realization that he was walking on the scattered bones of the gassed victims. Chełmno, which was completely demolished by the withdrawing Germans, had a special machine for breaking bones into tiny pieces; the result was one gigantic, open ossuary into which— unknowingly—the man had stepped. The story's object lesson was short: the most pressing need was to give the shattered bones a respectful burial.

Mass graves were excavated throughout Europe, unveiling the horror of the past. The bodies of victims were reburied in a dignified manner and some form of closure was reached. This type of necessary intervention was followed by an entire range of other intercessions, which subjected the Holocaust and its objectual world to the processes of their repossession,[2] arduous restaging, and museumization, as well as to complex political manipulations and debates. Arguably, one of the most damaging—in both its ethical and educational consequences—was the communist regime's decision not to append to the infamous inscription next to the gate to Auschwitz the information that Jews were not only among the murdered nationals in the camp, but that they, as a matter of fact, outnumbered the other groups. Such ideologization of the Holocaust was perhaps inevitable, yet it was by no means an innocent process. This type of appropriation was also observed in an entire range of other aspects of immediate postwar developments, to mention only the so-called camp literature in which the mass genocide became subjected to an ongoing representation. Among the earliest initiatives was, for example, Oficyna Warszawska na Obczyźnie in Munich,[3] which in 1946 published a collection of narratives entitled *We Were in Auschwitz* by three former inmates: Janusz Nel Siedlecki, Tadeusz Borowski, and Krystyn Olszewski.[4] All three men were imprisoned in both the Auschwitz and Dachau concentration camps. This information was made visible on the frontispiece of their book, in which the authors' names were preceded by their tattooed numbers. Besides validating their narratives, these numbers informed the reader how long each of the men spent in the camp: the shorter the number, the longer the imprisonment and the greater respect for seniority in survival. This hierarchy was also reflected in the order the names appeared in the volume. Authenticity of experience was inscribed in yet another aspect of this uncanny cover design: a small number of copies were bound in the original fabric recycled from the prisoners' striped uniforms (*pasiaki*).[5] Poignantly, the reader was informed that the striped fabric was, most likely, made of nettles, the most inferior raw material imaginable (Borowski et al. 2000, 94). This concept constituted yet another object lesson about the Nazi economic system, reminding the reader that the exploitation of prisoners was fused with the production and consumption of various *ersatze*. To acquire a copy of the book and, with it, a shred of *pasiaki*—which metonymically evoked the horror of the camp—allowed the reader to touch the authentic as a relic in its first protective layer. This relic, moreover, contained a narrative about the proximity between the fabric and the body of a prisoner. If this packaging was a speculation on Girs's part to sell the edition of altogether 10,000 copies quickly, it failed. Very few were interested in the Auschwitz stories, special bookbinding or not. Today, only a few copies of the edition remain in existence.

The authentication of written testimonies and packaging them as special objects in order to inform the world (which at that time remained unapprised of the genocide) in a persuasively tangible manner about the camps corresponded to another aspect of the authorial design. The authors shared the view that the emerging martyrological myths about the camps ought to be refuted. As survivors themselves, they aimed to portray a wholly authentic, demythologized document about "being in Auschwitz." Viewed together, the three differing contributions and perspectives created a sense of the collective experience. This collectivity, along with the commonality of the narrated experience of evil, buttressed what the authors insisted upon: the undignifying experience of inmates as truth about the camps. Although this concept constituted the core of the authorial project, the representation of survivors and survival as a nonheroic act had no impact at all on the camp legacy. The writer's post-Holocaust responsibility, as Borowski and his coauthors understood it, then, was to disseminate this message.[6] Not only did their idea find no adherents, but it instead acquired quite a few adversaries. As the history of Holocaust discourse demonstrated, what became the social doxa about survivors and nature of survival itself was in polar opposition to the authorial belief expressed in *We Were in Auschwitz*.

While the intent to preserve the framing of these testimonies with an authentic material sign went unquestioned, and the copies bound in the prisoners' clothes turned into sanctified relics years later, the collective experience narrated in the volume was, all the same, uniquely personal. The very fact that some of the "documents" (many written by Borowski) captured the attention of countless readers, while others, written in more conventional language, did not, indicated that even in mere documents there is no "zero degree" of style. The tension between figurative and historical narrations, which became one of the most powerful factors in the post-Holocaust axis of ethics and aesthetics, was already inherent in We Were in Auschwitz. The volume—conceived under the illusion that both the original experience of Auschwitz and its materiality could be preserved intact—represented one of the first instances of both the simultaneous representation and packaging of the Holocaust as a material event. Others followed suit.[7]

The anthropological spectrum whose extremes were traced by the anonymous and the personal co-constituted the postwar articulation of the genocide's material legacy. The volume, We Were in Auschwitz, oscillated narratively between a personalized account and one that outlined how individual experience was pushed into the collective anonymity of a bare life. This ambiguous approach transformed such personalized accounts into secondary and mediated versions of anonymity and, thus, into specific methods of representation. The incongruity present in the attempts at personalization prevailed in various commemorative sites. As a method, it chose to evoke a singular thing, picked up from the detritus left after the genocide, or to direct the visitor's attention towards an individual item, instead of a pile. Within the space of such a controlled and understated sphere of representation as the Auschwitz Museum, the curatorial decision to single out one item and display it in front of the pile of similar items creates a dialectic: such manipulation enhances the detritus effect, opposed to the solo performance of one thing selected and separated from an indistinct heap. In turn, a single item—and its potential personal tale—conditions the mound's anonymity and prompts a rethinking of its significance.[8] Instead of visual suspense, the piled objects tell the beholder that they contain a multitude of such potential individualized stories, all performed in past perfect.[9] Eliciting meditation, the synthesizing result of such a dialectical image is, thus, achieved or is inscribed as potential.

And yet, one encounters the most extreme instances of depersonalized objects in the accumulation of vestiges displayed today in Holocaust museums. The pitiful remnants of material possessions engage a peculiar perceptual mechanism, which shifts the mass genocide to a more readily comprehensible frame of reference. To put it in Susan Stewart's terms, here the miniature evokes the gigantic.[10] These Holocaust artifacts became involved in post-Holocaust visual performances of mediation; their extended, although fragmentary, type of existence was subjected to commemorative, educational, and epistemological demands. Since the power that enacted genocide has been removed, these objects, through their physicality, remain malleable and humble as they gesture, collectively, to a documented, described, and collected experience.

When approaching the factuality of the Holocaust today, those who study its history often employ a perspective that correlates the totality of mass murder with a mass of neutral facts and numbers. Thus, one type of reification is followed, out of necessity, by another. Although, on the one hand, this method may bring fragmented messages to the level of sheer abstraction, on the other, it points to these mounds' raison d'être: the totality of the Nazi depersonalizing project. The joint dynamic of the totalizing effect of such a display and the obfuscation (due to the passage of time) of individualizing signs inscribed in the objects visibly demonstrates the Nazis' desire to amass and accumulate, rather than to collect.

Performed within a museum space, these narratives—conditioned by an institutional framing presence, curatorial strategies, and survivors' advice—carry out seemingly limited messages concerning the objects' victimized owners. For Liliane Weissberg, who studies the visual aspects of the genocide, these artifacts, besides narrating their present uniformization, have very little—or nothing—to say about the lives of their original owners. For this reason, their restricted role has been to stand, in a metonymical manner, for their owners' death (Weissberg 2003, 401). Therefore, she compares the amassed suitcases, which often bear their owners' names, dates of birth, and other bits of biographical information, with coffins. Indeed, the inscriptions can be read like any sepulchral text marking loss. Out of almost four thousand of them, over two thousand have inscriptions that claim ownership and bear other personalizing signs. These inscriptions tell us how the owners protected them from being lost but, above all, they speak of an overpowering human desire to live.

The story of a thing continues as long as it maintains its capacity to serve its owner. A discomforting effect of the objects on display in Holocaust museums reverses the order of this relationship: beholders confront lifeless items that were in usable condition when separated from their owners and, thus, encounter in these vestiges not only their owners' tragic end, but also stories of their will to survive. Furthermore, one can see that the representational incapacity on the part of these relics is not total; their not yet obliterated significations can be decoded, providing a modest amount of personalized information. Herein lies the ambiguity of the vestigial sign, which arises from the interplay of negated and present aspects of objects. A skillful anthropologist, endowed with a detective's discriminating gaze, can decipher from the traces inscribed on the surface of items their owner's age, gender, wealth, place of origin and, occasionally, even profession.[11] An excavation of these material remainders may bring to light a signifier and signified that are still close to each other. The fact that these signs remain unread does not mean that they are illegible; it is, rather, largely due to the longstanding curatorial tradition of displaying such remains en masse, in anonymous piles.

The effect of arranging this kind of display in concentration camp museums makes for the creation of a necropolis of things collected and shown within an original, older, and larger necropolis composed of the ashes of victims, remnants of camp infrastructure, as well as extant documentation found on the premises of concentration and extermination camps.[12] If sites of remembrance, such as the Dachau or Buchenwald museums, are cemeteries within cemeteries, they suggest, in their double role, not only the mass murder, but also the fact that the things amassed and displayed there lost their use-value as they approach termination. The maintenance of a pile of eyeglasses costs the Auschwitz museum considerable and expensive effort and, thus, reveals a striking dissymmetry: what was considered a spoil and a source of profit during the war acquired, in the postwar years, a museum value that demands constant attention. Even the sole fact that Dachau's mesh wire fence had to be replaced several years ago makes us more and more aware of the impermanence of the displayed objects, whose unique phenomenality is gradually subtracted. The deterioration of these historical dumping grounds are governed by what Eric L. Santner refers to as creaturely life, that is, by the fact that the detritus acquires "an aspect of mute, natural being" (2006, 16). As Holocaust detritus becomes more natural, it loses its specific referential and historical orientation. One day this may be lost entirely, at which point the trajectory of the Holocaust object will be concluded in the stage of simulacrum.

The Holocaust object may also disappear according to another prevailing scenario, engulfed by the obscurity of unknowing or unintentional oblivion. Survivors seldom kept their uniforms, clogs, and other items as mementos of that horrible time; the suppression of traumatic memories was often the best way of coping with them. While mementos of this type ruptured the process of healing and forgetting, their documentary value prompted the owners to give them to museums. It is, therefore, the poet's task to rescue a personal Holocaust object, revealing its obfuscated origin.

Such is the purpose of Tadeusz Różewicz's "Professor's Penknife." On the surface, this poetic cycle narrates, unhurriedly and in a slightly disjointed, conversational style, the story of both the penknife and its maker.[13] The poet uncovers its story casually, in bits and pieces. The maker happens to be the poet's close friend, Mieczysław Porębski, an illustrious art critic and art historian, who manufactured the penknife while imprisoned in a concentration camp. Today, the strange-looking penknife—"dziwny nożyk," as Różewicz calls it—lies on the professor's desk, one item among many, lost amid papers, books, pens, and pencils (the usual clutter that, nonetheless, looks quite orderly). For those who do not know its history, the penknife can be easily overlooked, despite being displayed. Yet the knife attains new meaning as life goes on and the two survivors, the poet and his professor friend, contemplate its aspects over breakfast. Brought from the camp by Porębski, it became a small particle of his private life. Now it is present, openly, in his own dwelling and serves, for the initiated, as a marker of the professor's former identity as a camp prisoner.[14]

This inauspicious camp penknife reminds me, in its style, of an *objet-trouvé* or a rustic tool, if you will. It is rough-looking, in fact, handmade by Porębski from a barrel's hoop. Its camp-value was the same as any other penknife: it cut, severed, and peeled potatoes. It was a useful extension of its maker's apt hand. However, it was the penknife's meta-functional feature that mattered most, since it was illegal and punishable to own a sharp tool in a camp. Its possession made the owner's life precarious and turned him into a transgressor. For this reason, he used to hide it in the fold of his *pasiak*. Other ambiguities pushed this penknife into the grey zone of Holocaust things. For example, by Porębski's own admission, it helped him to survive. Crucial for the marking of his identity, the penknife does not function only as a sign of his dexterity and desire to stay alive, since it also bridges survival with memories of death. Between the two friends there is no need to speak about these memories, because this vestige can bring them back, as if it were a souvenir from afar.

Of course, it is not a souvenir, but a memento of camp life, a peculiarly modernist *momento mori*. The camp penknife, once the professor's handy extension, now disrupts its owner's benevolent and quiet everyday existence, opening a space for bereavement. It sharply cuts into the simple pleasure of sharing breakfast with an old friend and, in doing so, becomes more than merely the subject of their conversation. Suturing the rupture caused by the iron knife's mnemonic potential becomes a daily labor at a table where he can chat with his poet friend about the secrets of preparing soft-boiled eggs. Neither a nostalgically informed souvenir, nor a museumed, depersonalized referent to genocide, this vestige, unlike the other traces I have discussed, remains in close proximity to its maker: it has always been with him, in the fold of his *pasiak* and at his home. It has dwelled with him and in him. In this way, this relic cannot be extricated completely from the present moment. Neither can it be forgotten. Arguably, the hand-crafted tool placed at the survivor's hearth is of singular importance as the only such personal Holocaust object.

It is also Różewicz's arduous task to leave the therapeutic effect of the everyday and to resist the irreversible fate of those Holocaust objects that have been recycled or have simply vanished. His work of mourning extends his poetic symbolization beyond realistic boundaries. For Różewicz, the *recykling* (recycling)[15] of gold removed from the mouths and other orifices of Holocaust victims, ostensibly reduced to a mere commodity, remains as if unrecycled and endowed with a supernatural capacity of revealing its true origin. As a story that resists separation between the victims and their possessions, Różewicz's *recykling* claims a permanent stigma that cannot be erased from gold even through melting. The bullion, made of victims' dentures, coins, and jewelry and hidden in Swiss banks, acquires

features of an extraordinary representational space, in which the spectral identity of its rightful owners, their voices and memories, cannot be simply blotted
out. It is, thus, the weakness of recycling as a transformative force that ushers in
and allows for the triumphant return of Essential Design, phantasmagorically
resurrected in Różewicz's poem. One can say that both the identity of murdered
people and the gold bullion into which their valuables have been cast formed a
living unity whose function is both accusatory and commemorative. In this Holocaust poem, Różewicz endows matter with additional significance, for it cannot be separated from the soulfulness of the victims. This return of neo-hylozoism
in the poem has some recuperative purpose: the representational space of the
poem recovers what is lost and long dead. Its deceptive duration attains another
shade of moralistic meaning in that Różewicz locates this uncanny gold in the
cultural context of the contemporary consumerist society. The thoughtless dis-
posal of material goods produced and acquired in excess, which commonly
identifies such a society, indicates in the poem that the Holocaust object lessons
of accretion have been forgotten.

✻   ✻   ✻

To say that Holocaust writers preserved their proximity with the world of objects through representation, while post-Holocaust writers rescue the vestigial
signs of what used to be a whole and material proximate would be too simple
a conclusion. Holocaust writers experienced and preserved both proximity
and vestiges of their crumbling world: the ashes and the peculiar smell of soap
along with fragmented copies of poems, the material letter *J* as well as un-
burned photographs. Nonetheless, what we have inherited are shreds. Therefore, I conclude this book in an open-ended way by pointing to the main
objectual developments that occurred after the war, when changes concurred
with or contradicted the inheritance. One observation is unequivocal: the
post-Holocaust material world is the domain of both traces and vestiges entrusted to us to read them and grant continuation.

ACKNOWLEDGMENTS

M Y HEARTFELT THANKS go to Professor Harriet Murav for giving me an opportunity, in 2004, to present my then fledgling project to an inquisitive audience at the University of Illinois at Urbana-Champaign. I extend my gratitude to my colleagues Beth Holmgren, Madeline G. Levine, Agata Bielik Robson, and Ryszard Nycz, whose opinions I greatly value and whose friendship I cherish.

I owe special thanks to Dean of the Humanities Division at the University of Chicago Martha Roth for bestowing on me the honor to deliver the 2009 Jean and Harold Gossett Lecture in Memory of Holocaust Victims Martha and Paul Feivel Feingold. The University of Chicago has been an ideal place to have conversations related to my book with my colleagues. In particular, I acknowledge Bill Brown, David Nirenberg, Bob von Halberg, Shrikanth Reddy, and Samuel Sandler. Also, I am indebted to George Grinnell and Sean Lawrence for their illuminating remarks regarding the shifting approaches to the utilization of the body.

I am grateful to my husband Dave for reminding me that the Holocaust scholar should resist, at all costs, the temptations of populist thinking. Without his patience and generosity, this book would have been much more difficult to finish. I am very grateful to Project Editor Nancy Lightfoot for her unstinting support in this endeavor.

Finally, I thank Antje Postema for her editorial skills, which made this book much more readable.

Permissions

An earlier version of chapter 3 appeared under the title "Dziwne mydło: Zofia Nałkowska i gospodarka Zagłady," in *Teksty Drugie* 5 (2007): 62–73, in Kinga Maciejewska's translation.

Some earlier parts of the book appeared under the title "Własność i właściwość w sferze doświadczenia żydowskiego" in *(Nie)obecność: Pominię-*

cia i przemilczenia w narracjach XX wieku, Hanna Gosk and Bożena Karwowska, eds. (Dom Wydawniczy Elipsa: Warsaw, 2008), 447–455.

The following are reprinted by permission: "Campo di Fiori" (from "Ocalenie," 1945) and "Biedny chrześcijanin patrzy na getto" (from "Ocalenie," 1945); works into English include "Campo dei Fiori" (from *Rescue*, 1945) in Luis Iribarne and David Brooks's translation; "A Poor Christian Looks at the Ghetto" (from *Rescue*, 1945) in Czeslaw Milosz's translation; Ocalenie © 1945, by The Czeslaw Milosz Estate; *Rescue* © 1973, 1988 by the Czeslaw Milosz Estate. All rights reserved.

NOTES

The Totalized Object

All translations, if not indicated otherwise, are mine.

1. Despite strict quantity limitations imposed on deportees, the sheer quantity of things amassed can be illustrated by an archival photograph, in which piles of shoes were so high that a ladder was put into use; see the website of the Memorial and Museum at Auschwitz-Birkenau.

2. As the historian Jan T. Gross aptly put it: "The 'New Order' had no order." See Jan Tomasz Gross, *Polish Society under German Occupation: The Generalgouvernement, 1939–1945* (Princeton, N.J.: Princeton University Press, 1979), 92.

3. Jean Baudrillard, "Consumer Society," in *Selected Writings*, ed. and preface Mark Poster (Stanford, Calif.: Stanford University Press, 2003), 33.

4. The uninhibited hoarding instinct is well exemplified in Hermann Göring's growing greed, as he appropriated the choicest works of art from both European museums as well as private collections, and displayed these among his other trophies in his country estate in Carinhall.

5. On the subject of Nazi cultural politics and the art "collections" amassed by the upper echelon of Nazi leadership, see John Elsner and Roger Cardinal, eds., "Introduction," in *The Cultures of Collecting* (Cambridge, Mass.: Harvard University Press, 1994). The authors come to an astonishing conclusion: "Yet one wonders whether the latterday Nazi hunters, fifty years on, are not possessed of the same collector's zeal" (4).

6. The vast literature on the subject becomes quickly outdated due to ongoing changes in the restitution processes across Europe; the most recent data is discussed in Avi Beker, ed., *The Plunder of Jewish Property during the Holocaust: Confronting European History* (New York: New York University Press, 2001) and Martin Dean, *Robbing the Jews: The Confiscation of Jewish Property in the Holocaust, 1933–1945* (Cambridge: Cambridge University Press, 2008).

7. Emmanuel Levinas, *Totality and Infinity: An Essay on Exteriority*, trans. Alphonso Lingis (Pittsburgh.: Duquesne University Press, 1969), 162.

8. Jeremy Bentham, *Theory of Legislation*, trans. Richard Hildreth (London: Trubner & Co., 1814), 113. The book appeared first in French.

9. Hannah Arendt writes insightfully about this process in her *The Origins of Totalitarianism* (San Diego: Harcourt, 1985). German Jews functioned in Nazi Germany as "nationals," namely, as "second-hand citizens without political rights" (288).

10. "Decree Regarding the Reporting of the Jewish Property," in *A Holocaust Reader*, ed., intro., and notes Lucy S. Dawidowicz (West Orange, N.J.: Berman House, 1976), 50–51.

11. For example, in 1940 the Nazis created in Warsaw the Commissionary Board for the Secured Real Estate (Komisaryczny Zarząd Zabezpieczonych Nieruchomości), which took under its control almost all Jewish real estate over the course of six weeks. As in the Third Reich in the 1930s, a disorienting method was deployed: the name of the board did not augur dispossession, but connoted the "security" of one's property.

12. I should like to invoke here Saul Friedländer's new approach to Holocaust history, which foregrounds the individual voice of a witness. Saul Friedländer, "The Witness: Towards the Unifying History of the Holocaust," public lecture at University of Chicago, October 2008.

13. One such case was the Polish-Jewish modernist Bruno Schulz, who took great care to secure his manuscripts, paintings, drawings, and prints, mostly by employing the legal concept of *precarium* and entrusting them to friends who lived outside the Drohobycz ghetto. We know that, additionally, he also hid some of his archives within the ghetto. Even these precautions proved insufficient and only a portion of his texts were found; regrettably, the writer's unpublished novel, *The Messiah*, has not yet been found. See Jerzy Ficowski, *Regions of the Great Heresy: Bruno Schulz. A Biographical Portrait*, trans. and ed. Theodosia Robertson (New York: W.W. Norton & Co., 2003); see esp. the chapter "Works Preserved and Lost."

14. For example, the Auschwitz Sonderkommando's documents, interred in tin cans and, thus, protected, were found after the war, albeit partly damaged. See Gideon Greif, *We Wept without Tears: Testimonies of the Jewish Sonderkommando from Auschwitz* (New Haven, Conn.: Yale University Press, 2005).

15. Emanuel Ringelblum, *Kronika getta warszawskiego. Wrzesień 1939–styczeń 1943* (Chronicle of the Warsaw Ghetto: September 1939–January 1943), intro. and ed. Artur Eisenbach, trans. from Yiddish Adam Rutkowski (Warsaw: Czytelnik, 1988), 471.

16. Jacek Leociak, *Tekst wobec Zagłady (O relacjach z getta warszawskiego)* (Text versus the Holocaust [On reports from the Warsaw Ghetto]) (Wrocław: Fundacja na Rzecz Nauki Polskiej, 1997); see in particular the chapter "Losy tekstów" (The fates of texts), 83–96.

17. Leociak mentions that it was his amazement at encountering so many written testimonies of the genocide that motivated him to write his monograph, although "[a]ccording to the logic of the 'final solution,' they and their authors' slightest vestige should not have remained" (5).

18. Still, some chroniclers, such as the economist Ludwik Landau, were mainly concerned with this wider notion of actuality and its various aspects, in particular the military, political, or economic development across Europe. Although he recorded in detail aspects of daily life in Warsaw, Landau seemed to find hope in his extensive analyses of the theater of war; see Ludwik Landau, *Kronika lat wojny i okupacji* (Chronicle of the Time of War and Occupation) (Warsaw: Państwowe Wydawnictwo Naukowe, 1962–1963), 3 vols.

19. The Oyneg Shabes archives were buried in ten metal boxes and two milk cans. They were partly recovered after the war, in 1946 and in 1950. The documents in one of the milk cans, partially damaged by moisture, were illegible—another case of fragmentary Holocaust texts. The third and final part of the archive was never recovered from the apartment building at Świętokrzyska Street 36, despite several attempts. For the full account of the search, see Eisenbach, "Wstęp" (Introduction], *Chronicle of the Warsaw Ghetto: September 1939–January 1943*, 18–19.

20. For more on the subject of this intent, see the monograph by Samuel D. Kassow, *Who Will Write Our History? Emanuel Ringelblum, The Warsaw Ghetto, and the Oyneg Shabes Archive* (Bloomington: Indiana University Press, 2007).

21. Since Hungerford's analysis deals with post-Holocaust representation, it is pertinent to my discussion only to a degree. See Amy Hungerford, *The Holocaust of Texts: Genocide, Literature, and Personification* (Chicago: University of Chicago Press, 2002).

22. Dawid Graber's note included in the first part of the archives is quoted after Eisenbach, "Introduction," 18.

23. Emmanuel Levinas, *Otherwise Than Being or Beyond Essence*, trans. Alphonso Lingis (Pittsburgh: Duquesne University Press, 2002), 89. In this volume, the philosopher reaches a different understanding of proximity from *Totality and Infinity*, where he elaborates the hand's ability to govern and order objects through touch without delineating the gesture in terms of nearness.

24. As suggested by the early Jacques Derrida, *Of Grammatology*, corrected edition, trans., and intro. Gayatri Chakravorty Spivak (Baltimore and London: Johns Hopkins University Press, 1997). The conceptualization of the trace in his philosophy evolves into a concept nearly as broad and complex as his work itself.

25. Jacques Derrida, *Learning to Live Finally: An Interview with Jean Birnbaum*, trans. Pascale-Anne Brault and Michael Naas (Hoboken, N.J.: Melville House Publishers, 2007), 26.

26. The photographic documentation of the concentration camps is substantial. By contrast, as far as we know, only four pictures were taken of a death camp, two of which are entirely blurred; this erasure itself speaks for the void of lives of millions. This mission of documenting the crimes of Auschwitz-Birkenau was carefully planned by numerous individuals, some of whom were not imprisoned in Auschwitz. See also Teresa Świebocka, Jonathan Webber, and Connie Wilsack, eds., *Auschwitz: The History in Photographs* (Bloomington: Indiana University Press, 1995).

27. They also caused a debate between proponents of the Holocaust's essential, basic, and foundational unrepresentability and those who believe it capable of being represented. The debate, which involved such prominent public figures as Claude Lanzmann, is detailed by Georges Didi-Huberman (his opponent and supporter of representability) in the latter's *Images in Spite of All: Four Photographs from Auschwitz*, trans. Shane B. Lillis (Chicago: University of Chicago Press, 2008).

28. James E. Young comments persuasively on the overlapping of the figurative and the factual in his *Writing and Rewriting the Holocaust: Narrative and the Consequences of Interpretation* (Bloomington: Indiana University Press, 1990), 50–51.

29. David G. Roskies, "The Holocaust Literature According to the Literary Critics," *Prooftexts: A Journal of Jewish Literary History* 1, no. 2 (May 1981): 209–216.

30. Bill Brown, unpublished introduction to the Workshop on Material Object Culture at the University of Chicago, 2005–2006.

1. A Dandy and Jewish Detritus

1. Kazimierz Wyka, *Życie na niby. Pamiętnik po klęsce* (Life As If. A Memoir after Defeat) (Kraków: Wydawnictwo Literackie, 1982).

2. Władysław Szlengel, "Okolice Warszawy" (The Surroundings of Warsaw), in *Co czytałem umarłym. Wiersze getta warszawskiego* (What I Read to the Dead: Poems of the Warsaw Ghetto), ed. and intro. Irena Maciejewska (Warsaw: PIW, 1977), 79.

Although the title of this volume refers only to one collection of poems, Maciejewska managed to publish Szlengel's almost entire extant oeuvre in this volume.

3. On this occasion, one must remember Heidegger's misprision when he overlooked the fact that Van Gogh's painting, *A Pair of Shoes*, autobiographically represents the painter's old shoes and not, as the thinker believed, a poor peasant woman's footwear. For this reason, his reading of the painting is an imposition of his own vision; see Martin Heidegger, "The Origin of the Work of Art," in *Poetry, Language, Thought*, trans. Albert Hofstadter (New York: Harper and Row, 1975), 17–87, esp. 33–39. The philosopher's mishap caused subsequent discussions with Meyer Shapiro and Jacques Derrida; see Derrida's "Restitutions of the Truth in Pointing [pointure]," *The Truth in Painting*, trans. Geoff Bennington and Ian McLeod (Chicago: University of Chicago Press, 1987), 255–382.

4. Abraham Sutzkever, "A Load of Shoes," in *The Literature of Destruction: Jewish Responses to Catastrophe*, ed. David G. Roskies (Philadelphia: Jewish Publication Society, 1988), 493.

5. The Jewish Historical Institute.

6. See Kenneth Burke's discussion of metonymy in "Appendix D: Four Master Tropes," *A Grammar of Motives* (New York: Prentice Hall, 1945). In this work, he contends that spiritual and abstract words are metonymical in their derivation (503–517).

7. Some of his poems also convey a bitter sense of abandonment by his fellow Jewish artists abroad.

8. For a different view on Szlengel's poetry, see Frieda W. Aaron, *Bearing the Unbearable: Yiddish and Polish Poetry in the Ghetto and Concentration Camps*, foreword David G. Roskies (Albany: State University of New York Press, 1990). To my knowledge, Aaron's chapter is the only substantial interpretation of Szlengel in English; her approach to his poetry is based on textual explication.

9. This metaphor is vivid in the poems "Okno na tamtą stronę" (Window on the Other Side) and "Nowe święto" (A New Holiday).

10. This understanding of the Nazi atrocities as an attack against the civilized world was advanced early on during the Nuremberg trials. I perceive these acts, as well as the entire Holocaust, as committed *within* civilization; in doing so, I follow another point of view articulated by Hannah Arendt and Zygmunt Bauman, among others. For an eloquent discussion of these approaches, see Lawrence Douglas, "The Shrunken Head of Buchenwald: Icons of Atrocity at Nuremberg," in *Visual Culture and the Holocaust*, ed. and intro. Barbie Zelizer (New Brunswick, N.J.: Rutgers University Press, 2001), 275–299.

11. Charles Sterling, *Still Life Painting: From Antiquity to the Twentieth Century* (New York: Harper and Row, 1981).

12. "W porzuconych mieszkaniach / narzucone tobołki, / garnitury i kołdry, / i talerze, i stołki, / tlą się jeszcze ogniska, / leżą łyżki bezczynne, / tam rzucone w pośpiechu / fotografie rodzinne . . . " ("Things"; Szlengel 1977, 127).

13. Jan Steen and Adriaen Brouwer's canvases exemplify best the "art of describing" such scenes.

14. Both the French and Polish names for the genre—*nature morte/martwa natura* (dead nature)—deem this stasis literal.

15. In the original, "A na półce milczący, / zimny i martwy jej garnek" ("Monument"; Szlengel 1977, 83).

16. Szlengel favored puzzling conclusions in his poems: "pointa . . . ma zawsze dla mnie znaczenie." (a punch line . . . is always of importance to me) (*What I Read to the Dead*; Szlengel 1977, 37).

17. For Szlengel, there was nothing mystifying about the looting of Jewish property

that occurred in Warsaw, where the Nazis also organized the *Werterfassung* to supervise the accumulation of stolen goods. In his introductory essay to *What I Read to the Dead*, he makes the following equation: "Skarb Rzeszy rośnie. Żydostwo umiera" (The Reich's treasury is growing. The Jewry is dying) (Szlengel 1977, 49).

18. "Z Hożej i Wspólnej, i Marszałkowskiej / jechały wozy . . . wozy żydowskie . . . / meble, stoły i stołki / walizeczki, tobołki, / kufry, skrzynki i bety, / garnitury, portrety, / pościel, garnki, dywany / i draperie ze ściany. / Wiśniak, słoje, słoiki, / szklanki, plater, czajniki, / książki, cacka i wszystko / jedzie z Hożej na Śliską" ("Things"; Szlengel 1977, 125).

19. Aaron offers an extensive close reading of this poem (Aaron 1990, 41–53).

20. The disruptive act of moving homes exposes the home's hidden parts, as its innards are otherwise covered by walls and are inaccessible to the public or voyeuristic eye. In Bogdan Wojdowski's novel, *Bread for the Departed*, the narrator and protagonist feels shame and vulnerability as his family moves its meager belongings to the ghetto.

21. Speaking about the significance of objects in literature, Aleksander Nawarecki claims in his study that they have been sentenced to a life in the background since Aristotle's *Poetics*; see his *Rzeczy i marzenia. Studia o wyobraźni poetyckiej skamandrytów* (Things and Dreams. Studies on the Poetic Imagination of the Skamandrites) (Katowice: "Śląsk," 1993).

22. In their invaluable historical study, Engelkind and Leociak give a detailed, day-after-day reconstruction of the events of the *"wielka akcja wysiedleńcza"* (great deportation action); see Barbara Engelkind and Jacek Leociak, *Warszawskie Ghetto. Przewodnik po nieistniejącym mieście* (Warsaw: IFiS PAN, 2001), 661–689.

23. "In the elegant life, only superiority exists." Honoré de Balzac, *Les Parisiennes comme ils sont 1850–1848* suivi du "'Traité de la vie élégante,'" intro. and notes André Billy (Geneva: La Palatine, 1947), 201.

24. P. G. Konody, *The Painter of Victorian Life: A Study of Constantin Guys with an Introduction and a Translation of Baudelaire's Peintre de la vie moderne*, ed. C. Geoffrey Holme (London: Studio Ltd., 1930), 120.

25. Accordingly, in *Peintre de la vie moderne* Baudelaire speaks of the dandy's rule to show "the cold appearance that results from the steadfast resolution not to be moved" (Baudelaire 135) but to astonish others.

26. Roland Barthes, *The Fashion System*, trans. Matthew Ward and Richard Howard (New York: Hill and Wang, 1983), 256.

27. Zygmunt Bauman argues that national identity, including the "natural identity by birth" is a mere fiction. See his *Identity: Conversations with Benedetto Vecchi* (Cambridge: Polity Press, 2004), 20–23.

28. But there is one more intertext within this scene of writing—one that renders the poem's meaning still lighter and even more puzzling. According to Natan Gross, the poem was written to the melody of the old Polish song "Ty pójdziesz górą, a ja doliną" (You will go on the mountain, I will go in the valley), which laments the inevitable physical separation of two lovers who go their different ways. Natan Gross, *Poeci and Szoa. Obrazy Zagłady Żydów w poezji polskiej* (Poets and the Shoah. Images of the Annihilation of Jews in Polish Poetry) (Sosnowiec: OFFMAX, 1993), 91.

29. Michel Borwicz, *Écrits des condamnés à mort sous l'occupation allemande (1939–1945)*, intro. René Cassin (Paris: Presses Universitaires de France, 1954), 196–200. Writing about the satirical mode of speech and literature during the Holocaust, Borwicz observes that people retreated to wit under two conditions: first, to realize their predicament and, second, to detach themselves from it. He points out that people

in the ghetto, on the whole, maintained their sense of humor and that the production of satirical writing was plentiful, thereby complicating the stereotype that the mood of the victims was solemn and morbid.

30. *The Diary of Mary Berg: Growing Up in the Warsaw Ghetto*, ed. S. L. Shneidermann (Oxford: Oneworld, 2006), 104.

31. See Žižek's analysis of these films in "Laugh Yourself to Death! The New Wave of Holocaust Comedies," in *The Holocaust and the Historical Trauma in Contemporary Visual Culture*, http://www.arthist.lu.se/discontinuities/texts/zizek.htm.

32. Although the concept of comic distance in Holocaust literature often serves to delineate the boundaries between "different orders of reality," as Mark Cory puts it, this was not the case with Szlengel, who instantiated distance in various forms and media. Cory analyzes postwar literary expression on the Holocaust; see Mark Cory, "Comedic Distance in Holocaust Literature," in *Literature of the Holocaust*, intro. and ed. Harold Bloom (Philadelphia: Chelsea House Publishers, 2004), 195.

33. Krzysztof Kamil Baczyński's war poem "Ballada o wisielcach" (A Ballad on the Hanged Men) extends the existing constellation of poems linked to Villon's "La ballade des pendus." This Polish poet of Jewish background, distraught by the totality of death around him, imagines an entire landscape filled with scaffolds and hanged men. See Krzysztof Kamil Baczyński, *Utwory zebrane* (Collected Works), ed. Aniela Kmita-Piorunowa and Kazimierz Wyka (Kraków: Wydawnictwo Literackie, 1970), 1:3–4. For more, besides Szlengel, about the presence of various motives from Villon in the Holocaust poetry, see Borwicz 1954, 253–255.

34. The roundness, which the German advertising line "Juno sind rund" indicated, somewhat tautologically, also referred to the name Juno and its mythological bearer.

35. One finds this expression in "Kontratak" I (Counterattack I) (Szlengel, 135).

36. Anna Wierzbicka, *Semantics, Culture and Cognition: Universal Human Concepts in Culture-Specific Configurations* (New York: Oxford University Press, 1992); see the chapter "The Polish *Los*," 75–79.

37. According to Leociak, Szlengel was last seen on May 8th leaving the Szymek Kac bunker with its other inhabitants; in all probability, he was on his way to the Umschlagplatz (Leociak, 52). His claim is based on Leon Najberg's account in *Ostatni powstańcy getta* (The Last Insurgents of the Ghetto) (Warsaw: Żydowski Instytut Historyczny, 1993), 74. Szlengel was the last living Polish-language poet of the Warsaw Ghetto.

38. In this vein, one could easily link the gallows humor of "Top Hat" with François Villon's *Le petit testament*.

39. George Bataille discusses a similar type of humor in the essay "The Practice of Joy before Death," in *Visions of Excess: Selected Writings 1927–1939*, ed. Allan Stoekl, trans. Allan Stoekl with Carl R. Lovitt and Donald M. Leslie, Jr. (Minneapolis: University of Minnesota Press, 1985), 235–245.

40. Jean Amery, *On Suicide: A Discourse on Voluntary Death*, trans. John D. Barlow (Bloomington: Indiana University Press, 1999); see esp. the chapter "The Road to the Open," 123–153. Amery is also prone to connect suicide with dignity (43–44).

41. Plato, *Phaedo*, in *Plato*, trans. Benjamin Jowett (New York: P.F. Collier & Son, 1909), 2:112–113.

42. Ann Hartle, *Death and the Disinterested Spectator: An Inquiry into the Nature of Philosophy* (Albany: State University of New York Press, 1986).

43. Janusz Korczak, whose real name was Ludwik Goldszmit, was a popular psychologist, educator, and writer who organized orphanages for Jewish children and during the war strove against incredible odds to keep the sites operational.

44. Chaim A. Kaplan, "Scroll of Agony," in Roskies, 1988, 497.

45. Tadeusz Borowski, *This Way for the Gas, Ladies and Gentlemen*, selected and trans. Barbara Vedder, intro. Jan Kott, trans. and the translator's intro. Michael Kandel (London, New York, Toronto: Penguin Books, 1967), 44.

46. Giorgio Agamben, *Remnants of Auschwitz: The Witness and the Archive*, trans. Daniel Heller-Roazen (New York: Zone Books, 1999), 69. In this work, the philosopher refrains, mainly for etymological reasons, from using the term *Holocaust*.

47. Michał Głowiński, *Czarne sezony* (Warsaw: Open, 1999), 33.

48. Aaron offers a persuasive close reading of the poem and the issue of death with dignity; she also indicates that the poet repeatedly shows the glaring absurdity inherent in the application of prewar literary standards to occupation literature (1990, 152).

2. The Material Letter J

1. Sean Hides writes on problems resulting from the circular type of argumentation; see his "Material Culture and Identity," in *Experiencing Material Culture in the Western World*, ed. Susan M. Pearce (London and Washington: Leicester University Press, 1997), 2–35, here 13.

2. In this respect, the title of one of Kosinna's expositions, *Die deutsche Vorgeschichte—Eine hervorragend nationale Wissenschaft* (German Prehistory—a Predominantly National Science), is particularly telling.

3. Carl Schmitt, *Political Theology: Four Chapters on the Concept of Sovereignty*, intro. Tracy B. Strong, trans. George Schwab (Chicago: University of Chicago Press, 2005), 5.

4. Arendt analyzes how the statelessness of Jews resulted in the complete negation of their civic and human rights; see esp. the chapter "'The Nation of Minorities' and the Stateless People," 1985, 269–290.

5. Zuzanna Ginczanka, *Udźwignąć własne szczęście. Poezje* (To Bear One's Happiness. Poetry), intro. and ed. Izolda Kiec (Poznań. Książnica Włóczęgów i Uczonych, 1991), 141.

6. Her family spoke Russian at home.

7. Ginczanka was murdered, together with her high school girlfriend Blumka Fradis, in a prison courtyard on December 1944, just a few weeks before Kraków's liberation. According to Krystyna Garlicka, a fellow inmate, Ginczanka displayed great courage during the tortures she endured in prison. Garlicka also mentioned that Fradis, similarly tortured by the Gestapo, admitted that she and her friend were Jewish. See Izolda Kiec, *Ginczanka. Życie i twórczość* (Ginczanka. Life and Oeuvre) (Poznań: Obserwator, 1994), 160–163.

8. Although some Nazi informers were killed during the war by the underground, the Chomins, the self-imposed masters of the poet's destiny, were prosecuted only after the war for their crime (Kiec 1994, 156).

9. The poem was published as a centerpiece in the monthly *Odrodzenie* 12 (1946): 5.

10. According to Araszkiewicz, who conducted a phone interview with Stauber. See Agata Araszkiewicz, *Wypowiadam wam moje życie. Melancholia Zuzanny Ginczanki* (Warsaw: Fundacja OSKA, 2001), 163. The title of the monograph was taken from one of Ginczanka's poems and is considerably difficult to translate into English; one possibility is: "I take my life from you: Zuzanna Ginczanka's Melancholy."

11. See Anna Kamieńska, *Od Leśmiana. Najpiękniejsze wiersze polskie* (Since Leśmian. The Most Beautiful Polish Poems) (Warsaw: Iskry, 1974), 219.

12. The decision to give the poem a "name" was not a far-reaching editorial imposition because her poetic testament alludes to the lyrics of both Horace and Słowacki. Stanisław Zabierowski examines numerous references, as well as the variety of genres employed in "My Last Will." See Stanisław Zabierowski, "Testamenty poetyckie" (Poetic Last Wills), in *Księga ku czci Stanisława Pigonia*, eds. Teresa Podolska and Zygmunt Czerny (Kraków: Polska Akademia Nauk, 1961), 356–362.

13. In this case, I concur with Julian Przyboś, the poet and critic who first published the poem. Przyboś amended the poem by changing the last word *przerobi* (will remake) into *przemieni* (will transform). See Julian Przyboś, "Ostatni wiersz Ginczanki" (Ginczanka's Last Poem), *Odrodzenie* 15 (1946): 5.

14. In translation, "Jewish" (plural).

15. I have already discussed the danger of keeping any sort of records documenting Nazi atrocities. Przyboś, who compares the erasure of the adjective to the coding of smuggled prison messages, calls the erased word "a dangerous site" (1946, 5).

16. Anselm L. Strauss, *Mirrors and Masks: The Search for Identity* (New Brunswick: Transaction Publishers, 1997). Strauss proposes in his book, first published in 1959, the concept of identity as process or a transformation, thereby enhancing the understanding of identity that has become a characteristic postmodernist trope.

17. For other examples of textualizing Jewish identity, see *The Jew in the Text: Modernity and the Construction of Identity*, ed. and intro. Linda Nochlin and Tamar Garb (New York: Thames and Hudson, 1996).

18. Sara R. Horowitz discusses this forced muteness in her *Voices from the Killing Ground: Muteness and Memory in Holocaust Fiction* (Albany: State University of New York Press, 1997), 55–57.

19. As a letter sent to posterity, it is endowed with a further material feature.

20. Some insight regarding these uncertainties can be found in Kiec's biography.

21. More on the subject can be found in Jan Tomasz Gross, *Upiorna dekada. Trzy eseje o stereotypach na temat Żydów, Polaków, Niemców i komunistów. 1939–1948* (A Ghostly Decade. Three Essays on the Stereotypes of Jews, Poles, Germans, and Communists), intro. Antony Polonsky (Kraków: Universitas, 1998).

22. For the thorough analysis of the identity of those who survived on Aryan papers, see Małgorzata Melchior, *Zagłada a tożsamość. Polscy Żydzi ocaleni na "aryjskich papierach." Analiza doświadczenia biograficznego* (The Holocaust and Identity. Polish Jews Surviving on "Aryan Papers." An Analysis of a Biographical Experience) (Warsaw: Wydawnictwo IFIS PAN, 2004).

23. See Jacques Derrida's deliberations on the subject, "Materiality without Matter—Typewriter Ribbon: Limited Ink (2) ("within such limits"), in *Material Events: Paul de Man and the Afterlife of Theory*, ed. Tom Cohen (Minneapolis: University of Minnesota Press, 2001), 277–360.

24. Lacan writes: "By 'letter' I designate the material medium [*support*] that concrete discourse borrows from language." See Jacques Lacan, "The Instance of the Letter in the Unconscious or Reason Since Freud," in *Écrits. A Selection*, trans. Bruce Fink with Heloise Fink and Russell Grigg (New York and London: W.W. Norton & Co., 2002), 138–168, here 139.

25. Tzahi Weiss takes a different approach to Lacan's views of alphabetic letters as connected to the foundation of the world in Judaism; see his "On the Matter of Language: The Creation of the World from Letters and Jacques Lacan's Perception of the Letters as Real," *The Journal of Jewish Philosophy and Thought* 17, no. 1 (2009): 101–115.

26. Ginczanka's poem-palimpsest is remarkable not only for its precise use of a literary legacy in its echoes and inversions, but also for its fusion of several genres and subgenres, which include poetic last will, poetic letter, and enumeration.

27. Klara Sandberg died of a heart attack on the way to an extermination camp in Zdołbunów. Ginczanka's parents, divorced before the war, lived separately abroad. Ultimately, Ginczanka was survived only by her mother, who remarried and lived in Spain.

28. I discuss the postwar everyday objects and narratives of their provenance and circulation in "The Archeology of Occupation: Stefan Chwin on Danzig/Gdańsk," in *Framing the Polish Home: The Postwar Literary and Cultural Constructions of Hearth, Homeland, and Self,* ed. Bożena Shallcross (Athens: Ohio University Press, 2002), 116–132.

29. Indeed, the question of plundering the material world of the Holocaust abounds in literature: one need only to mention Ida Fink, Tadeusz Borowski, Chaim Kaplan, Henryk Grynberg, Bogdan Wojdowski, Louis Begley, and Władysław Szpilman.

30. Anne Jouranville, *La femme et la mélancolie* (Paris: Presses Universitaires de France, 1993), 227. However, the economy of the Holocaust produced another meaning that reverses Jouranville's claim: every victim was turned into a reified asset to the Reich, its useful possession.

31. Madeline G. Levine, "Home Loss in Wartime Literature: A Typology of Images." In Shallcross 2002, 97–115.

32. Here I am following Levinas's practice of distinguishing personal otherness (written with a capital "O") from objectual otherness, written with a lower-case "o" (Levinas 1969, 24–25).

33. In fact, in his poetry Leśmian—the most fascinating and totally untranslatable Polish poet—did not engage in allusions and associations to his Jewish roots or Judaism. On the other hand, Tuwim frequently thematized Jewish folklore, customs, and history, though usually in his abundant satirical poetry and cabaret lyrics. For both Tuwim and Słonimski, who observed the annihilation of the Jews from abroad, this historical catastrophe prompted a poetic return to their Jewish roots.

34. According to Bożena Umińska, Ginczanka's attitude toward her murderers— treating them as though they were close to her—expresses the poet's status as an assimilated Jewish woman. See Bożena Umińska, *Postać z cieniem. Portrety Żydówek w polskiej literaturze od końca XIX wieku do 1939 roku* (A Character with a Shadow. Portraits of Jewish Women in Polish Literature from the End of the Nineteenth century to the year 1919) (Warsaw: Sic!, 2001), 359. I do not find Umińska's claim sufficiently persuasive, because of the poet's sarcastic usage of the adjective.

35. This image is mentioned several times in the poem (lines 6, 19, and 22).

36. Martin Jay analyzes the historical-cultural privileged position of the gaze in his magisterial monograph *Downcast Eyes: The Denigration of Vision in Twentieth-Century French Thought* (Berkeley: University of California Press, 1994).

37. S. Czartkower, *Dziennik* (Diary); the citation from Mieczysław Inglot, "*Non omnis moriar* Zuzanny Ginczanki. W kręgu konwencji literackiej" (Zuzanna Ginczanka's "'Non omnis moriar.' Within the Sphere of Literary Convention"), *Acta Universitatis Vratislaviensis* 1876 (1996): 138.

38. Jacques Lacan, *Le séminaire. Livre 8. Le transfert, 1960–61,* ed. Jacques-Alain Miller (Paris: Editions Seuil, 1991), 177.

39. Plato, *Symposium,* trans. Robert Waterfield (Oxford and New York: Oxford University Press, 1994), 60. I coined the term *agalmatic,* since there is no such adjective in

English. I am indebted to Christopher Faraone, who also pointed out to me that there is no adjective *agalmatikos* in Greek.

40. Peter Stallybrass, "Worn Worlds: Clothes and Mourning," in *Cultural Memory and the Construction of Identity*, ed. Dan Ben-Amos and Liliane Weissberg (Detroit: Wayne State University Press, 1999), 31.

41. As manifested in such expressions as *trophy wife* and, more explicitly, in John Fowles's novel *The Collector*, where the libido is sublimated into an obsession, or, if you will, a perversion in which a woman's body is viewed as an object to be collected, not possessed sexually.

42. Jacques Lacan, *The Ethics of Psychoanalysis*, trans. Dennis Porter (New York: W.W. Norton & Co., 1992), 102.

43. In the sense of a free gift suggested by Derrida, for whom it is the hope or the expectation of objectual exchange that denies the gift; see Jacques Derrida, *Donner le temps. La fausse monnaie* (Paris: Galilée, 1991), in particular, the chapter "Folie de la raison économique: un don sans présent," 51–94. The thinker opposes Marcel Mauss's famous notion, espoused in his *Essai sur le don*, of a reciprocal gift that indeed *requires* an exchange.

44. As in the verses: "[M]eadows of . . . tablecloths, fortresses of invincible wardrobes, / vast bed sheets, precious beddings, / and dresses, light dresses" (141).

45. "The furniture from my grandparents' bedroom, undoubtedly, solid, bourgeois, but not particularly remarkable, was needed because in Pruszków they were furnishing a locum for some Hitlerite dignitary. Unbelievably, he was not disgusted by the contact with the objects taken from Jews and by the very fact, that they contaminated them by touch." Głowiński, 167.

46. Jacques Derrida, "Shibboleth: For Paul Celan," trans. Joshua Wilner, in *Acts of Literature*, ed. Derek Attridge (New York: Routledge, 1992), 309.

47. Jan Błoński observes that in Polish apocalyptic poetry, the fear of death undergoes the process of ironic sublimation. See his chapter "'Tradycja, ironia i głębsze znaczenie" (Tradition, Irony and a Deeper Meaning), in *Romans z tekstem* (A Romance with Text) (Kraków: Wydawnictwo Literackie, 1981), 68.

48. Under Ginczanka's pen, the ironic double meaning of the legacy and the legacy of the ironic double meaning remain central. In particular, the image of transformation that concludes her poem undergoes a sarcastic inversion.

49. There are other investigations of the material aspect of the word. For example, in her exploration of the prewar avant-garde treatment of the poetic word's materiality, Malynne Sternstein engages Peirce's linguistic system, and, in particular, his articulation of the relationship between the sign and the object. See Malynne Sternstein, *Will to Chance: Necessity and Arbitrariness in the Czech Avant-Garde: From Poetism to Surrealism* (Bloomington, Ind.: Slavica, 2006), 165.

3. Holocaust Soap and the Story of Its Production

1. Although I am interested in the phenomenology of the soap as an object, its chemical processing deserves to be briefly highlighted: "A cleansing and emulsifying agent that is made usually either from fats or oils by saponification with alkali in a boiling process or the cold process or from fatty acids by neutralization with alkali, that consists essentially of a mixture of water-soluble sodium or potassium salts of fatty acids, and that may contain other ingredients such as perfume, coloring agents, fluo-

rescent dyes, disinfectants or abrasive material." *Webster's Third International Dictionary* (1981), s.v., "soap."

2. Soap was known in ancient civilizations (Pliny the Elder thought it was invented by Gauls), yet the story of its modern production, defined above, harks back only to the nineteenth century. I am aware that soap is also produced from vegetable oils (coconut, palm kernel, etc.), but this type of raw material for saponification has been used for commercial production only since the 1950s.

3. Sigmund Freud, *Civilization and Its Discontents*, trans. James Strachey (New York: W.W. Norton & Co., 1961), 46.

4. Lawrence Douglas, "The Shrunken Head of Buchenwald: Icons of Atrocity at Nuremberg." In Zelizer 2001, 291.

5. These are *Romans Teresy Hennert* (Teresa Hennert's Romance, 1923); *Choucas* (1927); her most ambitious psychological novel *Granica* (The Border, 1935); and her greatest artistic achievement *Niecierpliwi* (The Impatient, 1938), in which she rejected the established formulae of a psychological novel. The novels also dealt with the social position of women.

6. After the war, only two members of his laboratory staff, compromised as collaborators, were arrested and interrogated by the Soviet and Polish secret police, as well as by the members of the Committee for Researching Hitlerite Crimes, including Nałkowska. A German prosecutor, who interrogated Spanner in 1948, dropped the case against the doctor. During the investigation, Spanner denied making such soap; his denial was consistent with the fact that he treated his wartime experiments in soap production as a secret operation disguised as a manufacture of anatomical specimens for medical students.

7. As Nałkowska put it in her *Dzienniki* [Diaries] 6 *1945–1954*, Part I (1945–1948), ed. Hanna Kirchner (Warsaw: Czytelnik, 2000), VI: 150.

8. Aside from Spanner himself, numerous Holocaust revisionists deny that the production of soap from human fat ever took place; one can find an abundance of information about the subject on the Web; for example, Mark Weber, an American historian who denies the Holocaust, writes that reports about human fat soap were mere Holocaust propaganda.

9. The production of such soap was also mentioned by two Czech prisoners, Ota Kraus and Erich Kulka, in their book *Noc a mlha*. Additional evidence was provided by the British prisoners of war John Henry Witton and William Neely, who installed the machinery in Spanner's lab.

10. The Polish prosecutor who, in 2005, opened the case against the late Spanner, also found him not guilty of any crime. The only direct result of the revised case was a plaque mounted on the lab's façade to commemorate the unwilling subjects of this research.

11. Professor Andrzej Stolyhwo, a specialist in lipid chemistry, who conducted the tests, concluded that the soap also contained caolin, likely added for better exfoliation.

12. Zofia Nałkowska, *Medallions*, trans. Diana Kuprel. (Evanston, Ill.: Northwestern University Press, 2000), 10.

13. Robert Jay Lifton's magisterial monograph *The Nazi Doctors: Medical Killing and the Psychology of the Genocide* (New York: Basic Books, 1986) and Michael H. Kater's *The Doctors under Hitler* (Chapel Hill: University of North Carolina Press, 1989) are still the most comprehensive studies on the subject of Nazi medicine.

14. The collection was written almost entirely after the war, with the exception of "The Cemetery Lady." Among its seven reportages, this piece employs a *Jetztzeit* that differs from the postwar perspective Nałkowska applies elsewhere in the collection.

Here the author deliberately retains the concreteness and contemporaneity of the lived experience as reported by an old, antisemetic woman who takes care of graves in the Catholic Powązki Cemetery on edge of the Warsaw Ghetto walls. It takes place in 1943, during the Ghetto Uprising, as Nałkowska visits her mother's grave and is in close proximity to the ongoing killing on the other side of the wall.

15. See Julia Kristeva, *Powers of Horror: An Essay on Abjection*, trans. Leon S. Roudiez (New York: Columbia University Press, 1982).

16. "The individual must accomplish his or her specific action at a frenzied pace, often amidst a pool of blood." Daniel Pick, *War Machine: The Rationalization of Slaughter in the Modern Age* (New Haven, Conn.: Yale University Press, 1993), 184.

17. After all, the cynical expression "mięso armatnie" (meat fodder) functions in many languages.

18. Emphasis in the original.

19. Stefan Essmanowski. "Dialogi akademickie. Rozmowa z Zofią Nałkowską" (Academic dialogs. A conversation with Zofia Nałkowska), *Pion* 10 (1934), quoted after Ewa Frąckowiak-Wiegandtowa, *Sztuka powieściopisarska Nałkowskiej (Lata 1935– 1954)* (The Novelistic Art of Zofia Nałkowska [Years 1935–1954]) (Wrocław: Wydawnictwo Polskiej Akademii Nauk, 1975).

20. This is a passage from Nałkowska's contribution to the 1933 survey entitled "Polish Writers and Soviet Russia," conducted by *Wiadomości Literackie* (Literary News); quoted after Frąckowiak-Wiegandtowa, 53.

21. As observed by Frąckowiak-Wiegandtowa.

22. With the exception of a brief passage in the article "Nowe żądania" (New Demands), published in *Kuźnica*, in which the writer seems to acknowledge the dangers inherent in modern science: "Science does not stop its experiments at the moment, when their paths seem to go off the straight lines and utilitarian directions." See Zofia Nałkowska, *Widzenia dalekie i bliskie* (Visions Close and Distant) (Warsaw: PIW, 1957), 72.

23. The question of the quantity of fat was addressed during the interrogation as a matter of fact: "One man gives maybe five kilos of fat" (Nałkowska 2000, 8).

24. "Psyche is extended, knows nothing about it." Freud wrote this last note of his on August 22, 1938, a year before his death. Sigmund Freud, *The Standard Edition of the Complete Psychological Works*, eds. James Strachey and Anna Freud, trans. James Strachey et al., 24 vols. (New York: W.W. Norton & Co., 2000), 23:300.

25. *Nota bene:* the sculpture of a human head on the jacket cover of the first Polish edition of *Medallions* refers to this aestheticized fragmentation of the body in her narrative.

26. As Frąckowiak-Wiegandtowa diagnosed the writer's thinking in her monograph (Frąckowiak-Wiegandtowa 1975, 145).

27. The skinscript was in Polish, which added more weight to the argument against connecting this phrase with the *Got mit uns* calling of the two World Wars; furthermore, its iconography, as recorded by Nałkowska, differs from its much better-known German counterpart. The phrase, inserted on belt buckles of German imperial army soldiers, was intended as part of an iconographic and ideological design, which included a laurel wreath and, as its most prominent sign, the imperial crown. The Wehrmacht soldiers' belt buckles consisted of a yet more complicated design: the very same religious expression, the *Hakenkreuz*, a laurel leaf wreath and an eagle.

28. In "Professor Spanner," the writer used the plural *we* to refer to committee members and their usher, which stood in polar opposition to the truncated cadavers addressed as *these*.

29. However, the critic did not speak of Nałkowska's *Medallions*.

30. William Shakespeare, *Macbeth*, in *The Complete Works* (New York: Avenel Books, 1975), 1060.

31. Boiling a human body was relegated by the medieval Church to the domain of the forbidden, because in 1300, Pope Boniface VIII issued a peculiar document that has an uncanny link to Spanner's practices. In his bull, entitled *De sepulturis*, he decreed that anyone engaged in boiling the bodies of Crusaders who perished in distant lands would be excommunicated. (Boiling the body to its bones facilitated transportation of the remnants home for burial.) Only later was the bull misunderstood as a prohibition of dissection. The papal bull, however, had little, if no, influence on limiting anatomical studies and dissections of cadavers. On this subject, see Charles H. Talbot, "Medicine," in *Science in the Middle Ages*, ed. David C. Lindberg (Chicago: University of Chicago Press, 1978), 391–428, esp. 408–409.

32. For example, there were 350 corpses in the morgue, in contrast to the anatomy institute's standard requirement of approximately 14, the number necessary to teach local medical students the craft of dissection. The abundance of corpses forced Spanner, anticipating their usefulness, to store some of them should there be future shortages or an expansion of his manufacture. This excess illustrates well the permissive aspect of totalitarianism.

33. Levi writes: "The prisoners were required to take a shower two or three times a week. However, these ablutions were not sufficient to keep them clean as soap was handed out in very parsimonious quantities: only a single 50-gram bar per month. Its quality was extremely poor; it consisted of a rectangular block, very hard, devoid of any fatty material but instead full of sand. It did not produce lather and disintegrated very easily, so after a couple of showers it was completely used up." Primo Levi with Leonardo de Benedetti, *Auschwitz Report*, ed. Robert S. C. Gordon, trans. Judith Woolf (London and New York: Verso, 2006), 45.

34. Francis Ponge, *Soap*, trans. Lane Dunlop (London: Jonathan Cape Ltd., 1969), 11.

35. Ponge's *Savon* serves as a case in point for Peter Schwenger, who persuasively relates the concept of the cosmetic and its poetic erasure to the death drive. See Peter Schwenger, "Words and the Murder of the Thing," in *Things*, ed. Bill Brown, *Critical Inquiry*, no. 1 (2001): 99–113.

36. The reader should not be mystified by this arguably frivolous statement since, during World War II, Ponge was also a soldier, an insurance worker, and a Resistance organizer.

37. Patrick Süskind, *Perfume: The Story of a Murderer*, trans. John E. Woods (New York: Pocket Books, 1991).

4. The Guilty Afterlife of the Soma

1. For more about Aszkenazy the prophet, see Jerzy Stempowski, *Eseje dla Kasandry* (Essays for Cassandra) (Kraków: Wydawnictwo ABC, 1981). Of course, that few believed these and many other prewar prophecies is reminiscent of the Cassandra effect.

2. Żagary was formed in 1931 in Wilno and is considered to represent the Second Avant-garde Movement. Its ideology was marked by leftist and antifascist orientations, fused with a catastrophic imagery and a strong sense of generational uniqueness. The group published the periodical *Żagary* and, later, *Pion*. In his introduction "Przypis po latach" (A Footnote after Many Years), Miłosz self-critically denied that these lyrics bore any greater artistic significance, considering them solely testimonial; see Czesław

Miłosz, *Wiersze tom 1, Dzieła zebrane* (Poems Volume 1, Collected Works) (Kraków: Znak, 2001), 15–16. *Żagary* became the subject of the monograph by Marek Zaleski, *Przygoda Drugiej Awangardy* (The Second Avant-garde's Adventure), 2nd ed. (Wrocław: Ossolineum, 2000).

3. For an analysis of the prewar catastrophic tendencies in Miłosz's poetry, see Stanisław Bereś, "Czeslaw Miłosz's Apocalypse," in *Between Anxiety and Hope: The Poetry and Writing of Czeslaw Miłosz*, ed. Edward Możejko (Edmonton: The University of Alberta Press, 1988), 30–87.

4. In 1942, he published a volume of his poems underground, using the pseudonym Jan Syruć, as well as the anthology *Pieśń niepodległa* (The Independent Song).

5. The ill-fated Warsaw uprising started on August 1, 1944; for a comprehensive study of this insurgency, see Norman Davies, *Rising '44: "The Battle for Warsaw"* (London: Macmillan, 2003).

6. Czeslaw Miłosz, "Zaraz po wojnie." Z Czesławem Miłoszem rozmawia Joanna Gromek (Just after the War. Joanna Gromek's Conversation with Czeslaw Miłosz), in *Rozmowy polskie 1979–1998* (Polish Conversations 1979–1998) (Kraków: Wydawnictwo Literackie, 2006), 756–802, here 774.

7. Both poems, written during the 1943 ghetto uprising in Warsaw, preserved the poet's outrage and pain caused by the destruction of the Warsaw Jewry. See Ewa Czarnecka and Aleksander Fiut, *Conversations with Czesław Miłosz*, trans. Richard Lourie (San Diego, New York, and London: Harcourt Brace Jovanovich, 1987), 88–89.

8. After the war ended, he began to work in the Communist diplomatic service, only to break with the regime in 1951, after which he decided to stay in the West. The volume of essays entitled *The Captive Mind* marked this ideological transition. From then, all of Miłosz's writings were banned in Poland, appearing only through an émigré publishing house in Paris. Despite the limited audience, the poet remained very prolific. Since 1980, when he received the Nobel Prize in Literature, he enjoyed worldwide attention and his works were translated into numerous languages; his writings also became easily accessible to readers in Poland.

9. *Three Winters* was the poet's second poetry volume, published in 1936.

10. By the Holy Inquisition's verdict, Giordano Bruno was executed with his tongue in a gag. Therefore, his muteness was literal and had nothing to do with the understanding of silence and inexpressibility in the Holocaust discourse.

11. In a thorough analysis of "Campo dei Fiori," Natan Gross discusses the subtle editorial changes Miłosz made to the poem's final version, which included a revision of the idea of shared language that, from the perspective of the victims, could not express this experience. See Natan Gross, *Poeci i Szoa. Obraz Zagłady Żydów w poezji polskiej* (Poets and the Shoah. The Image of the Jewish Genocide in Polish Poetry) (Sosnowiec: Offmax, 1993), see pp. 84–89. It must be added that the poet revised these and other lyrics for the final edition of his *Dzieła zebrane* (Collected Works).

12. The paratext in the Polish edition reads *Warszawa-Wielkanoc, 1943* (Warsaw-Easter, 1943), "Campo di Fiori," (Milosz 2001b, 1:191–193, here 193); the English translation reads "*Warsaw, 1943*," Czeslaw Milosz, "Campo dei Fiori," *New and Collected Poems (1931–2001)* (New York: Ecco Press, 2001), 33–35, here 35.

13. Likewise, Michel Borwicz observes that poetry of this time belongs to prewar literature, on account of its style, although its thematic content is different. For this reason, he claims, so many poems failed to grasp the complexity of the Holocaust linguistically. I believe that the poems discussed in this volume stand out as an exception to Borwicz's claim.

14. Czeslaw Milosz, *The Witness of Poetry* (Cambridge, Mass.: Harvard University Press, 1983), 80.

15. Zdzisław Łapiński, *Między polityką a metafizyką. O poezji Czesława Miłosza* (Between Politics and Metaphysics. On Czesław Miłosz'z Poetry) (Londyn: Odnowa, 1981), 18–19.

16. Such was Miłosz's suggestion, followed by Aleksander Fiut, that the contiguity of historical events endows the lyric with the quality of a journalistic writing (*publicystyka*); see Aleksander Fiut, *The Eternal Moment: The Poetry of Czeslaw Milosz*, trans. Theodosia S. Robertson (Berkeley: University of California Press, 1990), 11.

17. It reads *Warsaw, 1943* (Milosz 2001a, 64); the Polish edition does not include this information.

18. The extent of the demolition executed under Stroop's command was such that, after the war, the territory of the former ghetto was beyond rebuilding.

19. The shift from representational to nonrepresentational reality was a move that revolutionized Western art in the twentieth century. The nonrepresentational visual vocabulary did not concern European painters until the early part of this century, but certain discrete or inadvertent realizations of (non)representational tension can be found in a number of individual styles—that of William Turner and Eugene Delacroix, to name a few.

20. Gaston Bachelard, *Le droit de rêver* (Paris: Presses Universitaires de France, 1970), 55.

21. See the mysterious little book on ashes by Jacques Derrida, *Feu la cendre* (Paris: Des femmes, 1987).

22. In his study on the eighteenth-century Father Baka, Aleksander Nawarecki analyzes Miłosz's connection with Baka: *Czarny karnawał: Uwagi śmierci niechybnej księdza Baki. Poetyka tekstu i paradoksy recepcji* (Black Carnival: Father Baka's Notes on Unavoidable Death. The Text's Poetics and the Paradoxes of Reception) (Wrocław: Zakład Narodowy Ossolińskich, 1991).

23. Bees, unlike their relative, wasps, are hardly meat eaters, although some of them are parasitical. In terms of their laborious and collective type of life, bees hold characteristics in common with ants. Additionally, several types of bees, again like ants, burrow tunnels for nesting in the ground. Moreover, there is a subfamily of bees bearing the name of a "digger" or "mining bee" (*Antophorinae*). For what it is worth, this information sheds light on the relevance to the natural order displayed by the poem's unusual biological imagery.

24. These lines are italicized in the original (Miłosz 2001b, 213–214, here 213). The emphasis is omitted in the English translation: "Ants build around white bone" (Milosz 2001a, 63–64, here 63).

25. One wishes that Ewa Czarnecka, Miłosz's interlocutor, had probed Miłosz on this issue a bit further.

26. Leonard Nathan and Arthur Quinn, *The Poet's Work: An Introduction to Czesław Miłosz* (Cambridge, Mass., and London: Harvard University Press: Cambridge, and London, 1991), 17.

27. As Caroline Walker Bynum observes, "a hybrid forces contradictory or incompatible categories to coexist and serve as commentary each on the other." See Caroline Walker Bynum, *Metamorphosis and Identity* (New York: Zone Books, 2005), 31.

28. This division into what is invisible and what is visible is reminiscent of Maurice Merleau-Ponty's similar splitting up of the ocular field.

29. I deliberately do not take into account many other precedents of creating the

spatial vision of eternity in the Polish poet's output, in particular, his translation of his uncle, Oscar de Lubicz Miłosz's "November Symphonie," a Swedenborgian rendering of life after death, which is significant for Miłosz's subsequent development of the "second space," as he called the noumenon in one of his last volumes of poetry.

30. Miłosz often describes the constellation of his favorite poets with whom he, for a variety of reasons, identifies or whose impact he acknowledges at various stages of his career: Adam Mickiewicz, Oscar de Lubicz Miłosz, Robinson Jeffers, Józef Czechowicz, among others, constitute the main core of the group. Although he remains silent about them, there are several poets, such as Francis Ponge and R. M. Rilke, who also played a significant role in his poetic growth.

31. To invoke Santner's concept; see Eric Santner, *On Creaturely Life: Rilke, Benjamin, Sebald* (Chicago: University of Chicago Press, 2006).

32. For the thorough analysis of the visual dimension invoked in the poet's writings, see Kris van Heuckelom's monograph, *"Patrzeć w promień od ziemi odbity." Wizualność w poezji Czesława Miłosza* ("To Look in the Ray Reflected by the Ground." Visuality in Czesław Miłosz's Poetry) (Warsaw: Instytut Badań Literackich, 2004).

33. In the original *tęczujący opar* (rainbow-like vapor).

34. Rudolf Steiner, "Knowledge of the State between Death and a New Birth," www.rsarchives:Articles/org/.

35. In her discussion of the poem, Aaron identifies this space in a strictly historical and nonmetaphysical manner as "a sewer strewn with corpses of badly burned Jews who jumped out of the windows of flaming buildings and who died of their burns while attempting to reach the 'Aryan side' of Warsaw. Indeed, so badly burned are they that they form an undifferentiated mass of ash" (Aaron 1990, 186).

36. Marian Stala, *Trzy nieskończoności. O poezji Adama Mickiewicza, Bolesława Leśmiana i Czesława Miłosza* (Three infinities. On the poetry of Adam Mickiewicz, Bolesław Leśmian, and Czesław Miłosz) (Kraków: Wydawnictwo Literackie, 2001), 138.

37. Jan Błoński, *Biedni Polacy patrzą na getto* (Poor Poles are Looking at the Ghetto) (Kraków: Wydawnictwo Literackie, 1994), 17. The critic's reading is strongly corroborated by the fact that in T. S. Eliot's "The Waste Land," so expertly translated by Miłosz at that time, there appears the line: "I will show you fear in a handful of dust." T. S. Eliot, "The Waste Land," in *Collected Poems and Plays 1909–1935* (New York: Harcourt, Brace and World, Inc., 1971), 38.

38. In the same spirit, Norman O. Brown cautions in his *Life against Death:* "We must not be misled by the flat antinomy of the sacred and the secular; and interpret as 'secularization' what is only a metamorphosis of the sacred." Norman O. Brown, *Life against Death: The Psychoanalytic Meaning of History* (Middletown, Conn.: Wesleyan University Press, 1959), 105.

39. For reasons unknown to me, this stanza is omitted in the English edition of *New and Collected Poems*; "Mgła zimowa na szybie ta sama, / Ale nie wejdzie nikt. / Garstka popiołu, / Plama zgnilizny wapnem przysypana / Nie zdejmie kapelusza, nie powie wesoło: / Chodźmy na wódkę." See Miłosz, "Kawiarnia"; Miłosz 2001b, 1:212–213, here 212.

5. The Manuscript Lost in Warsaw

1. See Anna Synoradzka, *Andrzejewski* (Kraków: Wydawnictwo Literackie, 1997), 56–57.

2. One of his wartime works deserves mention here: "Przed sądem" (At the Court).

The author presented this short story, as well as *Holy Week*, at underground meetings in the Warsaw literary scene. In both cases, he did not meet the expectations of the audience: as we find out from Nałkowska's *Diary*, "Holy Week"—read aloud in Kazimiera Morawska's apartment—provoked an unfriendly reaction. (Synoradzka, 56–57).

3. Jarosław Iwaszkiewicz, *Dzienniki 1911–1955* (Diaries 1911–1955), introduction Andrzej Gronczewski, ed. and annoted Angnieszka and Robert Papieski (Warsaw: Czytelnik, 2007). Iwaszkiewicz, one of Andrzejewski's closest friends, did not voice any opinion at the time of the reading, but he recorded his thoughts in his wartime diary notes.

4. The second version was written during August and September 1945; an excerpt appeared in the collection of short stories entitled *Noc* (Night).

5. In Kott's cautious formulation. See Jan Kott, "Droga do realizmu" (A Road to Realism), *Po prostu. Szkice i zaczepki* (Just So. Sketches and Provocations) (Bydgoszcz-Warszawa: "Książka," 1946), 134–144. Quotation *in extenso* after Kott: Malecki had "a humiliating awareness of a hazy, nondescript co-responsibility for the immensity of cruelty and crime to which amidst the silent consent of the whole world the Jewish nation was subjected. The feeling of guilt he held inside like a wound in which the whole evil of the world seemed to inflame. He was cognizant that there was more anxiety and terror than genuine love to those helpless people, surrounded from everywhere, alone in the world, whom fate was depriving of the dishonored but truly existing brotherhood." According to Kott, Malecki's uncertainties and the incapacity of action are "qualified" as the character's most compromising quality (143). This passage from the originary text could have been easily incorporated into the postwar reinscription of the novella.

6. Jerzy Andrzejewski, *Książka dla Marcina* (A Book for Marcin) (Warsaw: PIW, 1956), 103.

7. His father, an Auschwitz prisoner, survived because he managed to escape during the camp's evacuation (Synoradzka 1997, 77).

8. Similarly, Jarosław Iwaszkiewicz confessed a loss of his interwar diaries during World War II, only to correct this statement later, saying that he had never kept such diaries and, thus, never lost them. By fabricating this account, the author wanted to join a chorus of voices that complained about individual bereavement and destruction (Gronczewski, 9).

9. I am using here the pseudonym under which Andrzejewski appeared in Miłosz's renowned collection of essays, *The Captive Mind*, an analysis of the communist system and the compromising adherence of several Polish intellectuals to the new political order in Poland. One chapter, "Alpha," depicts Andrzejewski's ideological conformism as a communist.

10. Andrzejewski's defense of Polish Jewry, fused with his humanistic spirit that led him to condemn antisemitism, was also expressed in his essay "Zagadnienia polskiego antysemityzmu" (Problems of Polish Antisemitism); see *Martwa fala. Zbiór artykułów o antysemityzmie* (Dead Wave: A Collection of Articles on Antisemitism), intro. Stanisław Ryszard Dobrowolski (Warsaw: Spółdzielnia Wydawnicza, 1947), 20–50.

11. Andrzejewski's last ideological shift turned him to the fledgling Polish dissident movement. From 1976, he was a member of the dissident group KOR (The Committee of the Defense of Workers) and coeditor of the underground periodical, *Zapis*. His novel, *Miazga* (Pulp), was published in 1979 in the underground press.

12. Another passage from the first version appeared in 1946 in *Żołnierz Polski*. The hope is that research in Kott's archives may yield some unexpected results. Since the critic quotes from the first version, he must have had access to it.

13. Joanna Rostropowicz Clark, "Holy Week. A Novel of the Warsaw Ghetto Uprising," *The Sarmatian Review* 27 (2007): 7.

14. Tomasz Szarota, *Okupowanej Warszawy dzień powszedni. Studium historyczne* (The Everyday in Occupied Warsaw: A Historical Study) (Warsaw: Czytelnik, 1973), 63.

15. Henri Lefebvre, *The Production of Space*, trans. Donald Nicholson-Smith (Oxford: Basil Blackwell, 1991).

16. "After they have given up their last breath they often remain lying on the street for long hours, no one bothers about them" (*The Diary of Mary Berg* 2006, 16).

17. Mistranslated in the English translations as "merry-go-round."

18. Rostropowicz Clark considers the presence of the roundabout in Andrzejewski's novel to be fictional. However, its factuality is proven not only by Miłosz and Andrzejewski, but is also evidenced by the photograph of the spot, which Rostropowicz Clark describes in detail.

19. For example, Szarota mentions that the installation of an amusement park in July 1942 coincided with the deportations of the Warsaw Jews to the Treblinka death camp (Szarota 1973, 386).

20. That both writers turned their attention to the Nazi use of the roundabout as a tool in the propaganda war can be attributed to their intellectual closeness at that time and the exchange of ideas by means of letters sent from one end of Warsaw to another; this correspondence was published by Miłosz in *Legends of Modernity*.

21. The unhealthy curiosity of one excited boy, for whom the shooting was as unreal as if it were projected on a screen, also indicates, albeit mildly, Andrzejewski's critical assessment of such spectatorship.

22. Michel Butor emphasized another, entirely historical aspect of Balzac's objects, defining them as "bones of time" and, thus, giving them a strong paleontological qualification. Butor uses the word *ossements*, which means the bones of the dead. See Michel Butor, "La philosophie d'ameublement," in *Essais sur le roman* (Paris: Gallimard, 1964), 68.

23. Jean Baudrillard, *The System of Objects*, trans. James Benedict (London: Verso, 2005). His treatment of objects is both historically and systemically indebted to Benjamin's "The Work of Art in the Age of its Technological Reproducibility" and to Roland Barthes's *The Fashion System*.

24. Such a modernist interior was made famous through Gombrowicz's parody in his novel *Ferdydurke*.

25. In the neighborhood of Bielany, where the Andrzejewskis themselves lived.

26. In particular, the Warsaw Polytechnic.

27. Among the architects associated with *Praesens* were Szymon Syrkus, Helena Syrkusowa, Bohdan Lachert, and Józef Szanajca.

28. Except projects such as the Żolibórz section of Warsaw, located not far from the Malecki's neighborhood, where the architects experimented in their new architectural idiom.

29. On the concept of functionalism for the masses, see Le Corbusier, *Towards a New Architecture*, trans. Frederick Etchells (New York: Dover Publications, 1986).

30. On the concept of privacy and its history, see Witold Rybczynski, *Home: A Short History of an Idea* (New York: Viking Penguin, 1986).

31. The Zamoyskis are one of the oldest Polish aristocratic families.

32. Jerzy Andrzejewski, *Holy Week. A Novel of the Warsaw Ghetto Uprising*, intro. and commentary Oscar E. Swan, foreword Jan T. Gross (Athens: Ohio University Press, 2007), 16. This translation was a course project undertaken by Swann and his students; thus, no individual translators are mentioned.

33. In the parlance of the time, he has the *zły wygląd* (wrong appearance).

34. As Teresa Walas observes in "Zwierciadła Jerzego Andrzejewskiego" (Jerzy Andrzejewski's Mirrors), in *Prozaicy dwudziestolecia międzywojennego. Sylwetki* (The Prose Writers of the Interwar Period. Silhouettes), intro., ed. Bolesíaw Faron (Warsaw: Wiedza Powszechna, 1972), 23–48, here 39.

35. Jean Baudrillard, *Simulacra and Simulation*, trans. Sheila Faria Glaser (Ann Arbor: University of Michigan Press, 2006), 12.

36. According to the Nazi law, every person who helped Jews was to be punished by death.

37. On the Jewish female characters in Polish literature, see Umińska.

38. In the Jewish literary tradition, Esther is connected to the foundational myth of the Jewish minority on Polish territories.

39. In the Yiddish version of the legend, Esther is married to the Polish king. For the comprehensive study, see Chone Shmeruk, *Legenda o Esterce w literaturze jidysz i polskiej* (The Legend of Esther in Yiddish and Polish Literature) (Warsaw: Oficyna Naukowa, 2000).

40. The critics and readers who were Andrzejewski's contemporaries considered Wanda Wertenstein to be the prototype for Irena. (Wertenstein and Maria Koral found shelter in the apartment shared by Andrzejewski and his wife-to-be, Maria Abgarowicz. According to Synoradzka, Koral, who after the war left for the States, was supporting the writer and his family and used to visit them [Synoradzka, 71]). Contrary to this perception, Andrzejewski claimed that Janina Aszkenazy, daughter of Szymon Aszkenazy, served as his model for the novella's female lead.

41. Clare Cavanagh, in her review of the English translation of *Holy Week*, perceives all characters in Andrzejewski's novel to be unsympathetic. Clare Cavanagh, *BookForum* 13, no. 4 (December 2007): 39.

42. This episode compromises Malecki, who is concerned only with the possibility that Irena's suitcase may have contained some of their correspondence, which could cause him trouble in the case of a Gestapo investigation. Upon learning that Irena had inadvertently disposed of his letters, Malecki's contentment indicates a desire to censor his life and erase any vestiges of the past that would jeopardize his stability and security.

43. The ancient saying, "I carry with me all that is mine," is enigmatic in defining what is carried. Are these a few material possessions or virtues? Here the saying attains an accusatory tone and refers directly to Irena's dispossessed status quo.

6. Things, Touch, and Detachment in Auschwitz

1. The Penguin selection of Borowski's short stories, *This Way for the Gas, Ladies and Gentlemen*, is based on his *Wybór opowiadań* (Selected Short Stories) (Warsaw: PIW, 1969). These short stories are often anthologized and are, therefore, the foundation of the writer's fame in the West. Only in encountering an absence of Borowski's work in Agamben's *Remnants of Auschwitz: The Witness and the Archive* does one realize how narrow is the universe within which his name bears recognition.

2. Before his imprisonment, in 1942 he published a volume of poetry in the underground press, entitled *Gdziekolwiek ziemia* . . . (Wherever the Earth . . .). Six other poems appeared in another mimeographed war publication during his imprisonment, *Arkusz poetycki* (A Poetic Sheet of Paper), edited by Stanisław Marczak-Oborski, who received the manuscripts from Borowski's father.

3. However, the poet could not recreate some of his poems from memory.

4. It was written as a poem-message and copied on the page of the inmate's Bible, with hope that the inmate, once free, would convey it to his mother. Borowski de-

scribed this inmate twice: in "Opowiadanie z prawdziwego życia" (True Story) and "Chłopiec z biblią" (A Boy with the Bible).

5. These manuscripts—found by the indefatigable Tadeusz Drewnowski—were given in 1945 to Jerzy Turowicz, editor in chief of *Tygodnik Powszechny*, who subsequently published several of them.

6. Besides the coauthored volume, *Byliśmy w Oświęcimiu* (We Were in Auschwitz), among his greatest accomplishments are *Pożegnanie z Marią* (Farewell to Maria) and *Kamienny świat* (The World of Stone).

7. For a comprehensive discussion of the heated debate sparked by the publication of Borowski's short stories, see Tadeusz Drewnowski, *Ucieczka z kamiennego świata* (An Escape from the World of Stone) (Warsaw: PIW, 1977), 152–210. Also see Andrzej Werner, *Zwyczajna apokalipsa. Tadeusz Borowski i jego wizja świata* (A Casual Apocalypse. Tadeusz Borowski and His Vision of the World, Warsaw: Czytelnik, 1977). The latter monograph, which owes its inspiration to Hannah Arendt, though published more than thirty years ago, still retains its validity amid the vast scholarship on camp literature. Very much in the spirit of Arendt's view of the Holocaust, Werner argues against Andrzej Wirth's understanding the prisoners' lack of alternatives as their new tragic position, indicating that while some alternatives did exist, they were ethically unacceptable (113–114). See Andrzej Wirth, "A Discovery of Tragedy: (The Incomplete Account of Tadeusz Borowski)," *Polish Review* XII, no. 3 (1967): 43–52.

8. Maurice Blanchot, *La communauté inavouable* (Paris: Les Éditions de Minuit, 1985); see in particular pp. 9–47. I am taking Blanchot's expression out of its original positive context.

9. Stanisław Buryła, *Prawda mitu i literatury. O pisarstwie Tadeusza Borowskiego i Leopolda Buczkowskiego* (The Truth of a Myth and Literature. The Writing of Tadeusz Borowski and Leopold Buczkowski) (Kraków: Universitas, 2003), 225.

10. See in particular his chapter "Fenomenologia systemu" (The Phenomenology of the System), 60–116.

11. Unlike his creation, Tadek, the real Tadeusz Borowski was not compromised as a prisoner more than any other inmate.

12. So much for the circulation of the news from other camps among the Auschwitz prisoners.

13. For example, a Ukrainian prisoner carved little wooden folk trinkets indicative of his cultural background.

14. The argument that the Final Solution was a part of Hitler's economic plan to appropriate Jewish capital was made after the war by Gerald Reitlinger and Hannah Arendt. See Gerald Reitlinger, *The Final Solution: The Attempt to Exterminate the Jews of Europe 1939–1945* (New York: Viking Press, 1960) and Hannah Arendt, *Eichmann in Jerusalem: A Report on the Banality of Evil* (New York: Penguin, 1994).

15. Hannah Arendt, *The Human Condition* (Chicago: University of Chicago Press, 1958), 72.

16. Borowski offers a rather jolly glimpse into the collapsed split between public and private in camp life, which has to do with the camp's arrangements of physiological necessities: "The latrines were built for the men and the women jointly, and were separated only by wooden boards. You sat there by the hour conducting love dialogues with Katia, the pretty little latrine girl. No one felt any embarrassment or thought the set-up uncomfortable. After all, one had already seen so much" ("The People Who Walked On," Borowski 1967, 93–94).

17. Yet one of the most disturbing types of the Holocaust gaze, not mentioned by

Borowski, is the panoptic and quintessentially detached gaze of the Nazi medical personnel, usually physicians, who observed the gassing of victims through small openings or windows. For a detailed account of the medical scientists' collaboration in the extermination program, see Robert Jay Lifton's *The Nazi Doctors*. Arendt mentions that Eichmann claimed that he was invited, during his visitation of the camp sites, to observe death by gassing, but refused. Hannah Arendt, *Eichmann in Jerusalem: A Report on the Banality of Evil* (New York: The Viking Press, 1963), 81–82.

18. Aristotle, *On The Soul and On Memory and Recollection*, trans. Joe Sachs (Santa Fe: Green Lion Press, 2004).

19. As Jodi Cranston writes in her "The Touch of the Blind Man: The Phenomenology of Vividness in Italian Renaissance Art," in *Sensible Flesh: On Touch in Early Modern Culture*, ed. Elizabeth D. Harvey (Philadelphia: University of Pennsylvania Press, 2003), 224–242.

20. Often the perpetrators' gaze is bluntly pejorative. For instance, the Kapo's eyes "glisten dangerously" or his stare is "lifeless, vacant" ("A Day at Harmenz"; Borowski 1967; 72, 75).

21. In the Leibnizian terms: "The monads have no windows through which something can enter or leave" (68). G. W. Leibniz, "The Principles of Philosophy, or, the Monadology (1714)," in *Discourse on Metaphysics and Other Essays*, eds. and trans. Daniel Garber and Roger Ariew (Indianapolis: Hackett Publishing Co., 1991), 68–81.

22. The act of touching regains importance at the end of the short story, when the *Schreiber* and the other men selected for gassing stand in the truck, "weeping and cursing their fate" and holding on to each other, but only "to keep from falling out." The final image, misunderstood by the narrator in "The Man with the Package," reinforces my argument that Borowski indicates how the spontaneous religious unity is overlooked: the Jewish men, with the *Schreiber* in their midst, sang "some soul-stirring Hebrew song which nobody could understand" (Borowski 1967, 151). Thus, the narrator consistently views all developments from his shallow perspective of the stronger man and the one who survives.

23. In certain cultures it is still a standing tradition, for example, among Serbs, whose coffins are equipped with plates, razors, or small amounts of money.

24. Benjamin, in "Unpacking My Library," also articulates another, equally radical, idea: the hand touching books brings new life to them and invigorates the owner as well; for Benjamin, touching books (contact) prevails over reading them.

25. The concentration camp lingo still awaits a comprehensive linguistic analysis. In this respect Borowski is a veritable gold mine, as he compiled two short dictionaries, one of an eschatological nature (which he did not want to publish). The other, entitled "Określenia Oświęcimskie" (Auschwitz Phrases), was added to the collection *Byliśmy w Oświęcimiu* (We Were in Auschwitz) by Borowski, Tadeusz 119198, Olszewski Krystyn 75817, Siedlecki Nel Janusz 5543. See the English translation, Borowski, Tadeusz 119198, Olszewski Krystyn 75817, Siedlecki Nel Janusz 5543, *We Were In Auschwitz*, trans. Alicia Nitecki (New York: Welcome Rain Publishers, 2000).

26. Primo Levi, who describes in detail the Monovitz camp prisoners' clothes, underscoring their "unbelievably bad condition," mentions another source for inmates' clothing: "many of the foot-cloths and the underpants had obviously been made out of the 'tallit'—the sacred shawl with which Jews cover themselves during prayers." Primo Levi with Leonardo de Benedetti, 39, 38. At the request of the Soviets, Levi and de Benedetti coauthored this richly informative report right after their liberation from the camp.

27. A mark was made for each truckload of people going to gas chambers.

28. Such as "bundles of every description" ("This Way for the Gas, Ladies and Gentlemen", Borowski 1967, 37).

29. Tadeusz Borowski, "Kamienny świat," *Proza* ("The World of Stone," *Prose*), ed. Sławomir Buryła; *Pisma w czterech tomach* (Writings in Four Volumes), eds. Tadeusz Drewnowski, Justyna Szczęsna, and Sławomir Buryła (Kraków: Wydawnictwo Literackie, 2004), I:258.

30. Dominick LaCapra, in his critique of the camp as understood by Agamben, advances the concept of the camp's sublime. See Dominick LaCapra, "Approaching Limit Events: Siting Agamben," in *Witnessing the Disaster: Essays on Representation and the Holocaust*, ed. Michael Bernard-Donals and Richard Glejzer (Madison: University of Wisconsin Press, 2003), 262–304.

31. It is also striking how close Lifton is to Borowski's notion of "biological emotions" when the former speaks of "psychic closing" that "can serve a highly adaptive function. . . . We may thus say that the survivor initially undergoes a radical but temporary diminution of his sense of actuality in order to avoid losing this sense completely and permanently; he undergoes a reversible form of symbolic death in order to avoid a permanent physical or psychic death" (Lifton 1986, 442).

32. See Janusz Nel Siedlecki, "Homo Sapiens and Animal" (2000, 17–21). In this survivor's account, the opposition between human and inhuman is blurred in the camp. In a polemical and inadequately substantiated gesture, Žižek insists on the opposite approach, which emphasizes the humanity of such an inhuman condition. Slavoj Žižek, *The Puppet and the Dwarf: The Perverse Core of Christianity* (Cambridge, Mass.: MIT Press, 2003),158–159.

33. Imre Kertész, *Dziennik galernika*, trans. Elżbieta Cygielska (Warsaw: W.A.B., 2006), 219–220, the title of the original *Gályanapló* (A Diary of a Galley-slave). Lacking the English version of the Hungarian original, I refer to the Polish translation.

34. Anticipating the Soviet Army's liberation of Auschwitz, the camp's commandant ordered the prisoners to be transferred to other camps. Borowski was among those directed to Dachau; during the transfer, later termed "The March of Death," numerous prisoners perished.

35. Bruno Bettelheim, *The Informed Heart* (New York: The Free Press, 1960), 152.

36. "Muzułmanin jest więc idealnym, z punktu widzenia władcy, modelowym obywatelem społeczeństwa obozu—jego byt ma charakter wyłącznie przedmiotowy." (A Muselmann is therefore an ideal, from the master's point of view, model citizen of the camp community—his existence has solely a reified character) (Werner 1971, 84).

37. His conceptualization sheds a different light on the question of genocide's inaccessibility than Lyotard's. See Dorota Głowacka, "Doświadczenie niemożliwe" (An Impossible Experience), in *Nowoczesność jako doświadczenie* (Modernism as an Experience), ed. Ryszard Nycz and Anna Zeidler-Janiszewska (Kraków: Universitas, 2006), 208–218.

38. Primo Levi, *The Drowned and the Saved*, trans. Raymond Rosenthal (New York: Random House, 1989), 84.

Coda

1. Instytut Pamięci Narodowej and Komisja do Badań Zbrodni Hitlerowskich, respectively.

2. A rare development took place after the war in France, where Jews returning to

Paris were able to retrieve some of their belongings on the basis of their descriptions, drawings, or extant photos; see Leora Auslander, "Coming Home? Jews in Postwar Paris," *Journal of Contemporary History* 40, no. 2 (2005): 237–259.

3. The Warsaw Press in Exile was a reopened by Anatol Girs, proprietor of the prewar Oficyna Warszawska.(Warsaw Press).

4. The authors and the publisher dedicated the volume to the 7th American Army, who "brought them freedom from concentration camp Dachau-Allach."

5. In the same fashion, copies of the recent English translation of *We Were in Auschwitz* are bound in the rough, bluish-gray cloth that emulates the striped uniforms used for the original volumes.

6. With regard to this view, Kott makes this claim: "The identification of the author with the narrator was the moral decision of a prisoner who had lived through Auschwitz—an acceptance of mutual responsibility, mutual participation, and mutual guilt for the concentration camp." See Kott, Introduction (1967, 21–22).

7. For example, the American representation of the Holocaust, often inflected by mass culture tropes, is the subject of several studies, to mention only Alvin Rosenfeld, *Americanization of the Holocaust* (Ann Arbor: Jean and Samuel Frankel Center for Judaic Studies, University of Michigan, 1995) and Annette Insdorf, *Indelible Shadows: Film and the Holocaust* (Cambridge: Cambridge University Press, 2002), 3rd edition.

8. Understood as a spatial dialectical image, the term is a modified version of Benjamin's temporal dialectical image. See Susan Buck-Morss, "Dream World of Mass Culture: Walter Benjamin's Theory of Modernity and the Dialectics of Seeing," in *Modernity and the Hegemony of Vision*, ed. David Michael Levin (Berkeley: University of California Press, 1995), 309–338.

9. Weissberg perceives them as a peculiar form of the sublime. See Liliane Weissberg, "In Plain Sight," in *The Holocaust: Theoretical Readings*, ed. Neil Levi and Michael Rothberg (New Brunswick, N.J.: Rutgers University Press, 2003), 396–403, here 401.

10. Susan Stewart, *On Longing: Narratives of the Miniature, the Gigantic, the Souvenir, the Collection* (Baltimore: Johns Hopkins University Press, 1994).

11. On the detective method, see Carlo Ginzburg's essay, "Morelli, Freud, and Sherlock Holmes," in Umberto Eco and Thomas A. Sebeok, eds., *The Sign of Three: Dupin, Holmes, Peirce* (Bloomington: Indiana University Press, 1983), 81–118.

12. For example, the Płaszów death camp was built on two former Jewish cemeteries.

13. Tadeusz Różewicz, *Nożyk profesora* (Wrocław: Wydawnictwo Dolnośląskie, 2001).

14. After his arrest for conspiratorial activities, Porębski was imprisoned in Gross-Rosen and Sachsenhausen.

15. Tadeusz Różewicz, *Zawsze fragment. Recykling* (Always a Fragment. Recycling) (Wrocław: Wydawnictwo Dolnośląskie, 1999), esp. 96–105.

BIBLIOGRAPHY

Aaron, Frieda W. 1990. Bearing the Unbearable: *Yiddish and Polish Poetry in the Ghettos and Concentration Camps*. Foreword David G. Roskies. Albany: State University of New York Press.

Abramsky, Chimen, Maciej Jachimczyk, and Antony Polonsky, eds. 1986. *The Jews in Poland*. Oxford: Basil Blackwell.

Adorno, Theodor. 1981. *Prisms*. Trans. Samuel Weber and Shierry Weber. Cambridge, Mass.: MIT Press.

Agamben, Giorgio. 2000. *Means without End: Notes on Politics*. Trans. Vincenzo Binetti and Cesare Casarino. Minneapolis: University of Minnesota Press.

———. 1999a. *The End of the Poem: Studies in Poetics*. Trans. Daniel Heller-Roazen. Stanford, Calif.: Stanford University Press.

———. 1999b. *Remnants of Auschwitz: The Witness and the Archive*. Zone Books: New York.

———. 1998. *Homo Sacer: Sovereign Power and Bare Life*. Trans. Daniel Heller-Roazen. Stanford, Calif.: Stanford University Press.

———. 1993. *Stanzas: Word and Phantasm in Western Culture*. Trans. Ronald L. Martinez. Minneapolis: University of Minnesota Press.

Amery, Jean. 1999. *On Suicide: A Discourse on Voluntary Death*. Trans. John D. Barlow. Bloomington: Indiana University Press.

Andrzejewski, Jerzy. 2006. *Holy Week: A Novel of the Warsaw Ghetto Uprising*. Introduction and commentary Oscar E. Swan. Foreword Jan T. Gross. Athens: Ohio University Press.

———. 1993. *Wielki Tydzień*. Warsaw: Czytelnik.

———. 1956. *Książka dla Marcina*. Warsaw: PIW.

Andrzejewski, Jerzy, et al. 1947. «Zagadnienia polskiego antysemityzmu.» In *Martwa fala. Zbiór artykułów o antysemityzmie*. Introduction Stanisław Ryszard Dobrowolski. Warsaw: Spółdzielnia Wydawnicza.

Appudarai, Arjun, ed. 1986. *The Social Life of Things: Commodities in Cultural Perspectives*. Cambridge: Cambridge University Press.

Araszkiewicz, Agata. 2001. *Wypowiadam wam moje życie. Melancholia Zuzanny Ginczanki*. Warsaw: Fundacja OSKA.

Arendt, Hannah. 1985. *The Origins of Totalitarianism*. San Diego: Harcourt.

———. 1963. *Eichmann in Jerusalem: A Report on the Banality of Evil*. New York: The Viking Press.

———. 1958. *The Human Condition*. Chicago: University of Chicago Press.

Aristotle. 2004. *On the Soul and On Memory and Recollection.* Trans. Joe Sachs. Santa Fe: Green Lion Press.

Auschwitz: The History in Photographs. 1995. Ed. Teresa Świebocka, Jonathan Webber, and Connie Wilsack. Bloomington: Indiana University Press.

Auslander, Leora. "Coming Home? Jews in Postwar Paris." *Journal of Contemporary History* 40, no. 2 (2005): 237–259.

Bachelard, Gaston. 1970. *Le droit de rêver.* Paris: Presses Universitaires de France.

———. 1969. *The Poetics of Space.* Trans. Maria Jonas. Boston: Beacon Press.

Baczyński, Krzysztof Kamil. 1970. *Utwory zebrane.* Ed. Aniela Kmita-Piorunowa and Kazimierz Wyka. Kraków: Wydawnictwo Literackie.

Balzac, Honoré de. 1947. *Les Parisiennes comme ils sont 1850–1848,* suivi du «Traité de la vie élégante.» Introduction and notes André Billy. Geneva: La Palatine.

Barthes, Roland. 1983. *The Fashion System.* Trans. Matthew Ward and Richard Howard. New York: Hill and Wang.

Bataille, Georges. 1985. *Visions of Excess: Selected Writings 1927–1939.* Ed. Allan Stoekl. Trans. Allan Stoekl, Carl R. Lovitt, and Donald M. Leslie, Jr. Minneapolis: University of Minnesota Press.

Baudrillard, Jean. 2006. *Simulacra and Simulation.* Trans. Sheila Faria Glaser. Ann Arbor: University of Michigan Press.

———. 2005. *The System of Objects.* Trans. James Benedict. London: Verso.

———. 2003. *Selected Writings.* Ed. and preface Mark Poster. Stanford, Calif.: Stanford University Press.

Bauer, Yehuda. 2001. *Rethinking the Holocaust.* New Haven, Conn.: Yale University Press.

Bauman, Zygmunt. 2004. *Identity: Conversations with Benedetto Vecchi.* Cambridge: Polity Press.

———. 1989. *Modernity and the Holocaust.* Ithaca, N.Y.: Cornell University Press.

Beker, Avi, ed. 2001. *The Plunder of Jewish Property during the Holocaust: Confronting European History.* Foreword Edgar Bronfman and Israel Singer. New York: New York University Press.

Ben-Amos, Dan, and Liliane Weissberg, eds. 1999. *Cultural Memory and the Construction of Identity.* Detroit: Wayne State University Press.

Benjamin, Walter. 1999. *Selected Writings.* Ed. Michael Jennings, Marcus Bullock, Howard Eiland, and Gary Smith. 4 vols. Cambridge, Mass.: Belknap-Harvard University Press.

———. 1968. *Illuminations.* Ed. and introduction Hannah Arendt. Trans. Harry Zohn. New York: Harcourt, Brace and World.

Bentham, Jeremy. 2001. *An Introduction to the Principles of Morals and Legislation.* Holmes Beach, Fla: Gaunt.

———. 1814. *Theory of Legislation.* Trans. Richard Hildreth. London: Trubner & Co.

Berenbaum, Michael, and Israel Gutman, eds. 1994. *Anatomy of the Auschwitz Death Camp.* Bloomington: Indiana University Press.

Bereś, Stanisław. 1988. "Czeslaw Milosz's Apocalypse." In *Between Anxiety and Hope: The Poetry and Writing of Czesław Miłosz,* ed. Edward Mozejko. Edmonton: University of Alberta Press, 30-87.

Bernard-Donals, Michael and Richard Glejzer, eds. 2003. *Witnessing the Disaster: Essays on Representation and the Holocaust.* Madison: University of Wisconsin Press.

Bettelheim, Bruno. 1960. *The Informed Heart.* New York: The Free Press.

Blanchot, Maurice. 1986. *The Writing of the Disaster. L'Ecriture du désastre.* Trans. Ann Smock. Lincoln: University of Nebraska Press.

———. 1985. *La communauté inavouable*. Paris: Les Éditions de Minuit.

Bloom, Harold, ed. 2004. *Literature of the Holocaust*. Philadelphia: Chelsea House Publishers.

Błoński, Jan. 1994. *Biedni Polacy patrzą na getto*. Kraków: Wydawnictwo Literackie.

———. 1990. "The Poor Poles Look at the Ghetto." In Polonsky, 34–48.

———. 1981. *Romans z tekstem*. Kraków: Wydawnictwo Literackie.

Borowski, Tadeusz. 2004. *Pisma w czterech tomach*. Ed. Tadeusz Drewnowski, Justyna Szczęsna, and Sławomir Buryła. Kraków: Wydawnictwo Literackie.

———. 1991. *Utwory wybrane*. Introduction and ed. Andrzej Werner. Wrocław: Zakład Narodowy im. Ossolińskich.

———. 1967. *This Way for the Gas, Ladies and Gentlemen*. Trans. Barbara Vedder. Introduction Jan Kott. New York: Penguin.

Borowski, Tadeusz, 119198, Olszewski Krystyn 75817, Siedlecki Janusz Nel 5543. 2000. *We Were in Auschwitz*. Trans. Alicia Nitecki. New York: Welcome Rain Publishers.

Borwicz, Michel. 1954. Introduction by Rene Cassin. *Écrits des condamnés à mort sous l'occupation allemande (1939–1945)*. Paris: Presses Universitaires de France.

———. 1947. *Pieśń ujdzie cało. Antologia wierszy o Żydach pod okupacją niemiecką*. Warsaw: Centralna Żydowska Komisja Historyczna w Polsce.

Brown, Bill. 2005. Unpublished introduction to the Workshop on Material Object Culture, University of Chicago.

———. 2003. *A Sense of Things: The Object Matter of American Literature*. Chicago: University of Chicago Press.

———, ed. 2001. "Thing Theory." In *Things. Critical Inquiry* 1 (2001): 1–22. .

Brown, Norman O. 1959. *Life against Death: The Psychoanalytic Meaning of History*. Middletown, Conn.: Wesleyan University Press.

Buck-Morss, Susan. 1995. "Dream World of Mass Culture: Walter Benjamin's Theory of Modernity and the Dialectics of Seeing." In *Modernity and the Hegemony of Vision*, ed. David Michael Levin. Berkeley: University of California Press, 309–338.

Burke, Kenneth. 1945. *A Grammar of Motives*. New York: Prentice Hall.

Buryła, Sławomir. 2003. *Prawda mitu i literatury. O pisarstwie Tadeusza Borowskiego i Leopolda Buczkowskiego*. Kraków: Universitas.

Butor, Michel. 1971. *Powieść jako poszukiwanie*. Trans. Joanna Guze. Warsaw: Czytelnik.

———. 1964. *Essais sur le roman*. Paris: Gallimard.

Bynum, Caroline Walker. 2005. *Metamorphosis and Identity*. New York: Zone Books.

Cavanagh, Clare. 2007. Review of *Holy Week, BookForum* 13, no. 4 (2007): 39.

Chwin, Stefan. Nd. *Samobójstwo jako doświadczenie wyobraźni*. Gdańsk: Wydawnictwo Tytuł.

Cohen, Barbara, Tom Cohen, J. Hillis Miller, and Andrzej Warminski, eds. 2001. *Material Events: Paul de Man and the Afterlife of Theory*. Minneapolis: University of Minnesota Press.

Comay, Rebecca, ed. 2002. *Lost in the Archives*. Toronto: Alphabet City.

Cory, Mark. 2004. "Comedic Distance in Holocaust Literature." In *Literature of the Holocaust*, ed. Harold Bloom. Philadelphia: Chelsea House Publishers, 193–204.

Cranston, Jodi. 2003. "The Touch of the Blind Man: The Phenomenology of Vividness in Italian Renaissance Art." In *Sensible Flesh: On Touch in Early Modern Culture*, ed. Elizabeth D. Harvey. Philadelphia: University of Pennsylvania Press, 224–242.

Czarnecka, Ewa, and Aleksander Fiut. 1987. *Conversations with Czeslaw Milosz*. Trans. Richard Lourie. San Diego: Harcourt.

Davie, Donald. 1986. *Czeslaw Milosz and the Insufficiency of Lyric.* Knoxville: University of Tennessee Press.

Davies, Norman. 2003. *Rising "44": The Battle for Warsaw.* London: Macmillan.

Davis, Lennard J. 2005. "Visualizing the Disabled Body: The Classical Nude and the Fragmented Torso." In *The Body: A Reader,* ed. Mariam Fraser and Monica Greco. London: Routledge, 165–181.

Dawidowicz, Lucy S., ed. 1976. *A Holocaust Reader.* West Orange, N.J.: Berman House.

De Man, Paul. 1996. *Aesthetic Ideology.* Ed. Andrzej Warminski. Minneapolis: University of Minnesota Press.

Dean, Martin. 2008. *Robbing the Jews: The Confiscation of Jewish Property in the Holocaust, 1933–1945.* Cambridge: Cambridge University Press.

Derrida, Jacques. 2007. *Learning to Live Finally: An Interview with Jean Birnbaum.* Trans. Pascale-Anne Brault and Michael Naas. Hoboken: Melville House Publishers.

———. 2005. *On Touching—Jean-Luc Nancy.* Trans. Christine Irizarry. Stanford, Calif.: Stanford University Press.

———. 2001. "Materiality without Matter—Typewriter Ribbon: Limited Ink (2) ('within such limits')." In Cohen et al., 277–366.

———. 1997. *Of Grammatology.* Trans. Gayatri Chakravorty Spivak. Baltimore and London: Johns Hopkins University Press, corrected edition.

———. 1992. "Shibboleth: For Paul Celan." Trans. Joshua Wilner. In *Acts of Literature,* ed. Derek Attridge. New York: Routledge.

———. 1991. *Donner le temps. La fausse monnaie.* Paris: Galilée.

———. 1987a. *The Truth in Painting.* Trans. Geoff Bennington and Ian McLeod. Chicago: University of Chicago Press.

———. 1987b. *Feu la cendre.* Paris: Des femmes.

The Diary of Mary Berg: Growing Up in the Warsaw Ghetto. 2006. Ed. S. L. Shneidermann. Oxford: Oneworld.

Didi-Huberman, Georges. 2008. *Images in Spite of All: Four Photographs from Auschwitz.* Trans. Shane B. Lillis. Chicago: University of Chicago Press.

Dobroszycki, Lucjan, ed. 1984. *The Lodz Ghetto Chronicle, 1941–1944.* New Haven, Conn.: Yale University Press.

Douglas, Lawrence. 2001. "The Shrunken Head of Buchenwald: Icons of Atrocity at Nuremberg." In *Visual Culture and the Holocaust,* ed. Barbie Zelizer. New Brunswick, N.J.: Rutgers University Press, 275–299.

Drewnowski, Tadeusz. 1977. *Ucieczka z kamiennego świata. O Tadeuszu Borowskim.* Warsaw: PIW.

Eco, Umberto, and Thomas Sebeok, eds. 1983. *The Sign of Three: Dupin, Holmes, Peirce.* Bloomington: Indiana University Press.

Eisenbach, Artur, intro. and ed. 1988. Trans. from Yiddish Adam Rutkowski. Emanuel Ringelblum, *Kronika getta warszawskiego. Wrzesień 1939–styczeń 1943.* Warsaw: Czytelnik, 5-27.

Eliot, T. S. 1971a. *Collected Poems and Plays 1909–1935.* New York: Harcourt, Brace and World, Inc.

———. 1971b. *The Complete Poems and Plays, 1909–1950.* New York: Harcourt.

———. 1921. *The Sacred Wood: Essays on Poetry and Criticism.* New York: Knopf.

Elsner, John, and Roger Cardinal, eds. 1994. *The Cultures of Collecting.* Cambridge, Mass.: Harvard University Press.

Engelkind, Barbara, and Jacek Leociak. 2001. *Warszawskie Ghetto. Przewodnik po nieistniejącym mieście.* Warsaw: IFiS PAN.

Essmanowski, Stefan. 1934. "Dialogi akademickie. Rozmowa z Zofią Nałkowską." *Pion* 10 (1934).

Ezrahi, Sidra DeKoven. 2004. "Questions of Authenticity." In *Teaching the Representation of the Holocaust*, ed. Marianne Hirsch and Irene Kacandes. New York: Modern Language Assn., 52–67.

Faron, Bolesław, intro. and ed. 1972. *Prozaicy dwudziestolecia międzywojennego. Sylwetki*. Warsaw: Wiedza Powszechna.

Felstiner, John. 2001. *Paul Celan: Poet, Survivor, Jew*. New Haven, Conn.: Yale University Press.

Ficowski, Jerzy. 2003. *Regions of the Great Heresy: Bruno Schulz. A Biographical Portrait*. Trans. and ed. Theodosia Robertson. New York and London: W.W. Norton & Co.

Fink, Ida. 1987. *A Scrap of Time and Other Stories*. Trans. Madeline Levine and Francine Prose. New York: Pantheon Books.

Fiut, Aleksander. 1998. *Moment wieczny: Poezja Czesława Miłosza*. Kraków: Wydawnictwo Literackie.

———. 1990. *The Eternal Moment: The Poetry of Czeslaw Milosz*. Trans. Theodosia S. Robertson. Berkeley: University of California Press.

———. 1985. "W obliczu końca świata." In *Poznawanie Milosza. Studia i szkice o twórczości poety*, ed. Jerzy Kwiatkowski. Kraków and Wrocław: Wydawnictwo Literackie. 174–188.

Fraser, Mariam, and Monica Greco, eds. 2005. *The Body: A Reader*. London: Routledge.

Frąckowiak-Wiegandtowa, Ewa. 1975. *Sztuka powieściopisarska Nałkowskiej (lata 1935–1954)*. Wrocław: Wydawnictwo Polskiej Akademii Nauk.

Friedländer, Saul. 1993. *Memory, History and the Extermination of the Jews of Europe*. Bloomington: Indiana University Press.

Freud, Sigmund. 2000. *The Complete Psychological Works*. 24 vols. New York: W.W. Norton & Co.

———. 1961. *Civilization and Its Discontents*. Trans. James Strachey. New York: W.W. Norton.

Fuss, Diana. 2004. *The Sense of an Interior: Four Writers and the Rooms that Shaped Them*. New York: Routledge.

Genette, Gérard. 1982. *Palimpsestes: la littérature au second degré*. Paris: Seuil.

Gilman, Sander L. 1998. *Creating Beauty to Cure the Soul: Race and Psychology in the Shaping of Aesthetic Surgery*. Durham, N.C.: Duke University Press.

Ginczanka, Zuzanna. 1991. *Udźwignąć własne szczęście. Poezje*. Ed. Izolda Kiec. Poznań:Książnica Włóczęgów i Uczonych.

Ginzburg, Carlo. 1983. "Morelli, Freud, and Sherlock Holmes." In *The Sign of Three: Dupin, Holmes, Peirce*, ed. Umberto Eco and Thomas A. Sebeok. Bloomington: Indiana University Press, 81–118.

Głowacka, Dorota. 2007. "Wsłuchując się w ciszę. Estetyka pamięci o Zagładzie według J.-F. Lyotarda," *Teksty Drugie*, no. 1/2 (2007): 41–59.

———. 2006. "Doświadczenie niemożliwe." In Nycz and Zeidler-Janiszewska, 208–218.

Głowiński, Michał. 2005. *The Black Seasons*. Trans. Marci Shore. Evanston, Ill.: Northwestern University Press.

———. 1999. *Czarne sezony*. Warsaw: Open.

Greif, Gideon. 2005. *We Wept without Tears: Testimonies of the Jewish Sonderkommando from Auschwitz*. New Haven, Conn.: Yale University Press.

Gronczewski, Andrzej. 2007. Introduction. In Iwaszkiewicz, Jarosław. *Dzienniki 1911–1955*. Ed. and annotations Agnieszka and Robert Papieski. Warsaw: Czytelnik.

Gross, Jan Tomasz. 1998. *Upiorna dekada. Trzy eseje o stereotypach na temat Żydów, Polaków, Niemców i komunistów. 1939–1948*. Intro. Antony Polonsky. Kraków: Universitas.

———. 1979. *Polish Society under German Occupation: The Generalgouvernement, 1939–1945*. Princeton, N.J.: Princeton University Press.

Gross, Natan. 1993. *Poeci i Szoa: obraz zagłady Żydów w poezji polskiej*. Sosnowiec: OFFMAX.

Grynberg, Henryk. 2001. *The Jewish War and the Victory*. Trans. Madeline Levine. Evanston, Ill.: Northwestern University Press.

Grynberg, Michał. 1988. *Pamiętniki z getta warszawskiego. Fragmenty i regestry*. Warsaw: PWN.

Hart, Kevin, and Geoffrey H. Hartmann. 2004. *The Power of Contestation: Perspectives on Maurice Blanchot*. Baltimore: Johns Hopkins University Press.

Hartle, Ann. 1986. *Death and the Disinterested Spectator: An Inquiry into the Nature of Philosophy*. Albany: State University of New York Press.

Harvey, Elisabeth D., ed. 2003. *Sensible Flesh: On Touch in Early Modern Culture*. Philadelphia: University of Pennsylvania Press.

Heidegger, Martin. 1975. *Poetry, Language, Thought*. Trans. Albert Hofstadter. New York: Harper and Row.

———. 1962. *Being and Time*. Trans. John Macquarrie and Edward Robinson. New York: Harper & Row.

———. 1959. *Gelassenheit*. Tubingen: Verlag Gunther Neske Pfullingen.

Heuckelom, Kris van. 2004. *"Patrzeć w promień od ziemi odbity." Wizualność w poezji Czesława Miłosza*. Warsaw: Instytut Badań Literackich PAN.

Horowitz, Sara R. 1997. *Voicing the Void: Muteness and Memory in Holocaust Fiction*. Albany: State University of New York Press.

Hungerford, Amy. 2002. *The Holocaust of Texts: Genocide, Literature, and Personification*. Chicago: University of Chicago Press.

Hutman, Bill. 1990. "Nazis Never Made Human-Fat Soap," *Jerusalem Post*, April 24, 1990: 2.

Inglot, Mieczyslaw. 1996. "Non omnis moriar Zuzanny Ginczanki. W kręgu konwencji literackiej." *Acta Universitatis Vratislaviensis* no. 1876 (1996): 138.

Insdorf, Annette. 2002. 3rd edition. *Indelible Shadows: Film and the Holocaust*. Cambridge: Cambridge University Press.

Iwaszkiewicz, Jarosław. 2007. *Dzienniki 1911–1955*. Intro. Andrzej Gronczewski, Ed. and annotations Agnieszka and Robert Papieski, Warsaw Czytelnik.

Jackson, Leonard. 1991. *The Poverty of Structuralism: Literature and Structuralist Theories*. London: Longman.

James, Ian. 2006. *The Fragmentary Demand: An Introduction to the Philosophy of Jean-Luc Nancy*. Stanford, Calif.: Stanford University Press.

Jankelevitch, Vladimir. 1996. "Should We Pardon Them?" *Critical Inquiry* 22, no. 3 (1996): 552–572.

Jay, Martin. 1994. *Downcast Eyes: The Denigration of Vision in Twentieth-Century French Thought*. Berkeley: University of California Press.

Jouranville, Anne. 1993. *La femme et la mélancolie*. Paris: Presses Universitaires de France.

Kamieńska, Anna. 1974. *Od Leśmiana. Najpiękniejsze wiersze polskie*. Warsaw: Iskry.

Kaplan, Chaim A. 1988. "Scroll of Agony." In *The Literature of Destruction: Jewish Re-*

sponses to Catastrophe, ed. David G. Roskies. Philadelphia, Jewish Publication Society, 435–449.

Karp, Ivan, Christine Mullen Kreamer, and Steven D. Lavine, eds. 1992. Museums and Communities: The Politics of Public Culture. Washington, D.C.: Smithsonian Institution Press.

Karwowska, Bożena. 2005. "Obozy Zagłady jako doświadczenie cielesne—przypadek Stanisława Grzesiuka." Przegląd Humanistyczny 2 (2005): 63–80.

————. "Redefiniowanie kategorii ciała. Doświadczenie stawania się kobietą—świadectwo dojrzewania w obozie koncentracyjnym (w Przejściu przez Morze Czerwone Zofii Romanowiczowej)," unpublished manuscript.

Kassow, Samuel D. 2007. Who Will Write Our History? Emanuel Ringelblum, the Warsaw Ghetto, and the Oyneg Shabes Archive. Bloomington: Indiana University Press.

Kater, Michael H. 1989. The Doctors under Hitler. Chapel Hill: University of North Carolina Press.

Kertesz, Imre. 2006. Dziennik galernika. Trans. Elżbieta Cygielska. Warsaw: W.A.B.

Kiec, Izolda. 1994. Ginczanka. Życie i twórczość. Poznań: Obserwator.

————. Intro. and ed. 1991. Ginczanka, Zuzanna. Udźwignąć własne szczęście. Poezje. Poznań: Książnica Włóczęgów i Uczonych.

Konody, P. G. 1930. The Painter of Victorian Life: A Study of Constantin Guys with an Introduction and a Translation of Baudelaire's Peintre de la vie moderne. Ed. C. Geoffrey Holme. London: The Studio Ltd.

Kopytoff, Igor. 1986. "The Cultural Biography of Things: Commodization as Process." In The Social Life of Things: Commodities in Cultural Perspectives, ed. Arjun Appudarai. Cambridge: Cambridge University Press, 64–91.

Korczak, Janusz (Henryk Goldszmit). 1978. Ghetto Diary. New York: Holocaust Library.

Kott, Jan. 1967. Introduction. This Way for the Gas, Ladies and Gentlemen, by Tadeusz Borowski. Trans. Barbara Vedder. New York: Penguin, 11–26.

————. 1946. Po prostu. Szkice i zaczepki. Bydgoszcz-Warsaw: "Książka."

Kristeva, Julia. 1982. Powers of Horror: An Essay on Abjection. Trans. Leon S. Roudiez. New York: Columbia University Press.

Kubler, George. 1962. The Shape of Time. Remarks on the History of Things. New Haven, Conn.: Yale University Press.

Kuchinsky, Neil. 1990. "Human Fat Soap." Jerusalem Post, May 20, 1990: 4.

Kugelmass, Jack. 1992. "The Rites of the Tribe: American Jewish Tourism in Poland." In Museums and Communities: The Politics of Public Culture, ed. Ivan Karp, Christine Mullen Kraemer, and Steven D. Lavine. Washington, D.C.: Smithsonian Institution Press, 382–427.

Kwiatkowski, Jerzy, ed. 1985. Poznawanie Miłosza. Studia i szkice o twórczości poety. Kraków-Wrocław: Wydawnictwo Literackie.

Lacan, Jacques. 2002. Écrits. A Selection. Trans. Bruce Fink with Heloise Fink and Russell Grigg. New York London: W.W. Norton.

————. 1992. The Ethics of Psychoanalysis. Trans. Dennis Porter. New York: W.W. Norton.

————. 1991. Le Séminaire. Livre 8. Le transfert, 1960–61. Ed. Jacques-Alain Miller. Paris: Editions Seuil.

LaCapra, Dominick. 2003. "Approaching Limit Events: Siting Agamben." In Witnessing the Disaster: Essays on Representation and the Holocaust, ed. Michael Bernard-Donals and Richard Glejzer. Madison: University of Wisconsin Press, 262–304.

————. 1994. *Representing the Holocaust: History, Theory, Trauma*. Ithaca, N.Y.: Cornell University Press.

Landau, Ludwik. 1962–1962–1963. 3 vols. *Kronika lat wojny i okupacji*. Warsaw: Państwowe Wydanictwo Naukowe.

Lang, Berel. 1990. *Act and Idea in the Nazi Genocide*. Chicago: University of Chicago Press.

Langer, Lawrence L. 1995. *Art from the Ashes*. New York: Oxford University Press.

————. 1975. *The Holocaust and the Literary Imagination*. New Haven, Conn.: Yale University Press.

Lawrence, D. H. 1931. *Apocalypse*. Florence: G. Orioli.

Le Corbusier. 1986. *Towards a New Architecture*. Trans. Frederick Etchells. New York: Dover Publications.

Lefebvre, Henri. 1991. *The Production of Space*. Trans. Donald Nicholson-Smith. Oxford: Basil Blackwell.

Leibniz, G. W. 1991. *Discourse on Metaphysics and Other Essays*. Ed. and trans. Daniel Garber and Roger Ariew. Indianapolis: Hackett.

Leociak, Jacek. 1997. *Tekst wobec Zagłady. O relacjach z getta warszawskiego*. Wrocław: Fundacja na Rzecz Nauki Polskiej.

————, and Barbara Engelkind. 2001. *Warszawskie Ghetto. Przewodnik ponieistniejącym mieście*. Warsaw: IFiS PAN.

Levi, Neil, and Michael Rothberg, eds. 2003. *The Holocaust: Theoretical Readings*. New Brunswick, N.J.: Rutgers University Press.

Levi, Primo. 2002. *Survival in Auschwitz: The Nazi Assault on Humanity*. Trans. Stuart Woolf. Cambridge: ProQuest Information and Learning.

————, and Leonardo de Benedetti. 2006. *Auschwitz Report*. Trans. Judith Woolf. Ed. Robert S. C. Gordon. London and New York: Verso.

————. 1989. *The Drowned and the Saved*. Trans. Raymond Rosenthal. New York: Random House.

Levinas, Emmanuel. 2002. *Otherwise Than Being or Beyond Essence*. Trans. Lingis Alphonso. Pittsburgh, Pa.: Duquesne University Press.

————. 1969. *Totality and Infinity: An Essay on Exteriority*. Trans. Alphonso Lingis. Pittsburgh: Duquesne University Press.

Levine, Madeline G. 2002. "Home Loss in Wartime Literature: A Typology of Images." In *Framing the Polish Home: The Postwar Literary and Cultural Constructions of Hearth, Nation, and Self*, ed. Bożena Shallcross. Athens: Ohio University Press, 97–115.

Lifton, Robert Jay. 1986. *The Nazi Doctors: Medical Killing and the Psychology of Genocide*. New York: Basic Books.

Lindberg, David C., ed. 1978. *Science in the Middle Ages*. Chicago: University of Chicago Press, 391–428.

Lyotard, Jean-François. 1988. *The Differend: Phrases in Dispute*. Trans. George Van Den Abbeele. Minneapolis: University of Minnesota Press.

————. 1984. *The Postmodern Condition: A Report on Knowledge*. Trans. Geoff Bennington and Brian Massumi. Manchester: Manchester University Press.

Łapiński, Zdzisław. 1981. *Między polityką a metafizyką. O poezji Czesława Miłosza*. London: Odnowa.

Maciejewska, Irena, ed. 1988. *Męczeństwo i zagłada Żydów polskich*. Warsaw: Krajowa Agencja Wydawnicza.

————, intro. and ed. 1977. *Co czytałem umarłym. Wiersze getta warszawskiego*. Warsaw: PIW.

Mauss, Marcel. 1990. *The Gift: The Form and Reason for Exchange in Archaic Society.* Trans. W. D. Halls. Foreword Mary Douglas. New York: W.W. Norton.

Melchior, Małgorzata. 2004. *Zagłada a tożsamość. Polscy Żydzi ocaleni na "aryjskich papierach." Analiza doświadczenia biograficznego.* Warsaw: Wydawnictwo IFIS PAN.

Miłosz, Czesław. 2006. "Zaraz po wojnie," Z Czesławem Miłoszem rozmawia Joanna Gromek. In *Rozmowy polskie 1979–1998.* Kraków: Wydawnictwo Literackie, 756–802.

———. 2005. *Legends of Modernity.* Trans. Madeline G. Levine. New York: Farrar Straus Giroux.

———. 2001a. *New and Collected Poems 1931–2001.* New York: Ecco-Harper.

———. 2001b. *Wiersze,* vols. 1 and II. *Dzieła zebrane.* Kraków: Znak.

———. 1983. *The Witness of Poetry.* Cambridge, Mass.: Harvard University Press.

———. 1981. *The Captive Mind.* Trans. Jane Zielonko. New York: Random House.

Miłosz, Czesław, and Jerzy Andrzejewski. 1996. *Legendy nowoczesności: eseje okupacyjne: listy-eseje Jerzego Andrzejewskiego.* Kraków: Wydawnictwo Literackie.

Moczarski, Kazimierz. 1997. *Rozmowy z katem.* Ed. Andrzej Krzysztof Kunert. Warsaw: PWN.

Modernity and the Hegemony of Vision. 1995. Ed. David Michael Levin. Berkeley: University of California Press,

Morgan, Michael L., ed. 2001. *A Holocaust Reader: Responses to Extermination.* New York: Oxford University Press.

Mozejko, Edward, ed. 1988. *Between Anxiety and Hope: The Poetry and Writing of Czeslaw Milosz.* Edmonton: University of Alberta Press.

Najberg, Leon. 1993. *Ostatni powstańcy getta.* Warsaw: Żydowski Instytut Historyczny.

Nałkowska, Zofia. 1975–2000. *Dzienniki.* 6 vols. Ed. Hanna Kirchner. Warsaw: Czytelnik.

———. 2000. *Medallions.* Trans. Diana Kuprel. Evanston, Ill.: Northwestern University Press.

———. 1957. *Widzenia dalekie i bliskie.* Warsaw: PIW.

———. 1931. *Ściany świata.* Warsaw: Nakład Gebethnera i Wolfa.

Nancy, Jean-Luc. 1997. *The Sense of the World.* Trans. Jeffrey S. Librett. Minneapolis: University of Minnesota Press.

———. 1992. *Corpus.* Paris: Seuil.

Nathan, Leonard, and Arthur Quinn. 1991. *The Poet's Work: An Introduction to Czeslaw Milosz.* Cambridge, Mass.: Harvard University Press.

Nawarecki, Aleksander. 1993. *Rzeczy i marzenia. Studia o wyobraźni poetyckiej skamandrytów.* Katowice: Śląsk.

———. 1991. *Czarny karnawał: Uwagi śmierci niechybnej księdza Baki. Poetyka tekstu i paradoksy recepcji.* Wrocław: Zakład Narodowy Ossolińskich.

Nel Siedlecki, Janusz 5543. 2000. "Homo Sapiens and Animal." In Borowski Tadeusz 119198, Olszewski Krystyn 75817. *We Were in Auschwitz,* trans. Alicia Nitecki. New York: Welcome Rain Publishers, 17–21.

Nochlin, Linda, and Tamar Garb, eds. *The Jew in the Text: Modernity and the Construction of Identity.* New York: Thames and Hudson, 1996.

Nycz, Ryszard, and Zeidler-Janiszewska, Anna, eds. 2006. *Nowoczesność jako doświadczenie.* Kraków: Universitas.

Ozick, Cynthia. 1987. *The Messiah of Stockholm.* New York: A.A. Knopf.

Pick, Daniel. 1993. *War Machine: The Rationalization of Slaughter in the Modern Age.* New Haven, Conn.: Yale University Press.

Plato. 1994. *Symposium.* Trans. Robert Waterfield. Oxford: Oxford University Press.

————. *Phaedo*. 1909. Trans. Benjamin Jowett. New York: P.F. Collier & Son, vol. 2.

Polonsky, Antony, ed. 1990."*My Brother's Keeper*": *Recent Polish Debates on the Holocaust*. London: Routledge.

Ponge, Francis. 1969. *Soap*. Trans. Lane Dunlop. London: Jonathan Cape Ltd.

Prekerowa, Teresa. 1986. "Relief Council for Jews, 1942–1945." In *The Jews in Poland*, ed. Chimen Abramsky, Maciej Jachimczyk, and Antony Polonsky. Oxford: Basil Blackwell, 161–176.

Przyboś, Julian. 1946. "Ostatni wiersz Ginczanki." *Odrodzenie* 15 (1946): 5.

Reitlinger, Gerald. 1960. *The Final Solution: The Attempt to Exterminate the Jews of Europe 1939–1945*. New York: Viking Press.

Rilke, Rainer Maria. 1967. *Selected Works*. Trans. J. B. Leishman. New York: New Directions.

Ringelblum, Emanuel. 1992. *Polish–Jewish Relations during the Second World War*. Trans. Dafna Allon, Danuta Dabrowska, and Dana Karen. Foreword Yehuda Bauer. Ed. and footnotes Joseph Karnish and Shmuel Krakowski. Evanston, Ill.: Northwestern University Press.

————. 1988. *Kronika getta warszawskiego. Wrzesień 1939-styczeń 1943*. Intro. and ed. Artur Eisenbach. Trans. Adam Rutkowski. Warsaw: Czytelnik.

Rose, Jonathan, ed. 2001. *The Holocaust and the Book: Destruction and Preservation*. Amherst: University of Massachusetts Press.

Rosenfeld, Alvin.1995. *Americanization of the Holocaust*. Ann Arbor: Jean and Samuel Frankel Center for Judaic Studies, University of Michigan.

Roskies, David G., ed. 1988. *The Literature of Destruction: Jewish Responses to Catastrophe*. Philadelphia: Jewish Publication Society.

————. 1984. *Against the Apocalypse: Responses to Catastrophe in Modern Jewish Culture*. Cambridge, Mass.: Harvard University Press.

————. 1981. "The Holocaust Literature According to the Literary Critics." *Prooftexts* 1, no. 2 (May 1981): 209–216.

Rostropowicz Clark, Joanna. 2007. "Holy Week. A Novel of the Warsaw Ghetto Uprising," *The Sarmatian Review* 27 (2007): 7, Sarmatia@ruf.rice.edu.

Rothberg, Michael. 2000. *Traumatic Realism: The Demands of Holocaust Representation*. Minneapolis: University of Minnesota Press.

————, and Neal Levi, eds. 2003. *The Holocaust: Theoretical Readings*. New Brunswick, N.J.: Rutgers University Press.

Royle, Nicholas. 2003. *The Uncanny*. New York: Routledge.

Różewicz, Tadeusz. 2001. *Nożyk profesora*. Wrocław: Wydawnictwo Dolnośląskie.

————. 1999. *Zawsze fragment. Recykling*. Wrocław: Wydawnictwo Dolnośląskie.

————. 1966. *Wycieczka do muzeum*. Warsaw: Czytelnik.

Rybczynski, Witold. 1986. *Home: A Short History of an Idea*. New York: Viking.

Sakowicz, Kazimierz. 2005. *Ponary Diary, 1941–1943: A Bystander's Account of a Mass Murder*. Ed. Yitzhak Arad. Trans. Laurence Weinbaum. New Haven, Conn.: Yale University Press.

Santner, Eric L. 2006. *On Creaturely Life: Rilke Benjamin Sebald*. Chicago: University of Chicago Press.

Schweitzer, Albert. 1931. *The Mysticism of Paul the Apostle*. Trans. W. Montgomery. London: A. & C. Black.

Schmitt, Carl. 2005. *Political Theology: Four Chapters on the Concept of Sovereignty*. Intro. Tracy B. Strong. Trans. George Schwab. Chicago: University of Chicago Press.

Schwenger, Peter. 2001. "Words and the Murder of the Thing." In *Things*, ed. Bill Brown. *Critical Inquiry* 1: 99–113.

Sebald, W. G. 1999. *On the Natural History of Destruction*. New York: Modern Library.

Shakespeare, William. 1975a. *The Complete Works*. New York: Avenel.

———. 1975b. "Macbeth." *The Complete Works*, 1045–1070.

Shallcross, Bożena. 2002. "The Archeology of Occupation: Stefan Chwin on Danzig/Gdańsk." In Shallcross, *Framing the Polish Home: Postwar Cultural Constructions of Hearth, Nation, and Self*. Athens: Ohio University Press, 116–132.

———. 1992. *Dom romantycznego artysty*. Kraków: Wydawnictwo Literackie.

———, ed. 2002. *Framing the Polish Home: Postwar Cultural Constructions of Hearth, Nation, and Self*. Athens: Ohio University Press.

Shelley, Lore. 1991. *Criminal Experiments on Human Beings in Auschwitz and War Research Laboratories: Twenty Women Prisoners' Accounts*. San Francisco: Mellen Research University Press.

Shilling, Chris. 1993. *The Body and Social Theory*. London: Sage.

Shmeruk, Chone. 2000. *Legenda o Esterce w literaturze jidysz i polskiej*. Warsaw: Oficyna Naukowa.

Siła-Nowicki, Jan Władysław. 1990. "A Reply to Jan Błoński." In Polonsky, 59–68.

Silverman, Lisa. 2003. "Repossessing the Past? Property, Memory and Austrian Jewish Narrative Histories." *Modern Humanities Research Association*, http://www.mhra.org.uk/Downloads/Silverman.pdf.

Stala, Marian. 2001. *Trzy nieskończoności. O poezji Adama Mickiewicza, Bolesława Leśmiana i Czesława Miłosza*. Kraków, Wydawnictwo Literackie.

Stallybrass, Peter. 1999. "Worn Worlds: Clothes, Mourning, and the Life of Things." In *Cultural Memory and the Construction of Identity*, ed. Dan Ben-Amos and Liliane Weissberg. Detroit: Wayne State University Press, 27–44.

Steiner, George. 1998. *Language and Silence: Essays on Language, Literature, and the Inhuman*. New Haven, Conn.: Yale University Press.

Steiner, Rudolf. "Knowledge of the State between Death and a New Birth." Rudolf Steiner Archives, an electronic library, http://wn.rsarchive.org/Articles/DeaBir_index.html.

Sterling, Charles. 1981. *Still Life Painting: From Antiquity to the Twentieth Century*. New York: Harper and Row.

Sternstein, Malynne. 2006. *Will to Chance: Necessity and Arbitrariness in the Czech Avant-Garde: From Poetism to Surrealism*. Bloomington, Ind.: Slavica.

Stewart, Susan. 1993. *On Longing: Narratives of the Miniature, the Gigantic, the Souvenir, the Collection*. Durham, N.C.: Duke University Press.

Strauss, Anselm L. 1997. *Mirrors and Masks: The Search for Identity*. New Brunswick, N.J.: Transaction Publishers.

Sutzkever, Abraham. 1988. "A Load of Shoes." In *The Literature of Destruction: Jewish Responses to Catastrophe*, ed. David G. Roskies. Philadelphia: Jewish Publication Society, 493–494.

Süskind, Patrick. 1991. *Perfume: The Story of a Murderer*. Trans. John E. Woods. New York: Pocket Books.

Synoradzka, Anna. 1997. *Andrzejewski*. Kraków: Wydawnictwo Literackie.

Szarota, Tomasz. 1973. *Okupowanej Warszawy dzień powszedni. Studium historyczne*. Warsaw: Czytelnik.

Szewc, Piotr. 1993. *Annihilation*. Trans. Ewa Hryniewicz-Yarbrough. Normal: Dalkey Archive.

Szlengel, Władysław. 1977. *Co czytałem umarłym. Wiersze getta warszawskiego.* Intro. and ed. Irena Maciejewska. Warsaw: PIW.

Sznapman, Stanisław. 1988. "Dziennik getta." In *Pamiętniki z getta warszawskiego. Fragmenty i regestry* by Michał Grynberg. Warsaw: PWN, 359–360.

Świebocka Teresa, Webber Jonathan, and Wilsack Connie, eds. 1995. *Auschwitz: The History in Photographs.* Bloomington: Indiana University Press.

Talbot, Charles H. 1978. "Medicine." In *Science in the Middle Ages,* ed. David C. Lindberg. Chicago: University of Chicago Press, 391–428.

Todorov, Tzvetan. 1996. *Facing the Extreme: Moral Life in the Concentration Camp.* Trans. Arthur Denner and Abigail Pollak. New York: Holt.

Umińska, Bożena. 2001. *Postać z cieniem. Portrety Żydówek w polskiej literaturze od końca XIX wieku do 1939 roku.* Warsaw: Sic!.

Van Alphen, Ernst. 2002. "Caught by Images: On the Role of Visual Imprints in Holocaust Testimonies." *Journal of Visual Culture* 1, no. 2 (2002): 205–221.

Wajdelota, J. (Tadeusz Sarnecki), ed. 1944. *Z otchłani.* Warsaw: ŻKN.

Walas, Teresa. 1972. "Zwierciadła Jerzego Andrzejewskiego." In *Prozaicy dwudziestolecia międzywojennego. Sylwetki.* Introduction and ed., Bolesław Faron. Warsaw: Wiedza Powszechna, 23–48.

Warminski, Andrzej, ed. 1996. *Paul De Man: Aesthetic Ideology.* Minneapolis: University of Minnesota Press.

Weissberg, Liliane. 2003. "In Plain Sight." In *The Holocaust: Theoretical Readings,* ed. Neil Levi and Michael Rothberg. New Brunswick, N.J.., 396–403.

———, with Dan Ben-Amos, eds. 1999. *Cultural Memory and the Construction of Identity.* Detroit.: Wayne State University Press.

Werner, Andrzej. 1971. *Zwyczajna apokalipsa. Tadeusz Borowski i jego wizja świata obozów.* Warsaw: Czytelnik.

Wierzbicka, Anna. 1992. *Semantics, Culture and Cognition: Universal Human Concepts in Culture-Specific Configurations.* New York: Oxford University Press.

Wirth, Andrzej. 1967. "A Discovery of Tragedy: (The Incomplete Account of Tadeusz Borowski)." *Polish Review,* Vol. XII, No. 3 (1967): 43-52.

Witnessing the Disaster: Essays on Representation and the Holocaust. 2003. Ed. Michael Bernard-Donals and Richard Glejzer. Madison: University of Wisconsin Press.

Wojdowski, Bogdan. 1997. *Bread for the Departed.* Trans. Madeline Levine. Evanston, Ill.: Northwestern University Press.

Wyka, Kazimierz. 1982. *Życie na niby. Pamiętnik po klęsce.* Kraków: Wydawnictwo Literackie.

Young, James E. 1990. *Writing and Rewriting the Holocaust: Narrative and the Consequences of Interpretation.* Bloomington: Indiana University Press.

Zabierowski, Stanisław. 1961. "Testamenty poetyckie." In Podolska and Czerny, 356–362.

Zaleski, Marek. 2000. *Przygoda Drugiej Awangardy.* 2nd edition. Wrocław: Ossolineum.

Zelizer, Barbie, ed. 2001. *Visual Culture and the Holocaust.* New Brunswick, N.J.: Rutgers University Press.

Žižek, Slavoj. 2003. *The Puppet and the Dwarf: The Perverse Core of Christianity.* Cambridge, Mass.,: MIT Press

———. 2000. "Laugh Yourself to Death! The New Wave of Holocaust Comedies." In *The Holocaust and the Historical Trauma in Contemporary Visual Culture.* http://www.arthist.lu.se/discontinuities/texts/zizek.htm.

———. 1992. *Looking Awry. An Introduction to Jacques Lacan through Popular Culture.* Cambridge, Mass.: MIT Press.

INDEX

Aaron, Frieda: as Milosz scholar, 154n35; as Szlengel scholar, 20, 142n8, 143n19, 145n48

Absence, 4, 40, 69, 72, 102, 120; of data, 7, 10, 39, 126, 141n26; deletion, 40, 42, 50, 79, 96; erasure from representation, 29, 36, 40, 42, 59, 75–77, 82–84, 100, 104, 141, 146n15, 152n35; exclusion of human presence, 23, 78; lack, 69; in trace, 10, 83. *See also under* Ellipsis

Accumulation, 3–4, 18, 67, 132, 142–143n17; accretion, 3, 123, 136; amassing, 3, 5, 18, 126, 133–134, 139nn1,5, 142–143n17; versus collection, 2–3, 133; of corpses, 67; piling, 18, 64, 123, 132–133, 139n1; heaps, 122; plethora of, 23, 48, 77; surplus of, 76, 123

Afterlife, 13, 71, 75, 78, 80–84, 153–154n29; eschatology, 65, 71, 78–79, 85; negation of, 65, 85; as specular concept, 80–83. *See also* Ashes

Agalma, 12; agalmatic (paradigm), 12, 47–48, 115–116; as coinage, 147–148n39; as desire, 12, 46–48; as dispossession, 58, 115–116. *See also* Lacan, Jacques

Agamben, Giorgio: on camp, 124, 127; on dignity, 32, 145n46; La Capra on, 125, 128, 160n30; on the *Muselmann*, 124; as a political philosopher, 41, 124; on witness, 126–128; *works by: Homo Sacer: Sovereign Power and Bare Life*, 124; *Means without End: Notes on Politics*, 124; *Remnants of Auschwitz: The Witness and the Archive*, 145n46, 157n1

Agency, 6, 17, 27, 31, 33, 48, 65, 75, 84, 110, 119–120

Amery, Jean: *On Suicide: A Discourse on Voluntary Death*, 30, 32, 128, 144n40

Anatomical, 67, 82, 149n6, 151n31

Andrzejewski, Jerzy: archives of, 96–97; as author, 95–98, 155n11; mimetic paradigm, 12; *works by:* "At the Court" (short story), 154n2; *A Book for Marcin* (autobiographical), 155n6; *A Heart's Order* (novel), 95; *Holy Week* (novel), 96–111, 154–155n2, 155nn5,12; *How I Became a Writer* (autobiographical), 97; "Night" (short story), 155n4; *Notes to the Autobiography* (autobiographical), 97; "Problems of Polish Antisemitism" (essay), 115n11, 155n10; *Pulp*, 155n11

Archives (archiving), 8–9, 18, 39, 57–58, 95–97, 73, 109, 113, 129–130, 139n1, 155n12; Oyneg Shabes (*Chronicle of the Warsaw Ghetto*), 8–9, 41, 140nn14,15,17,19, 141nn20,22. *See also Precarium*

Arendt, Hannah: on *homo sacer*, 124; on public-private opposition, 115; on totalitarian power, 124, 139n9, 142n10, 145n4; *works by: Eichmann in Jerusalem: A Report on the Banality of*

178

INDEX

98–101, 103, 140nn15,19, 144n37, 149–150n14, 152n7; in Vilna, 18; in Warsaw, 17, 21, 24, 26, 30–31, 44, 96, 98–99, 105–106, 108; at wartime, 96, 106, 108. *See also* Szlengel, Władysław

Ginczanka, Zuzanna, 8, 12–13; as Jewish, 38–43, 145n7; life of, 38–39, 145nn7,8, 147n27; poetry of, 39, 145nn5,6,7; *works by: About Centaurs*, 38; "My Last Will," 37–46, 48–51, 145nn9,10,11, 146nn12,13, 147n19, 148n48; "Non omnis moriar," 147n37

Gross, Jan Tomasz: as historian, 2, 139n2, 146n21; as historian of the Holocaust, 157n35; *works by: Polish Society under German Occupation: The Generalgouvernement, 1939–1945*, 139n2; *Upiorna dekada. Trzy eseje o stereotypach na temat Żydów, Polaków, Niemców i komunistów. 1939–1948*, 146n21

Haptic, 117. *See also* Tactile (tangible)

Holocaust text, 5–13, 19, 24, 39, 42–43, 74, 136, 140n16, 141n21; fragmentary, 39, 50, 140n19; incriminating, 41–42; itinerant, 18, 39, 72, 113; as material object, 6–9, 11, 24, 42–43, 50; its remainders, 9–10, 39, 72–73. *See also* Message(s); *Precarium*

Identification, 41, 76, 81–82, 83, 109, 113, 125, 128, 161n6; with Jews, 83; with *Muselmänner*, 126–128; of perpetrators, 41

Identity, 36, 79–80, 82, 99, 103, 108, 114, 122, 134–135; authorial, 40–41, 44; according to Bauman, 143n27; disguise of, 25 (*see also* Deception); Jewish, 26, 36–37, 42, 45, 50, 146nn14,17; in material culture, 146n1; of objects, 3,12, 49, 95, 101; according to Strauss, 146n16; of survivors, 146n22; transformation of, 146n16; of victims, 121, 135. *See also* Property

Inscription, 6, 18, 55, 74, 96, 130, 133; of Holocaust, 9; inscribed, 132; reinscription, 97–98, 155n5; skinscript, 64–66, 150nn278–279

Intimacy, 43–44, 95, 109, 118; of body, 12, 26; intimate, 70, 81; intimate bond with objects, 121; of self, 110; sphere, 43, 115; with text, 7–8. *See also* Privacy

Jew(s), 83, 95, 103, 105–107; annihilation of, 72, 143n28, 147n33; status in Germany, 145n4. *See also under* Body (bodies); Fat; Jewishness; Objects; Soap; Uprising, Jewish

Jewishness, 50; as identity, 3, 26, 37, 41, 46, 49; as stigma, 41

Jouissance, 19, 25, 27, 30, 39, 47, 49, 110; as laughter, 27; as vengeance, 47–48

Lacan, Jacques: on agalma, 46–48; his concept of letter, 42, 146nn24,25; *works by: Écrits. A Selection*, 146n24; *The Ethics of Psychoanalysis*, 148n42; *Le Séminaire. Livre 8. Le transfert*, 46, 147n38

Legacy, 2; artistic, 39, 49–50, 95, 147n26; material, 2, 43, 50, 132, 148n48; objectual, 13, 49

Letter: as genre, 147n26; of law, 41; material, 36, 40–42, 136, 146nn15,19,24,25; purloined, 47

Levinas, Emmanuel: on hand's touch, 121, 141n23; on object relations, 120; on object's identity, 3–4, 147n32; on proximity, 9, 139n7, 141n23; *works by: Otherwise Than Being or Beyond Essence*, 9, 141n23; *Totality and Infinity: An Essay on Exteriority*, 9, 121, 139n7, 147n32

Looting: of Jewish property, 2, 4, 17, 43–46, 139n6, 142–143n17, 147n29, 148n45; after liberation, 129; represented, 39, 42, 48, 115

Mark (marker): 159n27; on body, 40, 69, 78, 82, 84; of identity, 7, 13, 26, 41–42, 84, 134–135

Bożena Shallcross is Associate Professor of Slavic Languages and Literatures at the University of Chicago. She is the author of numerous articles, translations, and books, including *Rzeczy i Zagłada; Through the Poet's Eye: The Travels of Zagajewski, Herbert, and Brodsky;* and *Cień i forma. O wyobraźni plastycznej Leopolda Staffa.* She edited *The Effect of Palimpsest: Culture, Literature, History* (with Ryszard Nycz); *Polish Encounters/Russian Identity* (with David L. Ransel, Indiana University Press, 2005); *Framing the Polish Home: Postwar Cultural Constructions of Hearth, Nation, and Self; The Other Herbert;* and *Dom romantycznego artysty.*